TWENTIETH CENTURY CHURCH MUSIC

STUDIES IN CHURCH MUSIC

General Editor: ERIK ROUTLEY, B.D., D.Phil.

TWENTIETH CENTURY
CHURCH MUSIC

By

ERIK ROUTLEY

New York
Oxford University Press
1964

7P1.71
R P69t
103578

PRINTED IN GREAT BRITAIN

To
RONALD JOHNSON
Organist of St. Columba's Episcopal Church c.b.
Edinburgh
who knows, loves and interprets in the local congregation
Church Music of all ages.

Preface

IN church music there has been no age so full of surprises, and so full of creative promise, as our own. I should stand by this hazardous judgment in the face of any defender of the sixteenth century.

In the first place, church music is receiving more serious attention from musicians of proved excellence than it has received since the time of Palestrina.

Secondly (the converse) those who compose primarily for the church have proved to be musicians of higher standing and greater experimental imaginativeness than any since the days of Tallis's Forty Part Motet.

But thirdly—and here we go beyond the sixteenth century—this is an age of creative conflict, and, for the church, of the withdrawal of outward prosperity. The effect of this has been to breach the walls which surrounded the church's citadel in the past, and the going out and coming in has been entirely for music's good.

Fourthly (despite what the reader will hear later on from the pen of Messiaen) music has at last begun to catch up with the other arts in a process in which for fifty years the visual arts have been in the lead—a process of radical experiment, of deep and ruthless questioning, and of the sacrificial exploration of its relation to life. "Sacrificial" here implies that the explorers are, at last, indifferent to the possibility that history's verdict may be that they are investigating a blind alley. Had this book been written even ten years ago, its subject would have been far less interesting.

Now any author is tempted in his Preface to play a few strokes in the game of "beating the reviewers". I do not see why he should not. While I am sure there is much here that ought to be better and fuller and fairer, I must advise the reader that I have no hope here of being comprehensive, lexicographical or in any sense exhaustive. You have to put your deadline somewhere, of course: and things are now moving so quickly that if we put ours at 16th May, 1963, on which day this is being written, and on whose morrow this will be handed to the publisher, in the ensuing months anything may happen. That is an obvious hazard. But beyond that, I cannot hope to deal with, or even to be acquainted with, all the church music that has been written in the last sixty-three years. I do not think that for the present purpose it was necessary to attempt that. It has been necessary to select, and my selection of composers, and of their works, for comment will no doubt strike some as odd: not least such of these composers as are happily still alive. I hope this selection has not been injudicious; but I am ready to be told by anybody that had he been writing this book these are not the composers he would have selected, nor is this the selection of their works he would have mentioned, nor is this what he would have said about them.

7

For this book cannot possibly be history. It could be the basis of future history, even if it be used by a future historian as a demonstration of the curious opinions of a contemporary. A small minority of the composers mentioned here have finished their work: a judgment of some tentative sort can in such cases be made. But much of this book, and especially its last two parts, will inevitably read rather like some petrified news-letter. There seems to be no point in rigorously refraining from interim judgments on unfinished work: but obviously it would be impudence to claim anything in the way of objective permanence for any such judgments.

The purpose of these pages is to stir up interest in contemporary church music, to suggest, perhaps, lines along which future research would be worth pursuing, and to make some broad judgments about the social implications of some of the developments we shall encounter. "Church music" is here broadly liturgical music. Work on the oratorio-scale is better left to be dealt with in another study similar to this one which we hope to produce in this series; therefore here oratorios will (with one or two exceptions whose reason ought to be obvious) be only lightly touched on. What is normally likely to be heard in a church—any church, from a tin chapel to King's College—is our main subject, together with work that has been influenced partly by church customs and partly by secular movements. The central theme is the reconstruction of a very solid, serviceable and dignified structure of church music which in 1900 was virtually a symbol of Establishment. I am especially concerned with the radical protests that have come—from the German school, from the French organ school, and from the English "pop" experimenters—against the traditional image of church music.

This is the beginning of a conversation, not the record of a complete historical phase. I take responsibility, as I must, for all those defects of acknowledged purpose which it contains: but I must record my thanks to many who have advised me and helped me in its preparation: to many composers who have answered silly questions: to many friends who over the years have introduced me to music that made me feel that this study was worth undertaking: and to my friends of the Dunblane Church Music Group who have stimulated my otherwise sluggish perceptions of present-day social needs.

                                                                    E.R.

Contents

9

Part Four
GOING IN AND OUT

Acknowledgements

The author expresses his gratitude to the following owners of copyright for permission to quote from material under their control. Full details of the publications from which our music examples are taken will be found in the bibliographical index.

Oxford University Press, Music Department, 44 Conduit St., London, W.1.
Exx. 1, 2, 3, 6, 7, 8, 9, 12, 14, 16, 17, 18.

Curwen Edition, J. Curwen & Sons Ltd., 29 Maiden Lane, London,W.C.2.
Ex. 5.

Ascherberg, Hopwood & Crew Ltd., 16 Mortimer St., London, W.1.
Ex. 10.

Stainer & Bell Ltd., 29 Newman St., London, W.1.
Ex. 15.

Novello & Company Ltd., 160 Wardour St., London, W.1.
Exx. 19, 20, 21, 22, 23, 24, 25, 26, 27, 29, 30, 44.

Alfred Lengnick & Co. Ltd., 14 Sheraton St., London, W.1.
Ex. 28.

The Reverend Canon J. W. Poole, Precentor of Coventry Cathedral.
Ex. 31.

Mr. John Hotchkis.
Ex. 32.

Krompholz & Co., Bern, Switzerland.
Ex. 33.

Grail Publications, 58 Sloane St., S.W.1.
Ex. 34.

Artia Foreign Trade Corporation, Praha 2, 30 Ve Smeckach, Czechoslovakia.
Ex. 35.

Associated Music Publishers, New York.
Ex. 36.

Editions Salabert, 22 rue de Chauchat, Paris, IX, France.
Ex. 37.

United Music Publishers Ltd., 1 Montague St., London, W.C. 1.
Ex. 38.

Schola Cantorum, Paris.
Exx. 39, 40.

Josof Weinberger & Sons Ltd., 33 Crawford St., W.1.
Exx. 43, 45, 46, 47, 49, 50, 51, 52, 54, 55, 57, 58, 60.

The Reverend Ernest Marvin and A.B.C. Week-End Television Ltd.
  Ex. 61.

Mr. Charles Cleall.
  Ex. 64.

Mr. Peter Cutts.
  Ex. 65.

Introduction

QUEEN VICTORIA died on the twenty-second day of the twentieth century. The flowers sent to her funeral caused a major disturbance to the public arrangements for that ceremony; flowers at funerals were still something of an innovation in 1901. A restive horse delayed the procession from Windsor station to the Chapel of St. George in the Castle. The service began an hour and a quarter late. At that service they sang music by Purcell, S. S. Wesley, Spohr, Gounod and Tchaikovsky.[1]

E. H. Fellowes, who records this, tells us in another book[2] that a typical Cathedral list of the year 1896 contained within one week services by Sullivan, Stainer, Tours and Barnby, and anthems by Spohr, Stainer, W. H. Gladstone, Mendelssohn, Elvey, Goss, Barnby and S. S. Wesley, all of whom (Mendelssohn by adoption) may be called composers of the Victorian era.

It would have been a bold prophet who in 1901 had predicted that sixty years later, of the Victorians named above, only one, S. S. Wesley, would be likely to find his name in any Cathedral list (Anglican chants and hymn tunes apart) from one end of England to the other. It was only in academic circles that any questions were being asked about church music.

Music as a whole was just beginning to show a slight restlessness that was to prove to be the first stirring of a profound revolution. English music gathered itself round two vital and already-revered figures. One was Edward Elgar, who in 1901 was in his 44th year, and had in the year before produced *Gerontius*. The other was Henry J. Wood, twelve years younger, who in 1895, at 26, inaugurated the Promenade Concerts in London. That sets the scene tolerably well. Elgar, at the top of his form, showed himself the best translator into English of German music that the country had ever produced, and the most impressive craftsman since Purcell. Henry Wood struck oil in popular music-appreciation with the Proms. A recent writer, in an informed comment on non-Anglican church life, writes:

One has only to read the music criticism of George Bernard Shaw, written in the eighties and nineties, and scan the programmes of Henry Wood's first Promenade Concerts, to realise that the music then acceptable to mass audiences was clearly related to the music habitually sung by chapel choirs[3].

There was a great deal of music about, and so far as the ordinary music-hearer went, none of it was disturbing. Tchaikovsky had been dead eight years in 1901, Brahms four. Rachmaninov was to produce his C minor Piano Concerto later that very year, and everybody already knew his C sharp minor Prelude. Debussy had just completed his *Nocturnes*, and his best work was still to come. Stravinsky (19) had not yet been heard of, but a wild man called Schoenberg (27) was putting the finishing touches to his *Gurrelieder*, and most of those who had heard of him were foretelling a dire future for him if he did not mend his ways. Berg was setting down (according to one book of reference) his " first self-taught attempts at composition " at 15, and Webern (18) and Bartok (19) had still their names to make.

If anybody was whistling a tune in the street, it was, as likely as not, one of Sullivan's. He had died two months before the Queen. There was still the Music Hall for popular music, and those two enemies before which it was eventually to fall, the cinematograph and the gramophone, made their first appearances respectively in 1896 and 1897. In church the school of Mendelssohn reigned; the off-beat church music of those days was that of Sankey and his friends. There was plenty of music, plenty of publishing (although the Oxford University Press Music Department was not to come into being for another quarter of a century), plenty of amateur playing and singing. Singing Festivals, attended by choirs of large proportions and approximate virtuosity, were legion. The school of Curwen still conferred the benefits of sol-fa on enthusiastic choralists. Light opera and light church cantata alike flourished.

It needs a good deal of imagination now to place oneself in such an atmosphere as then reigned in music. It is not so much that we know nothing of that security and public euphoria which we attribute to the Edwardians. It is not, in this field, primarily a matter of being pre- or post–1914. The most remarkable difference that we should find if we were transported back to February 1901 is surely the absence of a certain kind of pedagogy, the absence of a certain strident class-consciousness in music, which is familiar to us, and has been familiar these sixty years.

It really seems that although there were leaders in music, there were not, as there are now, violent dissenters. Dissent was not yet showing its true colours, for you could not yet count Schoenberg. Who were the great teachers at that time? In London, Sir Alexander Mackenzie had reigned sixteen years at the Royal Academy of Music. In Cambridge, Stanford had been Professor since 1885, and at Oxford, Parry had held his appointment as Professor for three years alongside his directorship of the Royal College of Music in London. Of these three Mackenzie was an inconsiderable composer, but Parry and Stanford have retained, a generation after their deaths, the respect of singers and players. And what did Parry and Stanford teach their pupils? Why, they taught them to appreciate the accepted composers, and to write like craftsmen. They did not teach them that the composers of their own and the previous generation were handling an outdated idiom from which their pupils must divorce themselves. Parry was one of the finest composers England has produced—on his day. His opus numbers actually run beyond 200, and nine-tenths of his music now lies unsung and unplayed. But he had the *Songs of Farewell* (1918) in him, and *Blest Pair of Sirens*, and a good deal of organ music that was the best England had produced since Purcell—it might be safe to say, since Gibbons. In not a bar of this, however, did Parry challenge any fundamental assumption that Cherubini held. Stanford was almost as prolific as Parry; a little better at home in church music, a little less so, perhaps, in large choral works; a shade Irish in his more unbuttoned moments, but, again, a better craftsman, a more energetic imagination, than the country had seen for generations. But Schubert, had he been an Anglican, could have written *Stanford in B flat*, and Mendelssohn, on a really good day, might have risen to *Beati quorum via*. Not a paragraph in either composer shows any trace of the kind of dissent that Berlioz, who died in 1869, wrote into every bar of his music.

Where Parry and Stanford entered the limited field in which Dykes and Stainer and Barnby had worked with such universal acceptance, all they said was, "This, using the same materials and the same vocabulary, can be done better." No Victorian hymn tune composer wrote a better hymn tune than Parry's LAUDATE DOMINUM,[4] which was first heard in 1894 as the conclusion of a festival anthem; but any of them could have written it had they had Parry's clear sight. S. S. Wesley did not write Basil Harwood's hymn tune THORNBURY,[5] (1898) but hearing that tune, a listener of a later age could regard this as a mere accident.

It would be quite wrong to call these unoriginal composers.[6] They were not mere copyists by any means. They were capable of writing what had power and beauty. Very near the end of his life, Vaughan

Williams paid a generous tribute to Parry and Stanford as teachers; and in the course of this he said, "I fully believe—and keeping the achievements of Byrd, Purcell and Elgar firmly before my eyes—*Blest Pair of Sirens* is the finest musical work that has come out of these islands."[7] But this praise comes by way of exception to a more general statement of Parry as a composer: "Potentially, I believe, he was among the greatest. But something stood in the way of complete realisation." Vaughan Williams was a pupil of both; and among Stanford's pupils, and devoted admirers, is another of the architects of the English modern church music style, Herbert Howells. Parry and Stanford were, as these and many others testify, great teachers, over-prolific but not seldom distinguished composers, themselves conservative but in their influence on the new generation, wholly creative.

In 1901 there were other younger musicians whose work was beginning to give English church music a new self-confidence. There was, at Christ Church, Oxford, Basil Harwood, who at our zero date was 42, and lived into his 90th year. Harwood became a strictly "church" composer, specialising in choral and organ music, and in hymn tunes many of which showed a strange eccentricity. This way-wardness can be traced to his great personal admiration for S. S. Wesley's music. He had just that combination of a conservative manner with an instinctive impatience with certain conventions that Wesley had. The consequence is that his work is either, like the *Service in A flat*, pleasantly and competently romantic-cathedral in style or, like some of his organ-pieces and hymn tunes, so leisurely and lingering as to baffle the voice, the ear and the memory. Harwood had Stanford's disastrous tendency to use hymn tune subjects in large movements (see his C sharp minor organ sonata, which may be compared with Stanford's organ sonatas Op. 153–5), and his general tendency was to a slowness which could become muddy in the same way that a cathedral-organ of his time was designed precisely to make generalised and lingering, rather than clear and energetic, sounds for the hearer's delectation.

Ten years younger than Harwood was Henry Walford Davies, who in 1898 was appointed (aged 29) to the Mastership of the choir at the Temple Church. It is not now easy to write with enthusiasm of Walford Davies as a composer. Of all these Edwardian leaders he was most completely and exclusively the teacher and populariser. In later days he became one of the half dozen most famous broadcasters of the B.B.C.'s first decade. His most remarkable contribution to church music was his advocacy of "speech-rhythm" chanting of the psalms:

hardly less important was his championship of congregational hymn-singing (he was by birth a Congregationalist from the Marches). To Walford Davies, as to Harwood, church music was " a watchmaker's job": attention to minute detail in composition and in performance was their answer to the somewhat slapdash methods, especially in psalm-singing, that had prevailed in their predecessors' time. Their composi-tions, whatever their length, are essentially miniatures: a long composition is a string of miniatures. In Walford Davies's music a predilection for speech-rhythm induced a propensity for writing in irregular bars—which at the time was quite a gesture, but was soon to become a commonplace and even an affectation in the work of early twentieth century church composers.[8]

The conservative tradition of music continued, as we shall see, throughout our period in church music. The immediate question is: what was common to the outlooks of the leading church musicians in 1901? The evidence of these four composers, and of their immediate disciples (among whom we may for the present name Martin and Geoffrey Shaw and Charles Wood) shows that while they were indeed conservatives, they were engaged in a corporate gesture against the tendencies that had shown themselves to be corrupting the church music of the Victorian Age. Parry and Stanford were not primarily church musicians. Parry indeed was too much of a rationalist to be more than a marginal Christian, and his contribution to church music is very small: the *Songs of Farewell* are profoundly religious, but were not designed to be in the strict sense "church music"; and the organ works are church music only because of the church-associations of the instrument and of the subjects which the composer took for his chorale-preludes. These two were concerned with the condition of English music in general. Their comment on their immediate inheri-tance was not destructive; it was simply the comment of good musicians on the work of inferior musicians. All the four we have mentioned were, however, to some extent, *teachers*. It was as much the recovery of the craftsmanship of the classics as the making of new music that they advocated. Such as Walford Davies applied to the performance of music a new care for detail, a new craftsmanship in rhetoric. They did not wish to dig anything up by the roots.

It was people of this kind who inspired the boldly conservative revision in 1904 of the country's most famous hymn book, *Hymns Ancient and Modern*. And as I have said in another place, the relative failure of this book to capture the churchgoing public's imagination is largely due to its curiously pedagogic character.[9] It was not easy for

B

the ordinary person to see why what the new hymnal offered was much better than what the old one offered, because it did not seem that the new material was particularly different from the old. Why, yes, it contained some interesting new tunes by Parry and Stanford and B. Luard Selby, and some admirable revivals of old tunes, and plenty of S. S. Wesley that had not been given an airing in the editions of 1861, 1875 and 1889. But since this music was different from, and better than, the older selection only in ways that were evident to a professor of music or an experienced composer, people on the whole said, " Why change?" Only a small number were impressed—well, in all only about a million, which, by the standards the Proprietors of that book had become accustomed to, was poor going.[10] This is characteristic of the time. Conservative gestures in 1904 did not impress churchmen. Something "much the same but different in important details" was not strong enough to bring to repentance those whose taste had been conditioned by fifty years of pretentious vulgarity.

Vulgarity is not too strong a word. The folk-song of the English churches in the nineteenth century had become cheap beyond what any seventeenth century singer could have conceived. A cult of amateurism had ensured that mediocrity would be accepted: easy and cheap printing made the uncritical dissemination of music possible, and a substantial bourgeois population of churchgoers created a demand for what would undisturbingly adorn their acts of worship. Hearty singing in nonconformity went with a predilection for what was easy to sing; sol-fa sight-reading settled choral taste into a strictly 18th–19th century rut. Anybody who cared for plainsong and Tudor music was an eccentric; and the plainsong revival associated with the Oxford Movement was making very heavy weather under the faithful but lonely and far from expert helmsmanship of a few priest-musicians who treasured the memory of Redhead and Helmore.

When you place the music of Parry and Stanford alongside that of so much that went just before them, and continued alongside them, what you see at once is a *professional* touch. Barnby, Stainer and Sullivan were professional musicians—degree-holders who made their living by music. But their church music was, as it were, "amateurised" through their connection with the church. That is to say that a tradition had established itself by which not craftsmanship or imagination, but rather conformity to a certain set of conventions and the evocation of a certain well-defined atmosphere, presented themselves as the first necessities to the composer's mind. By the end of Victoria's reign, however, the impact on church music of those two wholly professional musicians, Parry and Stanford, was enough to call into question the conventional restrictions under which the true Victorians were content to work. When Parry wrote a hymn tune or an oratorio, this was a musician of high standing writing for the church what he was prepared to write for the concert-hall or the stage. When Sullivan wrote a cantata, he was not writing what he would have written for Savoy (except perhaps in that staggeringly incongruous setting of "We therefore pray thee, help thy servants" in the *Festival Te Deum* (1872)). Barnby did not write for anything but the church and the private glee club.

In the development of church music through the first sixty years of the twentieth century we are going to see first the effect of this new "professional" touch in a new interest taken by musicians of high standing in the requirements of the church, and by the church in the offerings of these composers. In the second place we are going to see the beginnings of a *rapprochement* between the church and music of a radically "dissenting" kind. In the third, we shall see the effect on church music of a social revolution of which only a few lonely prophets were dreaming in 1900.

NOTES TO INTRODUCTION

1. E. H. Fellowes, *Memoirs of an Amateur Musician* (Methuen, 1946) pp. 106–7.

2. E. H. Fellowes, *English Cathedral Music* (Methuen, 1941) p. 259.

3. C. P. Driver, *A Future for the Free Churches?* (S.C.M. Press, 1962) p. 77.

4. *Hymns A. & M.* (Revised edn., 1950) 376.

5. ib., 256.

6. On Stanford and Parry, see J. A. Fuller-Maitland, *The Music of Parry and Stanford* (Cambridge, Heffer, 1944).

7. U. Vaughan Williams and I. Holst (ed.), *Heirs and Rebels* (Oxford University Press, 1959) p. 97.

8. See E. Routley, *The Music of Christian Hymnody* (Independent Press, 1957) p. 136.

9. ib., p. 134.

10. W. K. Lowther Clarke, *A Hundred Years of Hymns Ancient and Modern* (Clowes, 1961) Chapter XI.

PART ONE

REPAIRING THE STRUCTURE

"It is indeed a moral rather than a musical issue. . . . Is it not worth while making a vigorous effort today for the sake of establishing a good tradition?"

R. Vaughan Williams, in the
Preface to the *English Hymnal* (1906).

I

Need for Reconstruction Noted

RALPH VAUGHAN WILLIAMS and Gustav Holst, lifelong friends, devoted admirers and acute critics of one another's work, were the pioneers of the first major English musical dissent of the twentieth century. Neither was precocious as a composer, and neither produced anything notable before the century opened. But of the two, Vaughan Williams was the more prolific and longer-lived: Holst, the more fastidious, the slower worker, the more involved in active propagation of music among the people of the country. Since Holst spent more time doing what men do not achieve great fame for doing, wrote less music, and certainly wrote less music that has ever been popular, his name is always in danger of being written in small type, as it were, under the bold letters of that of Vaughan Williams. But it is not only impossible to judge which was the greater composer: it would be repellent to the nature of either composer to call him greater than the other. Any attempt to do so is quickly stultified by reading the recently-published correspondence between the two which Mrs. Vaughan Williams and Miss Imogen Holst edited, to the great service of all music-lovers, in 1959 (see note 7 to chapter 1). In all their major enterprises in music the two went hand in hand until Holst died in 1934. Both made major contributions to the orchestral and choral literature of English music; and together they left an impression on church music which no responsible musician has been able to ignore.

Their dissent was a musical one. And it was made within an acceptance of certain musical axioms which others, like Schoenberg, were questioning. To put it plainly, Holst and Vaughan Williams were not, and never came within miles of being, atonalists or dodecaphonists. They were—and this is the radical difference between them and the revolutionaries—as much concerned with the development of ancient idioms as with the exploiting of new ones. It was the past to which they looked first—the remoter past—before they considered what intimations of the future they could convey.

But their dissent was from the whole harmonic and contrapuntal orthodoxy of the eighteenth and nineteenth centuries. An example

Ex.1.

O ALL YE WORKS OF THE LORD, BLESS YE THE LORD:

PRAISE HIM, AND MAGNIFY HIM FOR EV-ER.

from the maturity of Vaughan Williams (*Benedicite*, 1930) gives us, in a few bars, the whole argument. (Example 1)

That convenient example could be paralleled a hundred times in the work of either composer. Its chief points of controversy with the established idiom of 1700–1900 are obviously these:

(*a*) The near-axiomatic requisite of four-part harmony is questioned. For the traditional four-part harmony, or richer harmony adding more parts to weave a richer texture in the same material, Vaughan Williams constantly substitutes two-part or three-part writing, with parallel chords supporting the melodic lines. The whole of the above passage is essentially in two parts.

(*b*) The equally axiomatic cadences of "orthodox" music are abandoned in favour of cadences suggested by modality and linear writing: that in this example is characteristic.

(*c*) The associations of melody with the diatonic scale, emphasising the third and fifth, are replaced by associations with the modal scales whose "dominant" may be anywhere between the third and sixth of the scale.

(*d*) The rhythm, grouping of syllables under notes, and general shape of melody is divorced from the associations of four-bar-unit dance writing, and the result is a more melismatic melody which, when regular bars are used, as here, may cover an irregular number of them, or may divide a formal eight-bar group irregularly into five and three, or two, two and three, or in any other way. Another typical "Vaughan Williams" melodic phrase from the same work sung by the solo soprano, is this:

and a characteristic contrapuntal subject:

The sources of all this are not in any reaching out towards an unknown future, but in the reviving of an unknown past—of Tudor polyphony and of English folk music. Both these were, in 1900, areas of music known only to specialists: the vocabulary of both was communicated to the generality of musicians and listeners through the music of Vaughan Williams.

It is for this reason precisely that his influence on church music was so great: for Tudor polyphony gave of its best to the church, and English folk-song of the ballad kind was, by reason of the accident that the typical hymn-metre is still the metre of the ballads, carols and folk-songs of the late Middle Ages, easily adaptable for the congregational singing of hymns. Therefore in church music Vaughan Williams became the great populariser of a new idiom that was really ancient, whereas in his larger works he sounded, to secular listeners, like a "modern" composer. And indeed it was in these larger works that he developed his new-old vocabulary with an invention that made it something much more than an archaism.

In *Sancta Civitas* (1925), for example, he combines the style derived from the ancients with a great deal of very profound and suggestive "new music". The result of this combination is a strange kind of "humanity": for example, he so uses a variant of the common chord

Ex.4

(which also appears at "Lightnings and clouds" in the *Benedicite*, expressing elemental violence) as to give a picture of the Fall of Babylon, in St. John's Apocalypse, that suggests not only the terror of the judgment but also the grief that it brings on those who are lost:

Ex.5   BAB-Y-LON   THE GREAT   IS FALL-EN, IS FALL - - - - EN

Again, in *Sancta Civitas*, he makes use of the "fade" technique at the end—the unresolved discord disappearing into silence—that Holst used at the end of the last movement of *The Planets*, and that he himself used again in the last bars of his Sixth Symphony.

This has nothing to do with the Tudors, or with any other kind of archaism. It is impressionism, such as Debussy delighted in. And Vaughan Williams's use of it, and of so many other cunning devices to provide atmosphere surrounding argument, exposes the central dissent in his musical speech, around which all the others really gather: namely, that "not all good music is German or Italian in its vocabulary". This, of course, was the argument in his book, *National Music*. If only Englishmen would realise that in their blood there is as much French as German, and that the European influence in their culture did not begin with the Restoration of King Charles II, and above all that their own musical heritage is as upstanding as anybody else's they would realise that they need not go about assuming that they had no music in them.

When Vaughan Williams wrote homophonically, a " big tune" of a thoroughly popular kind not infrequently came out; and his facility with "big tunes" did much to endear him to the half-attentive public of the church, from the tune to " For all the saints" onwards. The *Te Deum* in G, (1928), "My soul, praise the Lord" (1936) and "O how amiable" (1940) have this texture; and his sense of occasion could prompt him to make dramatic and effective use of existing "big tunes", like the tune to "Our God, our help in ages past" in "Lord, thou hast been our refuge" (1921) and most famously in his treatment of the "Old Hundredth" in the 1953 Coronation Service. Here he showed a touch of the vulgar sense which Holst largely lacked: Holst's one famous "big tune" is, of course, in the "Jupiter" movement in *The Planets*—which, by his own co-operation, later became a hymn tune.

One remembers with some confusion one of Vaughan Williams's worst "big tunes"—written in an attempt to provide for the Second World War something like what Parry, in "Jerusalem", had provided for the first: this was "Hymn for Use in time of War" (1941), with words by G. W. Briggs, and was justly neglected by the general public. He could be forgiven for trying to emulate his old master—and indeed he atoned for this in one of his profoundest short compositions, which he wrote for the centenary of Parry's birth (1948). This is "Prayer to the Father of Heaven", a setting of words by John Skelton, and it carries the following dedication: "To the memory of my master, Hubert Parry, not as an attempt palely to reflect his incomparable art, but in the hope that he would have found in this motet (to use his own words) 'something characteristic'." Parry would indeed have found this—it is a Vaughan Williams version of the *Songs of Farewell*, but "characteristic" from it mysterious opening:

Ex.6

to its majestically solemn and complicated final cadence:

Ex.7

His cadences are, of course, a study in themselves; and no such study could overlook the most audacious, and the simplest, of them all: the final bars of the tiny motet, O *taste and see*, in the 1953 Coronation service:

Ex.8

The whole of this little work is quintessential "V-W": but who else, writing in an idiom so very nearly that of the romantics, would have dared those final consecutive octaves?

His sense of drama, which finds full expression in his operas, and in the masque, *Job*, found its way into church music not only in *Sancta Civitas* and *Dona nobis Pacem*, but in his two last church-pieces, *Hodie*

Ex.9

(1954), a Christmas cantata for three soloists, chorus and orchestra, and in the naïvely-titled *A Vision of Aeroplanes*, (1956), a motet for choir and organ with words from Ezekiel 1. On the whole it was not given to Vaughan Williams to make much dissent against the tradition that church music should move in grand, spacious and dignified measures— that is Britten's special contribution: but in the "Alleluia—Gloria" from *Hodie* there is a strong sense of the rustic and informal, and in such passages one sees where Britten gathered some of his inspirations: (Example 9)

A Vision of Aeroplanes is something of a *tour de force*: what aeroplanes have to do with it is not, and does not need to be, very clear. It is a typically violent yet abased setting of the most mysterious chapter in the Old Testament.

All this we write only to remind the reader of the great breadth of this composer's musical activity, even within our limited field. From the hymn tune (we shall say more of this at a later stage) to the large-scale cantata, he manifested an exact sense of what the occasion required: and in his *Mass in G minor* (1923) he equally showed an exact sense of what the liturgy required. He wrote enough music, lived long enough, and made a deep enough impression on the public consciousness through the manifold works of his genius (at the end of his life he became, and enjoyed being, one of the finest practitioners of the art of film-music) to ensure that his musical Dissent should be written firmly into the continuing musical tradition of the country.

Without the popularising genius of Vaughan Williams, without his constant encouragement and admiration, perhaps Holst would never have stood a chance. Holst's retiring nature, his aversion from the vulgar, his contentment in the kind of humble service of music that made him teach—successfully—a Byrd Mass to soldiers fighting at Gallipoli, made Holst a poor candidate in the musical rat-race. But the integrity of his music is for this very reason probably purer than that of Vaughan Williams. Apart from *The Planets*, he is still relatively little known and played. He shared with "V-W" an alert, questioning attitude to things religious, and a taste for the mysterious. His *Hymn of Jesus* (Op. 37), a work full of music of monumental power, is a setting of some of the most perverse literature that ever attempted to shelter under the church's wing—but it was that "off-beatness" that attracted him far more than the canonical literature of the Bible would have done. One of his most charming small works is his setting of an old Cornish carol, "Tomorrow shall be my dancing day"—his title comes from its refrain, *This have I done for my true love*. These words are now better known than they were in his time, because they are in the *Oxford Book of Carols*; but it was possible in the thirties for an Anglican vicar to be reprimanded by his bishop for displaying its words in his church. Its words were thought of as at best marginally Christian in that generation: it needed a broadening of Christian sympathies to receive them back into the canon of sacred song. It was this predilection for something less pedestrian and more spiritually demanding than the Christianity he was familiar with that led Holst to write little that can be called church music. But his contributions in hymnody to a book, *Songs of Praise*, which at the time of its publication was "off-beat" enough to appeal to him were, as will be shown, highly characteristic and notable. We shall not attempt to say the same for his well-known tune to the late nineteenth century Christmas song, "In the bleak midwinter", but we can say that, and much more, of his music to the Mystery Play, *The Coming of Christ*, first performed in 1928 in Canterbury Cathedral. He knew nothing whatever about "popularity", neither seeking it nor enjoying it. But in his relentless pursuit of the ideal of clear texture in music, of economy in resources even in his biggest scores, and especially in what he did through teaching, lecturing, and example, he was with "V-W" one of the pioneers of the new English music.

2

The Conservative Craftsmen

Not everybody, of course, at the time felt that Vaughan Williams and Holst had the last word in the new argument. Many were still prepared to support the German–English school of church music writing: and those who did so did it with remarkable skill.

It is, indeed, one of the many curiosities of this period that whereas in the nineteenth century German–English music was very clearly "minor" music-making (whom have we? Sterndale Bennett—S. S. Wesley—Sullivan: Sullivan wrote excellent Schubert, but did the others, and those behind them in the procession, write much beyond moderate Weber?)—in the twentieth century we have a number of musicians who wrote really fine music in the wholly conventional Bonn-Vienna style. Without any doubt the major German influence behind all the successors of Parry and Stanford was Brahms. Beethoven had laid traps for minor composers into which they had all fallen ignominiously, probably through making the elementary error that the greatness of Beethoven was in grandeur of diction. In church music the romantics had little to offer—except where Sullivan and one or two others hopefully tried to ecclesiasticise Schubert. But Brahms was accepted and fashionable during the formative years of Walford Davies, Harwood, Somervell, Charles Wood and Bairstow, and Parry himself—for example, in *I was glad* (1901), the finest piece of purely ceremonial church music of that generation—owed plenty to him.

These were all craftsmen of a more considerable sort then their immediate predecessors. Walford Davies was a teacher rather than a composer, and in his fairly small output of original church music shows a curious and not very well integrated combination of Brahms and new-found plainsong. To some extent the same is true of Harwood, who went on publishing until nearly the end of a very long life, but who was at his best when, too rarely, he found a Brahmsian energy, as in the anthem, "O how glorious", a relatively early work.

Arthur Somervell, a contemporary of Harwood, wrote a certain amount of church music again in a conventional style, of which the two longest works are *The Passion of Christ* (1924) and *Christmas* (1926).

In the *Passion* his master, in form and occasionally in content (as in the aria "My Lord and Master", pp. 35 ff) is Bach; indeed, his intention clearly was to write a simple cantata that church choirs could perform when they felt that the Bach Passions were too difficult, and Stainer's *Crucifixion* too sentimental, for their situation. In this there is much pleasant music, and some that is dramatic: and the whole ends with a hymn tune which has achieved a certain popularity in its own right (CHORUS ANGELORUM, to "Praise to the Holiest", which is in the Revised Edition of *Hymns Ancient and Modern*). The *Christmas* cantata is less successful: Somervell was not able to repeat the well-proportioned simplicity of the earlier work, and the result is somewhat heavily platitudinous. That is exactly the difficulty which these Georgian composers were up against: to write what was original, even English, in the idiom which had been so thoroughly worked over by so many secular masters: platitude was their constant enemy.

Charles Wood (born 1866) had more stamina and staying-power than any of these. He is worthy to set alongside Parry. His output was almost entirely church music, and his contribution to the literature in the first quarter of the century was excellent, generous and timely. He had, like Parry, a good eye for a suggestive text—Biblical or extra-Biblical—and a great sense of dignity. He was not a rhythmical experimenter, even to the extent that Walford Davies was, but his gift of melody and sonorous harmony, of sensing what would sound well in an English cathedral, and of underlaying these with an unerring traditional craftsmanship, ensured that he would find a warm welcome wherever a music was looked for that would say the familiar things with decorum and cogency. Moreover, it must be remembered, while we are considering the more conservative tradition of modern English church music, that these musical appointments which are now not only taken for granted in a cathedral foundation but are regarded by some as the centre of an over-cautious musical habit, were in the year of Charles Wood's birth (1866) hardly in existence, and in the years of his earlier maturity far from common. In the middle years of the nineteenth century it was still something unusual for a cathedral to boast an organ which had a full pedal-board: nowadays we can count on three or four manuals, pedals, and sixty speaking stops. In that period, again, the choir may well have been such as a decent parish church today would regard as beneath its notice. It was the achievement of the age in which Parry was a young man and Wood a boy, that conditions of this sort were improved, and church music taken seriously for the first time for at least a century.

C

Therefore there was a market in the churches, and especially the cathedrals, for music of exactly Wood's kind—church music that used these new resources and helped to build up a tradition of craftsmanship that revolutionised the praise-lists of the cathedrals between 1895 and 1930. This, for example from the opening of Wood's "O Thou the central Orb" (1915) is still one of the authentic "cathedral sounds" that remain in the memory of anybody who has attended evensong regularly:

Ex. 10

but when it was written it stood against the background of the theatrical trivialities of Barnby and Sullivan.

One of Wood's most remarkable contributions to church music is

the *St. Mark Passion* (1921). This is based on an ancient form of devotion
in which the reading of the Gospel is illuminated by responsive hymns.
The medieval service of "Tenebrae" is the origin of this device of
reading large portions of Scripture and interspersing choral responses.
The Service of Lessons and Carols, now familiar at Christmas time and
other seasons, is, of course, a modern development of the same form.
Wood's *Passion* differs from those of Bach and his imitators in containing no arias at all. It goes back rather to the Passion music of
Byrd and his school in confining itself to the narration and choral
singing of the Gospel. It is a work whose devotion shines through
every bar; the hymns are chosen with a scholarly sense of fitness, and
the Gospel narrative is introduced and concluded with the plainsong
Pange lingua. All the music is modest and (especially for this composer)
undemonstrative, but it increases in austerity of texture as it approaches
the climax of the Passion-story. When seen in its historical context it
is a work beyond all praise.

Wood also made many contributions in the "hymn-anthem" form
which will be dealt with in their place, and his settings of the service
canticles are still in regular and much-appreciated use. He is the only
composer of any eminence to have made a cathedral setting of the
metrical version of the Evening Canticles.

Perhaps the greatest of all the Brahmsians, however, was Sir Edward
Bairstow—that formidable administrator and highly gifted organist of
York Minster. Bairstow again gave the greater part of his attention to
church music. He was the archetypal English *Kapellmeister*, and he
could be remarkably dull and pedantic; but when imagination took a
hand, he could achieve real greatness.

The influence of Brahms is evident on nearly every page of what he
wrote. Whence else comes such a phrase as this, from his Mass in D?

Ex.11

He has a setting of "Though I speak with the tongues of men" (1934), from I Corinthians 13, which is reminiscent of the fourth of Brahms's *Serious Songs* (Op. 121), not only in its opening phrase—

Ex. 12

but also in that it makes almost exactly the same selection of verses, omitting the passage beginning "Charity suffereth long and is kind", that Brahms made.

He was another master of the "big cathedral" style, as his environment obliged him to be. He had greater respect for orthodox 18th–19th century music than for music of the older sort: so that when he wrote his dramatic setting of "Blessed city, heavenly Salem", the plainsong tune URBS BEATA

Ex. 13

comes out like this:

but the whole piece is a series of variations on the tune such as Brahms might have written, leaving no melodic suggestion unexplored and no opportunity of dramatic word-painting untaken. Again, his short Introit, "Let all mortal flesh keep silence" shows how far his imagination could reach into a text:

John Ireland, one of the most attractive of English minor composers (thus to be called because in the end his output was not large, and his style remained somewhat eclectic) made a few contributions to English church music, including a well known *Service in F* and an anthem, "Greater love hath no man than this". Ireland, unlike Bairstow and Wood, was an unwilling organist, who abandoned the loft as soon as he found more congenial work. His greatest gift was in song-writing, but in secular music he achieved one piano concerto and a good deal of choral music, including *These Things shall be*, a cantata with humanist-religious overtones. The music of this is rather like the "unreformed" Vaughan Williams of *Towards the Unknown Region* (1909)—bold, tuneful, and thoroughly romantic.

In "Greater love hath no man" (1912) he produced what was, for the period, an advanced and resourceful piece of church music. Its words are Biblical, but the collocation of texts from the Song of Solomon, St. John's Gospel, and First Peter is in itself interesting and, in public worship, edifying. Once again, it is the old idiom, but applied with professional skill, a sense of occasion, and the song-writer's dramatic touch. Other works of his will be found in carol-books and hymn books, and will be discussed later.

All these composers are men who could have written, and in some cases did write, music before 1900, but whose major output contributes to the early twentieth century. All are disciples of orthodoxy, though each has his original touch that makes his work still worth performing. What is to be primarily observed is this: that although this music is almost entirely derivative, music of this standard was new to the English Church at the time of its composition—at any rate in the period 1900–25. What these composers dissented against was the never-lessness of the late Victorians. They did not invent a new speech, but they spoke the old speech with an air which their predecessors could not affect. Romanticism lingered long before it gave of its best to English church music; at the time when it was producing masterpieces in continental secular music, it was producing only pale and sentimental and largely ineffective gestures in English music, sacred or secular. Bairstow was the last of the great romantics of the English organ loft, and the fairly short procession in which he is the last and most effective filled a gap in our church music by showing how intrinsically *well* the familiar speech could be spoken. If it is too much to say that they bridged the gulf between Vaughan Williams and Stanford, at least they provided transport that took the hearers some distance towards the further shore. For they re-established the church musician as a musician seriously to be reckoned with.

This is the kind of thing we mean. In the later years of the Second World War—it may have been about 1943—a film was released from Ealing Studios called "A Canterbury Tale". This romantic and domestic comedy concerned the realisation of the aspirations of two or three characters, set against the resistance of a Canterbury magistrate towards some of the consequences of wartime living (which issued in eccentric and anti-social acts that had to be exposed). One of the aspirants was a soldier waiting for embarkation. Towards the end of the film it emerged that he was an organist. The climax of the plot was set in Canterbury Cathedral, where the whole detachment of soldiers was to attend an embarkation service. Just before the service, the soldier was looking round the cathedral, and found himself in the path of the organist, making his way to the organ loft. The organist, a bent old gentleman of absent-minded air and surely some seventy years, dropped a piece of music, in picking up which the soldier-organist engaged him in conversation. The following dialogue ensued (approximately):

ORGANIST: Ha! so you're an organist? How much do they pay you, hey?
SOLDIER: Thirty a week.
ORGANIST: Hum! Not bad. When I was a boy I thought myself lucky to get twenty-two shillings a week . . .

And the next thing one saw was the soldier sitting at the console setting the stops for "Onward, Christian soldiers".

The point is this. In 1943 in the public mind a cathedral organist was an old gentleman who had not the education or general *savoir-faire* to know that a cinema organist could raise £30 a week in the thirties, and who thought that rates of pay even in the church had not altered in fifty years. (It is not to the point here to elaborate on the point that they had not altered very dramatically in that period.) Moreover, the organist of Canterbury Cathedral at the time was Mr. (now Dr.) Gerald Knight; his age was, in 1943, thirty-five and he was serving in the Air Force. Many distinguished organists were—and in responsible ranks (Sir William McKie, Dr. Dykes Bower and the late Dr. Boris Ord of King's College were among them). The film-producing profession, reflecting public opinion, still thought cathedral organists were elderly and absent-minded hacks. To some extent, in 1900, they were. The remarkable cultural change in this profession—which has not been matched by comparable increases in reward—is one of the sociological changes in the English Church that the twentieth century has brought: and this is due to two major forces—the foundation and continuing work of the Royal College of Organists, and the leadership of these craftsman-composers none of whom the secular musical world could ignore.

3

The Sons of the Craftsmen

TWO streams, then, were running in English music in the first quarter of the century. During the second quarter there are regions in which they converge, and others in which they run apart. It will be convenient here to follow on our discussion of the great "Georgians" by mentioning certain composers whose work in the following generation has chiefly followed the romantic and orthodox path.

Sir Sydney Nicholson's chief contribution to church music was in hymnody (see below p. 99). He wrote one Evening Service, in the unusual key, for such compositions, of D flat, which is still in frequent use; but apart from hymns, carols and short anthems he will be chiefly remembered for his foundation of the School of English Church Music in 1927—which is now the Royal School of Church Music, and the centre of musical culture and training for the Anglican Communion. At the time when he founded it he was organist of Westminster Abbey. Its influence now extends through all Anglican dioceses all over the world; it had had much influence on the latest Archbishops' Committee's Report (1951) on Church Music, and on the music of the Revised Edition (1950) of *Hymns Ancient and Modern*. By the activities of local chapters and diocesan level, and of commissioners who spend much time in teaching tours among parish church choirs, it has done more than any other single agency to establish and give continuity to the ideals of revival which Parry and Walford Davies and the other pioneers stood for.

As a composer, Nicholson used a conservative idiom, with occasional rhythmic irregularities that suggest the style of Walford Davies, but without any notable harmonic divergences from the beaten track.

The most prolific composer in the traditional style born between 1880 and 1900 is undoubtedly Sir William Harris, who first appears in English church music as one of those who contributed harmonisations to the *English Hymnal* (1906) but who in the second quarter of the century sent a steady stream of music into the church's libraries. Most of his best work is in the shorter forms, although he has written for chorus and orchestra. Broad melody and rich harmony are much to be found in his work. *Praise the Lord*, an extended setting of Psalm 103 for eight-part unaccompanied choir (1938), exhibits many of his best, and perhaps also his weakest points. This is a massive piece of choral writing, owing much to Parry in its use of enharmonic modulations, but producing an episodic and disjointed effect through its constant use of very brief subjects, and its insistence on a somewhat *Kappelmeister*-ish pedantry in their elaboration. The weakness in post-Parry church music is (as later composers have demonstrated by contrast) the tendency to crowd the score. Sir William has not always avoided this: and the temptation to make full use of the resources of such a musical establishment as that at St. George's Windsor are, of course, very strong.

In music of this kind a rhythmic energy is all-important; in meditative moods it can become thick and immobile. "Be strong in the Lord" (1948), an anthem for St. George's day, is full of fine music, largely homophonic, and using four parts (sometimes divided into eight) and organ, with plenty of incidental key-colour. "From a heart made whole" (1947) is a study in enharmonic modulation and effective block-chord writing for eight unaccompanied parts. A similar "Songs of Farewell" style is in "Love of love and light of light" (1934). On the other hand, the "big tune" technique with massive unison effects comes off very well in *Laudamus* (1945) an anthem celebrating victory in the 1939–45 War, in a unison setting of the poem "Vox Ultima Crucis", beginning "Tarry no longer" (1937), and in "The Lord my pasture shall prepare" (1944). In some of his latest work he adopts a less crowded style, as in the anthem "Lord of the worlds above" (1961), written for a parish church, which keeps to four undivided parts throughout, and makes much use of excellent orthodox counterpoint. His harmonies often evince an impatience with orthodox progressions, which in his best moments produces an effect of austere and slightly acid comment. The following passage from "O joyful light" (1939), an unaccompanied anthem which also makes effective use of speech-rhythm and irregular bars, is characteristic: (Example 16)

A first-class workman, W. H. Harris has never turned out anything shoddy or cheap: he is a central figure in that rehabilitation of orthodox cathedral music which the first half of our century has seen.

Harold Darke is another composer of this age who, at the time of writing, must be called a veteran. It is possible that his first published work is a hymn tune in the now obscure hymnal, *Worship Song*, whose publication fell in his eighteenth year (1905). Darke has been composing

Ex.16

steadily for over fifty years, and in his work there is a most notable sense of development. In the early days he was as romantic as any—as in his well-known setting (1911) of the carol, "In the bleak midwinter", which has, of course, much less innocence than Holst's. By 1929 he was writing such music as we hear in "Even such is time"—an unaccompanied 4-part anthem in the Parry-Harris style, including in its first phrase a consecutive fifth of which Vaughan Williams would no doubt have approved.

Ex.17

His contribution to the music at the Dedication of Coventry Cathedral (1962) included this most imaginative phrase to the first verse of Psalm 84 at the opening of the Communion service: (Example 18)

His working life has been spent, since 1916, at St. Michael's Church, Cornhill, London, whose music he raised to, and has maintained at, a cathedral standard. His contribution to church music has been considerable and continuous.

How amiable are thy dwell-ings, thou Lord of Hosts. My soul hath a de-sire and long-ing to en-ter in to the courts of the Lord, the courts of the Lord.

One of the more original minds in the business, again in a cathedral organist, has been that of Heathcote Statham, since 1928 organist at Norwich Cathedral. His style, in the modest output that he has given for church use, is lighter and more astringent than that of the post-Parry composers normally is. There is more here of Vaughan Williams, even occasionally a touch of Britten. His *Benedicite in G* (1957) and *Te Deum in F* (1956) are both remarkable for their clear scoring and free-ranging melody, and another excellent example is "Ye that know the Lord is gracious" (1960). His contributions to organ music and hymnody, as we shall see, are far from negligible.

Also from the classic organ-lofts has come church music from Sir Thomas Armstrong, formerly of Christ Church, Oxford, H. K. Andrews, formerly organist at New College, Oxford, Herbert Sumsion of Gloucester, and George Oldroyd. All these have written in a modern-traditional style, with judicious care rather than with prolixity. Oldroyd made a special contribution in writing anthems in a delicately archaistic style that owed much to a great love of plainsong. Sydney Campbell (Ely, Southwark, Canterbury and St. George's,

Windsor) has written music whose idiom is considerably more advanced, and clearly receives the orthodox tradition through such composers as Walton. Sir Ernest Bullock's contribution, very much of the older style, largely recalls his tenure of the organ-loft at Westminster Abbey.

These all come from our eminent organ-lofts and all from the Church of England. The most distinguished and prolific composer from English Dissent is Eric Thiman, whose work has been appearing with great regularity since about 1925. Dr. Thiman is, indeed, one of the few church musicians of national standing who has spent the whole of his working life in one denomination—the Congregational churches. He has produced several works of cantata-length, of which the best known are *The Last Supper* and *The Temptation of Christ* (1930); but for the better part of forty years he has regularly published anthems. His style is conservative: but it has been largely dictated by the modest —and indeed diminishing—musical resources of the nonconformist churches; and it is there that his work is chiefly heard.

Thiman in his day has had to be the Bairstow and the W. H. Harris of nonconformity. When he was young, the standard of nonconformist church music in Britain was, one cannot possibly deny, low and getting lower. The tradition of hearty singing, of congregational singing of anthems, of high-minded reformed piety which had little time or money to spare for such details as music because it wanted it all for the intellectual cult of sermons and the building of impressive places of worship, ensured that its aesthetic taste would be not so much conservative as obstinately reactionary. In consequence, the musical diet of nonconformity up to about 1940 was largely made up of scraps discarded from the Anglican table. Hymns and anthems which had been born, been used for a season, and then been ejected from the Anglican churches were hospitably received and sedulously kept alive in nonconformity. Stainer's *Crucifixion* is the most outstanding example; but the contents of the Dissenting hymn books of the period 1900–40 tell the same tale. Music that was easy to sing and easy to listen to, and gave quick returns in aesthetic amusement, made the required modesty of demand on attention which Dissent hoped to preserve for higher things.

Thiman's answer to this was to provide music which was still easy to sing and listen to, but which stood much higher in integrity of melody, harmony and texture than did the minor Victorians. One of his earliest anthems, and one of his most enduringly successful, is "Sing Alleluia forth in duteous praise" (1925). It is simply a good tune—

which shows that Dr. Thiman is of the Parry–Dyson tradition—
appearing in four different forms—unison, S.A.T.B., sopranos alone,
and unison, with varied organ accompaniment. There is not much to
learn, and the tune is catchy and memorable. At the time this was a real
gesture—half-way, as it were, between anthem and hymn. The
attempt of the Victorians to write elegant four-part harmony throughout an anthem, and to write a continuous setting which often they
had not the intellectual stamina to carry through without distressing
gaps in the musical argument, is replaced by a much more modest
aim—to provide music that is really easy, and also sound in argument
and musical logic.

Thiman's music is, then, *Gebrauchs* in the best sense—written with
the specific demands of a situation in mind. It is not a discipline which
permits of much variety of style: but Thiman has been imitated by
many other composers who have done the work less effectively. It
is the restriction on style that this manner of writing imposes, along
with his very large output in the anthem-form, that has caused Thiman
to receive a press in reviews that is not always enthusiastic in praise.
There is, it must be admitted, an almost obstinate lack of surprise in
his music. But fairness demands an historical recognition that to have
forced the pace on the entrenched reactionism of English nonconformity
of 1925 would have been to invite complete rejection. Dissent was at
that time simply not available to anybody who would speak strongly
to it about its music. What has happened—and in his own denomination this is due to such as Thiman—is the gradual overturning of a
good many accepted standards. Thiman's technique was not aggression
but infiltration. What is more, if there is now in nonconformity a
much more radical criticism of music, which may cause an east wind
to blow that withers some of the less robust branches of the Thiman
tree, Thiman's place in history is that he made this possible.

His idom is always completely unaffected and—except in a tendency
to finish a cheerful anthem with a somewhat vulgar organ-flourish—
urbane. His vocabulary is that of the romantics, but he always handles
it with the kind of unobtrusive skill that makes for grateful singing,
as in this passage from his anthem, "The Pilgrim's Prayer" (1951):
(Example 19)

Richard Aldridge, a somewhat younger composer, coming from
the same denomination, has produced some attractive short anthems.
W. S. Lloyd Webber, although coming from an Anglican background,
is, at the time of writing—and at the time when the majority of his
compositions have appeared—organist of the Central Hall (Methodist),

Ex.19

Westminster. His idiom is not unlike that of Thiman—conservative, romantic, but in places having a touch of richness, the merest touch also of modalised Brahms, that one does not find in Thiman. Among his longer works are *The Wondrous Cross* and *The Saviour*, a Passiontide cantata deliberately written (to quote its publisher) "in the tradition of Stainer's *Crucifixion*", to provide for choirs who could sing that work, but wanted a change for something no more difficult but somewhat less dated. Once again, we have here a musician battling with the entrenched philistinism of Dissent. It is, on the whole, in his organ music that Mr. Lloyd-Webber has done himself the best justice.

Methodism has produced a number of indigenous musicians who have done their best work as instructors rather than as composers. The late Frederick Luke Wiseman (1858–1945), a distinguished Methodist minister, did much pioneer work in his denomination's music. In the latter generation Francis B. Westbrook, a Methodist minister who holds both the D.Mus. of London and the Fellowship of the Royal College of Organists, has gathered round him a group of enthusiasts who in the Methodist Music Society have done much to raise standards. George F. Brockless, formerly organist at the Central Hall, Westminster, produced a certain amount of music and much musicianship, and his son, Brian Brockless is appearing as an organ composer in an advanced idiom. Similarly the Baptists have experienced a revival of musical consciousness, which is most greatly to be seen in their 1962 *Baptist Church Hymnal*. They have formed a music society. Since 1951 the Congregationalists have had a Guild of Organists and Choirmasters, and for a longer period the Presbyterian Church of England has had its Guild of Organists. The work of these groups is practical rather than in the field of composition, and they have not thrown up much music of an inventive kind. But what was most necessary they have all been doing: laying foundations upon which in another generation original work may be built up. If this book is rewritten in 1985, it may well contain several outstanding names of musicians in English Dissent.

A good deal of the revival of musical consciousness in the church during the first half of this century has been achieved through the lively musical education that children have received in the schools and that the general public has received through broadcasting. On the whole this again has been a matter of consolidating a decent conservative heritage rather than experimenting in new forms (although in these last years Peter Maxwell Davies has been producing some very remarkable contemporary music from an environment which until lately was a scholastic one).

The English Public Schools have long had, and have more recently made use of, an unrivalled opportunity for education in church music. The status of the Public School Director of Music has greatly advanced during the present century, and much excellent music has come into general use from this background. The three editions of the *Public School Hymn Book* (1903, 1919, 1949) show a fairly conservative tradition in music, but, within that tradition, laudable integrity. A tendency to sentimentality is not unexpected in this environment, and the broad unison effect and warm harmony of the Parry tradition is always acceptable in a large congregation of boys.

One of the earliest Public School composers to enter the choral field was Alexander Brent Smith (Lancing), who wrote perhaps five times as much music for informal use as found its way into print, but who published one or two anthems, inluding "My soul, there is a country" (1920), and an extended *Elegy*, written for the Three Choirs' Festival in 1939, but not performed until that Festival, cancelled in 1939, was reopened in 1945. He was a singular combination of Elgar, in his ceremonious music, with Sullivan, in his more informal moments: and if Elgar, then of course, Brahms as well. His remarkable gift for melody, which made him an excellent "Public School" musician, is exemplified in this quotation from the *Elegy*: (Example 20)

More prolific is the genius of C. S. Lang (Christ's Hospital) who has written many anthems and services, organ works, and a few larger-scale works for the church. A tendency to mannerism is noticeable in his more rhetorical passages, and his hymn tunes (of which the 1949 *Public School Hymn Book* contains a large number) are positively disfigured by emotional over-writing: but more often his music is imaginative and excellently proportioned.

W. K. Stanton, who was not only a Public School musician (Wellington), but also served on the B.B.C. and later became Professor of Music at Bristol University, is a more fastidious and astringent composer. He could affect the popular idiom in such simple works as "Christ is the world's true light" (1943), but his setting of the whole of Psalm 137, "By the waters of Babylon" (1940) is far more characteristic. He reacts radically against the more sentimental "public school" tradition (see below, p. 104 for a reference to him as the composer of one of the most truculent hymn tunes in existence).

Leonard J. Blake (Malvern) is a very good example of the unpretentious "working musician" whose services have steadily preserved the standard of public school music. He does not claim to be an original composer: but he writes what a large congregation of boys, supported by a decent choir, can easily and pleasurably sing, and his aim has been rather to fill obvious gaps in school-literature than to make a name as an inventive composer. This modest educationism is a force in contemporary church music whose unobtrusiveness must not cause it to be neglected.

Sir George Dyson (formerly of Winchester College) has written much choral music for the church, as well as for secular use. He is another master of Edwardian full-blooded melody, and his unison effects are always broad and easy on both voice and ear—as in "Praise" (1919), "Morning and Evening" (1933), and "I will worship" (1954).

Ex.20

"Hail, universal Lord" (1958) is as satisfying a "period piece" in this style as anybody could wish for: resolutely in the key of G major, it provides a continuous argument, beginning with the commanding phrase (Example 21) and going on through sixteen pages of vocal score without coming to a single perfect cadence in the home key, and reaching its home-cadence, by the plagal route, only in its very last

D

Ex.21

few bars. Dyson's music excels in this kind of long-paragraphed diction, and it was, of course, the peculiar virtue of Brahmsian music to do just this. Did not Brahms himself write some of the longest "tunes" in the literature (excelled only by Bach)? Later music is given to epigram, piercing poetry, colourful dashes of impressionism, or, in its extreme forms, a new kind of diagrammatic logic, but not the measured, balanced paragraphing of the earlier music. Without taut argument, the earlier music becomes windy and pretentious, but with it, it shows its finest qualities, and Dyson was a master of these. In the church style he wrote three long works, *The Canterbury Pilgrims* (1930), *St. John's Voyage to Melita* (1933) and *Nebuchadnezzar* (1935). Impatience with long works in this orotund style is now fashionable; but the craftsmanship is still to be respected, and the composer who could, in ninety seconds of music, express so great a sense of spaciousness as Dyson does in the *Confortare* in the 1953 Coronation service, is a composer whom it is unwise to treat lightly.

Of musical educationists the two best known in their generation were Martin and Geoffrey Shaw. As instructors and inspectors in English day-schools they did much to raise standards of appreciation and musicianship. Both had a command of melody which, with the occasional harmonic touch that showed their admiration for Vaughan Williams, caught the imagination of young people. Martin, the elder, lived longer and wrote more.

Much of this was designed for the ordinary parish church or the school choir, of limited resources. He wrote a good deal of parish-liturgical music, and also settings of prayers that would amplify this, or make a kind of liturgical setting possible within the framework of a school-assembly. "Go forth into the world in peace" (1927) and "Lord, make us instruments of thy peace" (1957) are examples. "With a voice of singing" (1923) and "Christ is our corner-stone" (1958) are typical examples of his work for choirs—diatonic, upstanding, no nonsense stuff, deliberately contrived to provide an unsubtle substitute for Victorian sentiment. Geoffrey took the same line: his best known choral piece is probably "Worship" (1923)—a broad tune to broad words ("O brother man, fold to thy heart thy brother")—warm-hearted enough to include an unintended quotation from the prologue to *Pagliacci*. (Example 22)

If there is something transitory and occasionally—to a modern ear—maddening in the music of the Shaws for church use, it is the result of their passionate educationism. It shows through nowadays: the music

Ex. 22

To WORSHIP   RIGHT-LY   IS   TO   LOVE   EACH   OTH-ER

is rather obviously "worthy", and designed to "improve", as well as to amuse, the singer: one turns with relief to such exquisite things in secular music as Martin Shaw's "Song of the Palanquin-Bearers", where he seems to shake off the cares of pedagogy and write his own music.

The historic place of Martin and Geoffrey Shaw in English music is comparable to that which we assigned to Thiman (p. 44) in the music of nonconformity. They have proved to be the kind of musicians who have made themselves expendable. If we now know that there is more in church music than a clean line and a good bass, it was the Shaws who largely taught us that we do at least need that. Martin Shaw wrote in 1923 a small book entitled *The Principles of Church Music Composition*, which was a manifesto against the Victorian techniques. It contains all manner of judgments which would now be regarded as over-cautious or even misconceived: and yet it needed to be written then. If one is primarily a teacher, or an improver, or a cleaner-out of overstocked music-warehouses, something in creative capacity must be allowed to lapse. The honour of the Shaws is that they made the world safe for music to sail on past them, and for critics to arise in a new generation who would have little to say in their personal praise.

PART TWO

ENLARGING THE WEST DOOR

David went and brought up the ark of God from the house of Obed-Edom into the city of David with gladness. And it was so, that when they that bore the ark of the Lord had gone six paces, he sacrificed oxen and fatlings. So David and all the house of Israel brought up the ark of the Lord with shouting, and with the sound of the trumpet.

And as the ark of the Lord came into the city of David, Michal, Saul's daughter, looked through a window, and saw King David dancing before the Lord: and she despised him in her heart.

Then David returned to bless his household. And Michal, the daughter of Saul, came out to meet David, and said, "How glorious was the king of Israel today, who uncovered himself today in the eyes of the handmaids of his servants, as one of the vain fellows shamelessly uncovereth himself!" And David said unto Michal, "It was before the Lord, which chose me before thy father, and before all his house, to appoint me ruler over the people of the Lord; therefore will I play before the Lord."

II Samuel 6. 12, 16, 20-1.

This story of David's ecstasy, and of his wife's contempt of his departing so far from religious decorum, was read in Coventry Cathedral at the Service of the Arts held a fortnight after the consecration of the new building (8th June, 1962).

Immediately after the reading of these words, a ballet was danced in the cathedral.

4

Masters of Ceremonies

THE composers mentioned in the last chapter were primarily church musicians who saw their task in terms of writing music that spoke soundly in a conservative idiom. Between these and the composers who are exploring the possibilities of the most comtemporary developments in music thare is a large group whose church music forms a bridge between the conservative and the *avant-garde*. We shall resist the temptation to call them the Liberals.

Within this large group there are two sub-groups: one is made up of those composers whose chief work, or a substantial part of whose work, was outside church music but who brought to the church a depth of musical experience and a breadth of invention which was the result of these wider activities; some of these have been composers purely, some of them principally teachers, and not a few combined both activities. The other group contains those who have chiefly written church music but have written it as members of a new generation moving towards the advanced style.

Perhaps the central figure, though not quite the senior, and not the most eminent outside church music, in the first group is Herbert Howells. Dr. Howells has combined a lifetime of teaching at the Royal College of Music and the University of London with a steady, though modest, output of composition, much but not all of which has been for the Church.

Howells stands centrally, and yet he is quite unclassifiable. He is one of those composers whose idiom is immediately recognisable from any couple of bars of his music: yet it has been a developing idiom, not a static one. There is in it always a strong dash of the romantic. He has always been a composer for whom beauty of sound is music's first requirement. In this he is the reverse of *avant-garde*, for *avant-garde* (as we shall see) does not see beauty as something contrived by the composer but as something, like Plato's "pleasure", supervening when idea becomes action. If the result of pure logic is judged beautiful, it is well: but for such a composer the deliberate contrivance of beauty is an assumption that a composer is forbidden to take on himself.

Howells's music is never anything but beautiful; he was a pupil of Stanford, and has never had anything but admiration for the best of the modern conservatives. Yet at its best his music has a strange astringency which comes from the Vaughan Williams stream; for his admiration for Vaughan Williams (and Vaughan Williams's for him) was equal to his admiration for Stanford. (Vaughan Williams wrote in a dedicatory note to his *Hodie*; that he had found, and was pleased to find, that he had "cribbed a phrase" in it from Howells's *Hymnus Paradisi*).

And thus to tap the Vaughan Williams stream implies that Howells is an admirer above all of the gentle and courtly musical idiom of the Tudors. This is where one needs to start when evaluating his music. The essence of his instrumental music—especially his organ music—is in the music of the harpsichord and clavichord; not only in its modality and its cultivation of courtly dance-rhythms but also in its actual technique. Take for example his six organ pieces, written between

1940 and 1945 and published as a set, containing two *Sarabandes*, a *Prelude Sine Nomine*, *Master Tallis's Testament*, *Fugue*, *Chorale and Variation*, and *Paean*. In these, *Master Tallis* is pure clavichord; the *Sarabandes* evoke all the courtesy of aristocratic early secular music in their rhythm. And the clusters of notes, high and deep, that one often finds in these pieces suggest at once the clear voice of the old keyboard insruments rather than the rich tone of the piano: and indeed they call for judicious organ registration. Two examples will show what we mean, first the development of the cadence in *Master Tallis* between the theme and the first variation (Example 23) and then in the development of the opening theme of the *Sarabande for the Morning of Easter* at the recapitulation:

Ex. 24 A

Ex. 24 B

But one has only to hear or play these pieces to recognise that this is no mere "cool antiquarianism". *Master Tallis* is a piece indeed for a hot summer's day; but the *Sarabande in Modo Elegiaco* is a most sinister, dark and strange piece, evocative of sombre ideas all through: harmonically knotted and ruthless in rhythm, it is one of his most emotionally demanding compositions. He is using ancient language with a modern accent to say contemporary things that make harsh hearing: yet never without a central poise of reason and beauty.

These are works of his maturity. In earlier organ works, notably the three *Rhapsodies*, Op. 17 (1938–39), he affected a more flamboyant style, and in these there is a tendency for the note-clusters to become thick and hard on the ear. This is partly because they do not show the sheer poise of modesty that his later works master. His *Psalm-Preludes*. which appeared in two sets, the first (composed 1915) in 1921, the second (1938–39) in 1940, show a similar development away from the experimental towards the assured; and a much later organ piece, *Siciliano for a High Ceremony* (1953–57) continues the development, past the 1940–45 set, towards a style of greater austerity without loss of the essential and characteristic warmth.

His vocal compositions for the church amount now to a long series of anthems, service-settings and cantatas. Among the earlier anthems, " My eyes for beauty pine" (1925–28) is a good example of his capacity for writing a unison tune in the Vaughan Williams tradition, and "When first thine Eies unveil" from *Three Motets* (1925–27: the composer gives the day before that of "My eyes" as the date of composition) is a gentle part song full of harmonic invention, with, towards the end, a remarkable (and in his music quite unusual) tonic pedal with which extends over eight bars, and then with a few bars interruption, continues to the end—but at the last moment becomes a mediant pedal in the true key of the piece (tonic C becoming pedal mediant of A minor). This is not the kind of device to which in his later years he has given much attention: there is always a very firm and unambiguous sense of key that binds together his sublest and remotest harmonic deviations. The *Four Anthems* of 1941–43, three composed in three January days, the fourth on Easter Day, are perhaps his most frequently heard church music: among them are "O pray for the peace of Jerusalem" and "Like as the hart", and the last is the spirited "Let God arise".

Since the Second World War, Howells has written a set of Cathedral services which are distinguished by special dedications to particular choirs. The earliest of these is the *Collegium Regale* setting of the Evening Canticles, written for King's College, Cambridge (1947). There have followed similar settings for Worcester (1953), St. Paul's, London (1954), Westminster Abbey (1956) and St. John's College, Cambridge (1958); for Christ Church, Oxford, he composed a Communion setting, *Missa Aedis Christi* (1961). The acoustic, the geographical setting, and the special choral traditions of the cathedrals and college chapels have influenced his approach to the settings in each case, but throughout the series runs a single devotional purpose. The Magnificat is always approached with restraint—with delicacy in *Worcester*, with solemn dignity in *St. Paul's* with almost incoherent awe in *Collegium Regale*; the tonality is always minor with strong modal associations; and in the *Gloria* there is always a decisive note of triumph. In *St. Paul's* and *Westminster* the Gloria is varied for the *Nunc Dimittis* —in *St. Paul's* through an approach from the subdominant, returning to the former score at "as it was in the beginning", and in *Westminster* simply through a dramatic remodelling of the ante-penultimate bar. The technique perfected by Stanford of using a short "motif" in various guises throughout each piece is here imitated: and the whole series is bound together by an emphasis in these motifs on the minor third:

The following brief quotation from *Westminster*[1] is as good an example as any of the style one finds throughout these works.

Ex.26

Of his larger works the most considerable—a work, indeed, deserving much wider recognition than it has received—is *Hymnus Paradisi* (1950). This is in effect a "free-text" Requiem, using words largely associated with the English Burial service, running 48 minutes and scored for double choir and full orchestra with optional parts for piano, organ and celesta.

This is a work full of rich scoring, expressive equally of grief and of hope. All its main musical themes are of plainsong-like flexibility, and here again we have that juxtaposition of modern-romantic, harmonic resources, classical counterpoint and archaic subject-matter which makes his work so homogeneous and indentifiable. In the following passage all his characteristic qualities, and the sources of their derivation, are to be seen together—the Vaughan Williams approach to melody and parallel note-clusters, combined with the enharmonic subtleties that come from the late romantics, and through it all, an almost medieval stillness. (Example 27)

Equally worth study are the *Three Motets* of 1958, especially the virile and brilliant "God is gone Up", and the recent *Sequence For St. Michael*, written like Michael Tippett's *Magnificat and Nunc Dimittis* (see below, p. 142) for the 450th anniversary of St. John's College, Cambridge (1961).

The central place here given to Howells in contemporary English church music is justified by the proportion of his output devoted to the church, but also by the fact that he has written plenty of music in other contexts. His integration of old and new, with a bias towards the old, has produced a style which has influenced many of his younger contemporaries, and which yet has had few direct imitators. Especially to be noted is his use of the organ, for which he writes with the greatest sensitiveness whether as a solo instrument or as an accompaniment. He is equally far removed from the pedagogic-conservative style, which makes concessions to the known limitations of singers' and players' ability and appreciation, and from the novel popular or experimental styles. His music has the limitations of his style: few

(Example 27)—continued

composers have written so much at so consistently scholarly a level, with so much invention, and yet with so little variety of vocabulary. It is probably fair to say of him that he is not a composer whose work one would best appreciate if one heard only his work for the whole of a full-length concert; but that he is a composer who cannot be omitted from any cathedral or choral repertory, or from any organist's repertory, without serious loss.

Another composer whose gracious style often reminds one of Howells, is Gerald Finzi, whose untimely death in 1956 was a serious loss to English music. His contribution to church music was not large, but *Dies Natalis* (1948) is a charming Christmas celebration that shows the best of his lyric and imaginative genius for musical miniature.

Church music has not been entirely outside the field of the English symphonists of our time. In recent years Sir Arthur Bliss has contributed to the celebrations of two English Cathedrals restored

(Example 27)—continued

after extensive war damage. At the opening of Llandaff Cathedral (1960) his extended anthem "Stand up and bless the Lord your God" was sung, and as part of the consecration celebrations at Coventry Cathedral (1962) his massive cantata, *The Beatitudes* received its first performance. The former of these is a relatively slight work in a somewhat *Kapellmeister*-ish style, but *The Beatitudes* is a large and imaginative score, in which the words of Matthew 5, 2–12 are contrasted partly with religious poetry and partly with prophesy: at the end a violent chorus in which the world's cruelty breaks in with the words "Revile him! Persecute him!" is followed by a quiet setting of a prayer from Jeremy Taylor and a triumphant "Amen". The effect of the work is gained by such sudden juxtapositions of moods, and the music follows the moods with an operatic eloquence that was appropriate to the occasion. A little more will be said about this occasion in itself in a moment (pp. 78-80).

William Walton has shown a singular aptitude for setting sacred texts ever since, at the age of 15, still a boy at Christ Church choir school, Oxford, he wrote a beautiful setting of Phineas Fletcher's poem, "Drop, drop, slow tears" (1917, published 1930 as "A Litany"). Of the work of his "middle period", contemporary with his celebrated First Symphony, his equally celebrated *Belshazzar's Feast* (1937) broke new ground in the imaginative setting of a really violent Old Testament text. This work stands on the very edge of our subject, and will be better treated elsewhere. A short wedding anthem, "Set me as a seal upon my heart" (1938) comes from the same period. The post-war years brought from him a contribution to the Coronation Service of 1953 in his ceremonial setting of the *Te Deum*, and in 1961 came his finest piece of church music, the great *Gloria*, for choir and full orchestra, commissioned for the 125th anniversary of the Huddersfield Choral Society.

Now Walton is a composer, *vis-à-vis* church music, typical of his age. Only the first of the four works we have named, and that a work almost of childhood, was not written as a commission. Church music is not his natural style, and indeed he has not lived, in the sense that Howells for example has always lived, in the climate of the church. His special place in this story is in that he is our finest example of a composer not naturally a churchman whose contributions to church literature are significant and remarkable as church music. There is not a bar in the two small anthems that does not contain a touch of that originality which he has always shown in his secular music. And when we hear the *Gloria* there is a quite remarkable evocation of the style of another composer of another age, who, equally far from church conventions or orthodox beliefs, brought at least once the whole of his genius to bear on a church text—Beethoven. The parallels with the *Gloria* of Beethoven's *Missa Solennis* are irresistible—among them the sounding of a final explosive "Gloria!" as the last bar of the piece, the very shape of the figure used at the second *"miserere"* (bars 388-393, treble and tenor), and above all the way in which every phrase of the text is separately and dramatically set. *"Miserere"* itself is set in all manner of ways—a descending second followed by an octave leap upward (bar 304), a downward rush in thirds, sometimes inverted (305-08), a solemn progress of minims (315, tenor), a wild plainsong-like melisma (326–34), a confused choral mutter (344 ff) and a Bach-like "sobbing" motif of apoggiaturas (398–400). "*Tu solus altissimus*" is a wild striding canon suddenly becoming a whirling vortex of sound, a *crescendo* followed (Beethoven-like again) by a precipitous *forte-piano*. All the abrupt, uncompromising, malicious vitality of Walton's secular music is in this extraordinary piece, on every page of which there is a surprise.

Edmund Rubbra, virtually a contemporary of Walton, provides an extreme contrast to this mood. That Rubbra is a child of Catholic faith is evident in all that he has written for sacred use. There are three liturgical Masses, a setting of *Lauda Sion* (1961), and two ceremonial settings of the *Te Deum*—the *Festival Te Deum* (1951) and a later setting (Op. 115) first performed in 1962. Nothing here is wild or incongruous or reminiscent of the harsh clangour of profane life. There is always something ruthlessly polished about Rubbra's music, which pursues its way with a rectitude that is always austere, and often beautiful, but never over-dramatic. The influence of neo-medievalism is nowhere more evident than here. Sometimes there is a strangely angular and astringent effect—often produced by the combination of tonalities or by simple "false relations", but it is the angularity of very early polyphonic music. You hear Byrd and Tallis less often than Dunstable when Rubbra is writing for the church, as in the massive restraint of the following homophonic passage in *Lauda Sion*

Ex.28

which sounds like a very ungainly and ponderous man treading with noiseless grace. The 1962 *Te Deum* and the *Lauda Sion*, like the Masses,

E

are in Rubbra's favourite *a capella* style, with much division and subtle manipulation of the voices.

Two composers of somewhat slighter but still not negligible stature, and of about the same generation, are Gordon Jacob and Armstrong Gibbs. Both have written with great effectiveness for church purposes. Jacob's inventiveness is best seen in his Christmas Cantata, *The New Born King* (1960), and in his festival anthem for the Feast of St. Cecilia, *Sing a Song of Joy* (1957). The cantata is scored for orchestral accompaniment, and the anthem makes very effective use of the resources of the organ, for which as a solo instrument he has also written well, as in *Prelude, Meditation and Fanfare* (1958). Armstrong Gibbs has made a contribution to Passion music worthy to stand beside that of Charles Wood, in *Behold the Man* (1955), for solos, choir and orchestra: this work, a Biblical Passion on a small scale, makes effective use of the Old Testament, and is marred only by the somewhat mournfully conventional specially-composed hymns which appear here and there (and for which other better known ones can, says the composer, be substituted: they should be). He has written many anthems, of which perhaps the finest is "I the prisoner of the Lord" (1948), written for the B.B.C. Singers. His "Easter" (1926) is a good early example of the influence of Vaughan Williams, and his setting of Psalm 150, "O praise God in His Holiness" (1953) is a capital example of what can be done with the limited resources of a two-part choir. Both Jacob and Gibbs show their best qualities in music which is optimistic even when it is grave, and write with a freedom that they owe to the influence of Holst and Vaughan Williams, although they do not attempt the profundities of choral resource. Both have made effective and welcome contributions to organ literature.

Roughly of the same generation are two distinguished teachers, two of whom came to Britain from Europe. Egon Wellesz, the pioneer scholar in Byzantine musical studies, has a *Mass in F minor* (1949) for choir and organ, largely homophonic and diatonic, with Bruckner rather than Brahms in the background. There are two other Masses and some motets; in these works there is little evidence that in fact he was a pupil and biographer of Schoenberg; he is, as a composer, equally at home in the Romantic and the twelve-tone tradition, but his sacred music is strictly practical—and of its kind, masterly.

Matyas Seiber, born in Hungary but naturalised in Britain from 1935, is another distinguished teacher whose interests run through the whole of the musical spectrum: his liturgical music includes a *Missa Brevis* of quite remarkable beauty and liturgical propriety.

The English musical Professors have made contributions, on a more modest scale than Parry, Stanford and Howells, in Arthur Hutchings (Durham), "Victim Divine" (1957), "Grant them rest" (1952) and *Communion service in* G (1958)—restrained evocations of the ancient *a capella* style, and Sir Jack Westrup's "God be merciful" (1962), an interesting brief essay in acompanied linear writing. And there are other contemporaries of the older generation of twentieth century church musicians too numerous to mention, all of whom have contributed something to the building up of a clear-minded tradition that ordinary choral singers will find approachable.

NOTE TO CHAPTER 4

1. The *Westminster* evening canticles from which Ex. 26 is quoted were composed for the Church Music Society Jubilee Festival Service in Westminster Abbey, 1956. The canticles for *Westminster Abbey* are in F sharp minor and were published in 1957.

5

Letting in More Air

THE great watershed in English music—sacred and secular—is in the work of Benjamin Britten. It is of course impossible to evaluate intelligibly the work of a composer who is still composing so industriously in so many forms, and whose development cannot possibly be said to have finished in his fiftieth year. But Britten has achieved, and achieved early, an international recognition which rarely in the past has been accorded to an English musician, and he is, without any competitors, the most sought-after English musican of our time.

It may be of interest to quote here a judgment of him recently made in France.

> Britten is one of the first "professional" English musicians, one of the first English musicians who has never envisaged any career but music; in consequence he is as a craftsman more guided by a technical assurance than by the waywardness of inspiration. . . .
>
> Britten began to work out his style in his earliest youth; his gifts were evident, but his first scores showed a somewhat weak personality. . . . But in 1940, with his *Sinfonia da Requiem*, Britten became suddenly a composer who commanded attention. In a word, he disclosed the reality of his talent in discovering the possibilities of the human voice in music. "One of my principal purposes," says the author of *Peter Grimes*, "has been to try to do justice to the musicality of the English language, to the vitality and freedom of which it has been completely deprived since Purcell's death."
>
> C. Samuel (ed.) *Panorama* (see
> note 1 to Chapter 10), p. 507.

That is an excellent non-partisan summary of Britten. There are some in his own country who say that England is still incapable of producing really contemporary music: and it will be seen a little later on how much *avant-garde* music comes from the Continent, and perhaps why. Britten is not a serial composer, even if occasionally a touch of that ethos appears in his later works. Other Englishmen have gone much further in that direction than he. But that is not the point about Britten. He is an English composer and he is a vocal composer; he is—at any rate as yet—incapable of that kind of renunciation which the "total-organisation" composers practise; that is, he is incapable of being unaware, and of making himself unaware, of the effect his music will have, On the contrary he is surely the most penetrating and assured judge of musical effects that we have ever produced. No doubt there is something a little cold, a little offhand, about some of his early work. *A Boy was Born*, Op. 3, (1932) even in its revised version of 1958, leaves an impression of intricate ingenuity, and sometimes of a cold draught not incompatible with the winter-legend of Christmas. The "Hymn to the Virgin" (1930–35) is charming, medieval in spirit, but perhaps hardly so suggestive of impressive musical invention as Walton's adolescent work which we mentioned a short while ago. And his secular music of the pre-1940 period is more notable for brilliance and wit than for the promise of genius.

It is then, from the point of view of the church, a piece of excellent fortune that so much of Britten's church music comes from after 1940. Nobody claims that that year of the *Sinfonia da Requiem* saw a dramatic change in Britten's outlook or talent; it is simply as a French critic put it, that after that work, nobody could afford not to take Britten seriously.

It is a notable series of works, in many forms—as many as the church could accommodate—that Britten has composed in the sacred context. *Ceremony of Carols* (1943), *Rejoice in the Lamb* (1943), *Festival Te Deum* (1945), *St. Nicolas* (1948), *Hymn to St. Peter* (1955), *Noye's Fludde* (1958), *Missa Brevis* (1959), and the *War Requiem* (1962)—this list by no means exhausts them: but consider its diversity: liturgical music, festival music, church opera in a form which he has virtually invented.

It is perhaps possible to come at the secret of Britten's remarkable success in church music if we consider him as making a third with the two other composers we have especially paused on—Howells and Walton. The three approach church music from three quite different directions. Howells is steeped in its tradition, and can approach it with a minimum of dissent. He comes to it with a mind already full of admiration and love for church music as church music. Walton comes to it bringing a musical idiom that runs from satire to passion: he comes as one who has hobnobbed with "Les Six", as the composer of *Façade* and the First Symphony. Invited in from an alien culture, he brings what he has, and once he has offered his *Gloria* and *Te Deum*, one sees how appropriate, not how incongruous, the ironic and violent idiom is to the contemporary human expression of praise. Britten is at a point equidistant from both: he neither consents to the traditional idiom as far as Howells does, nor dissents from it as obviously as Walton does.

Moreover, while he has a touch, but only a touch, of the romantic, and a touch, but hardly more, of the Tudor in him, he is singular in having so great a love for Purcell. Nobody else reincarnates Purcell as Britten does: and Purcell's genius is for producing amazing effects from accompanied vocal music. Purcell has the courtly touch, yet he is just preorthodox. So an admirer of him will not be preoccupied with a *a capella* polyphony; nor yet will he be writing Bach, Mendelssohn or Parry; nor again will he be affecting a French or Germanic idiom. He will be writing English music of a new kind, strange equally to Parry and to Vaughan Williams.

Not a few of Britten's choral works for the church use the organ; and while one cannot but give primacy to his treatment of the voice—as he does in his self-criticism, the listener and critic will miss much if they do not attend to his quite remarkably apt use of the organ. He uses it, for example in *Rejoice in the Lamb* and the *Missa Brevis*, every bit as aptly as he uses the voice, or as he uses the orchestra in his many symphonic works. He does not try to make the organ sound like anything but an organ: but every note of the organ part of the *Missa Brevis* is worth studying with care by anybody who would now write for that instrument: look at the devastating effect of the crescendo of dissonances over an ostinato bass in the *Agnus Dei*, or the clear jubilant sound that the instrument makes in the *Sanctus*.

It is Britten's quite uncanny gift for judging what sound he wants heard, and in what proportion, that gives him the rank of genius. And this is the consequence of that "professional" and "technical" background to which his French critic refers.

But there is another quality in Purcell that Britten has captured—a kind of detachment that is partly the result of courtly discipline and partly a simple confidence in the authority of music. The effortlessness of his best effects, and the understatement and economy which he constantly practises in his later scores, are similarly the consequence of an unerring eye for what *this* church wants and can manage on *this* occasion. All his more considerable church works are occasional works that have become classics: and you have only to compare the *look* of the score of *A Boy was Born* with that of *Rejoice in the Lamb* to see how the common human necessity of writing for an occasion (St. Matthew's, Northampton) has raised technical excellence to the level of genius. It is surely the possession of this gift of writing for *what is there* that not only makes Britten so effective a writer for children and choirboys, but also makes him welcome the chance to do so: as he did in *St. Nicolas* (for Lancing College), and later in *Noye's Fludde*—to say nothing of his celebrated operas. He appears to rejoice in taking a commonplace hymn tune—as he does three times in *Noye's Fludde*—and making it the basis of any amount of musical invention. The introduction of "Eternal Father, strong to save", a tune of J. B. Dykes at which Vaughan Williams sniffed contemptuously, into that work gives it an almost ludicrous humanity: well, humanity is ridiculous at times, and incongruous, and untidy.

This "detachment" has become in Britten a detachment from conventional solemnity. Writing for St. Matthew's Northampton, he sets not a Psalm or a passage from the Prophets but a mad poem by Christopher Smart which includes passages about cats and mice, a quaint runic passage about letters of the alphabet, and—when Britten handles it—an almost intolerably pathetic passage about the madman's loneliness. Writing his *Ceremony of Carols*, he stuns the listener on first hearing by his juxtaposition of a medieval plainsong opening with music of whimsical lightness which in places impresses first by the actual physical *speed* at which it is delivered.

Up to the opening of the year 1962 Britten had established himself as a master of effect, as a composer who seemed unable to write music that, whatever its colour, failed to glisten; it seems all to evince more than anybody else's the quality that St. Thomas Aquinas called *nitor*—coruscation. And along with this, humanity—a gift for communicating. And along with that a very curious and disturbing tendency towards operatic plots of a perverse and slightly horrid kind. Britten has his spooky side: he can be absolutely terrifying, as in the "Lyke Wake Dirge" in the *Nocturne* for Tenor solo and chamber group, Op. 31. Quite early on he showed a tendency towards political dissent and his generation's protest against the distortion of civilisation in his setting of Auden's poems in *On This Island*, Op. 11. This side of his thought he kept for the theatre and the concert room until 25th May, 1962, when at the dedication celebrations at Coventry his *War Requiem* (Op. 66) received its first performance.

The *War Requiem* is obviously his profoundest work so far. It is the most dramatic and unnerving setting of the *Requiem* since Verdi: and critics have already found that Verdi is the only composer he can here be compared with. Musically, this is—and may easily remain—Britten's greatest opera. The tragic theme is one which he was now ready to tackle, and to tackle with all the abandon that he showed in his lighter works, and in his less ceremonious approaches to death, terror and perversity. So he approaches the *Requiem* in anger, producing some of the most ravishingly beautiful sounds, and some of the most grotesque, that even he has yet achieved. (What other word than that can describe the terrifying appropriateness of his *"tuba mirum"* theme in the *Dies Irae*?) But—here is what brings the observer up all standing—he adds to the liturgical words a good deal of poetry by Wilfred Owen, who is a poet of the *First* World War. The minds of all who were present were already sated with recollections of martial terrors which were quite peculiar to the Second World War. Coventry became a symbol from the moment when on 14th November, 1940 it was destroyed by enemy action. But it is not bombs and aircraft and civilian deaths with which Britten's libretto deals. It deals with the mud and blood of the trenches of 1915. Was this a misjudgment? Or was Britten saying that if one must repent of war, one comes to such repentance better through the monumental aggregation of individual sufferings which was World War I, than through the symbolic and monstrous communal suffering of World War II? This we cannot know, unless he tells us one day. But what we do know is that the music reflects with piercing clarity this approach to war. It has the personal appeal of the massive operatic set-up, the virtuoso soloists, the great choir, the orchestra doing everything that a large orchestra can do by way of tone-painting. Few of his works are actually less mysterious, less forbidding, less elusive. Here is no under-statement, no *double-entendre*; the composer threw himself at that audience as he had never done before: and somehow it worked. Somehow nobody has felt that this was anything but the essential Britten.

In the face of that it seems quite idle to complain if Britten sounds conservative beside Krenek or Searle or even Stravinsky. When the French critic called him our first "professional" he said what we might vulgarly but not inaccurately put in the phrase, "This man knows what he is doing". What might have been affectation has, it seems safe to judge, transformed itself into eloquence. But we are probably still in Britten's "middle period". . . .

Britten's chief influence on composers of his generation has been of course, in directing their attention to new possibilities in vocal writing, and in encouraging them to economise in their rhetorical devices. It is not possible to say that he has any direct imitators, but obviously the new experiments in vocal effects in English church music that are being seen here and there at present are largely owed to his work. The manner in which dissonance, double-two-part writing, and an austere economy of rhetoric are being employed by such con-temporary young composers as Nicholas Maw and Mansel Thomas, for example, shows some debt to Britten. Along with other influences, he has clearly made some impact on Peter Maxwell Davies.

Probably the most significant composer of the years following Britten, at any rate in the church field, is John Joubert. One of his earliest compositions, "O Lorde, the maker of all things" (1953), though written for four voices and organ, is mainly an essay in austere double-two-part writing, and it established him at once as a composer to reckon with. This has been followed by a number of choral works on various scales, of which the most considerable is *Missa Beati Joannis* (1962), the *Credo* of this work is a remarkable study in suggestive tonal ambiguity. The key is firmly C major, but its leading motifs are these (vocal parts only in A and B).

Ex. 29 A

FAT-REM OM-NI-PO- TEN-TEM

Ex. 29 B

ET EX PA- TRE . NA-TUM. AN-TE

ET EX PA-TRE NA-TUM AN-TE

Ex. 29 C

ET IN SPI-RI-TUM SANCTUM, DOM-I-NUM ET VI-VI-FI- CAN-TEM

Equally characteristic is his trilogy of motets, collectively called *Pro Pace*, and individually, *"Libera Plebem," "O Tristia Secla Priora"* and

"*Solus ad Victimam*" (1956–60). These are for unaccompanied choir, and contain a good deal more contrapuntal writing than the *Mass*. As befits their subject, they are dark, sonorous and deeply serious. On the other hand, for light-hearted breakneck hilarity, his "Welcome Yule" (1957) has few competitors even among the compositions of Britten. This is a contrapuntal unaccompanied setting using only a single subject, and the only accidentals which appear from beginning to end of it are the sharpened fourth and, with demure, justice, the flattened seventh—and these, respectively, only on page 4 (plus two bars on page 5) and page 6 (plus one note on page 7) of an eight-page score.

Joubert is an intensely serious composer, who often writes what looks gnarled and forbidding but what emerges on acquaintance as remorselessly logical and technically brilliant. He has not yet aspired at all to the sheer beauty of sound with which Britten captivates the ear: beauty is here, as it is even more in *avant-garde* music, emergent rather than contrived.

A composer who in his secular music not infrequently shows a masterly ironic touch is Geoffrey Bush; he has written a good deal of chamber music and some film music, and to church music he brings an idiom which ranges from tenderness to exuberance without ever touching the traditional mood of stiff solemnity. His longest church work, *Christmas Cantata* (1948), for solo, chorus, strings and oboe, is a charming score, full of contrasts within an area that hardly goes beyond the range of chamber music. His festival anthem, "Praise the Lord, O my soul" (1956), with words from Psalm 103, is a very good example of the manner in which modern composers can, with their freedom from conventional inhibitions, come near to the barbaric ecstasy that lies near the surface of the Psalms. "Uninhibited" is certainly the word that occurs to the hearer when he compares this with what a romantic composer would have written for the words, or even with what an "old school" modern composer like Sir William Harris did write for them: after a full-throated opening, the music disperses into an ecstatic recitative for soprano solo—"Who saveth thy life from destruction": then the words "Praise the Lord" return, unison, pianissimo, and the following musical directions appear from there on: *poco a poco animando, poco a poco crescendo, accel., largamente declamando, Tempo I, con slancio, poco f energico, ritmico, poco f energico, brioso, poco a poco animando, mf, mp-cresc., piu mosso, trionfale, sempre animando, poco rall. allargando molto, Tempo I ff, lento ff, vivo* (shout), *fff possibile.* The last four notes are directed to be shouted. This composer's small but significant output is worth anybody's time to study, for it shows remarkably well how a versatile modern composer steers from serenity to violence without passing through complacency at any point. Modern church music constantly does this: and no doubt the effect is rather often restless, and makes the listener feel that when all is said, Parry and Stanford, Harris and Howells, have made the world safe for these dramatic gestures. But all this is part of the break-through of music into the church which by themselves the pioneers could not have achieved.

Kenneth Leighton, John Gardner and Anthony Milner are at the present time producing some notable church music. Leighton has appeared as a choral composer of singular gifts, especially in his cantatas, *The Light Invisible* (1958) and *Crucifixus pro Nobis* (1961), the second of which is perhaps the finest short passiontide cantata in the contemporary church idiom at present available. That he is an excellent keyboard composer is evident in his sensitive use of the organ, of which another example is in the extended anthem, "Alleluia, Amen" (1962). Milner is affecting a somewhat richer style. His *Salutatio Angelica*, Op. 1 (1948–57) showed something of the Howells-touch, and the sombre *City of Desolation* (1955–56) very fully draws out the poetry and menace of Ronald Knox's translation of Lamentations and Isaiah. Both are scored for choir and orchestra. The music of Brian Brockless, another young contemporary, shows some remarkable advances even on these: his organ *Prelude, Toccata and Chaconne* (1959) is one of the very few English organ works to display a twelve-tone row above its score; on the other hand his anthem, "Now blessed be thou, Christ Jesu" (1960) is obviously the work of somebody who knows intimately the contents of *Musica Britannica*:

Ex.30

This is a foretaste of the contact between the farthest past of polyphony and the farthest reach of totally-organised music on which in a later chapter we shall comment further.

It has been the misfortune of Scotland to be somewhat laggard in musical progress during this century, and to be dependent on visitors from the South for a good deal of its enterprise in church music. It is still true that English guests in Scotland are doing much to make music come alive in that country—the Edinburgh Festival is, of course, not the only example. But young Scottish composers are now making their mark: the most eminent is perhaps Iain Hamilton, who practices the advanced techniques in his orchestral and chamber scores. One of the liveliest native church composers is Cedric Thorpe-Davie of St. Andrews University, and Professor Robin Orr of Glasgow University is not only the composer of some very attractive church music but the encourager of many younger composers (such as his assistant, Frederick Rimmer, for whom see p.230) to go as far as they can into the advanced techniques.

Argur Oldham, organist at St. Mary's Roman Catholic Cathedral, Edinburgh, is nurturing at that cathedral a very polished singing-tradition, and his *Laudes Creaturarum*, (1961) a cantata based on words from St. Francis, is a particularly striking and vivacious piece of modern choral writing. The experimental work being done in the Music Faculty of the University of Aberdeen, under Mr. Reginald Barrett-Ayres, Head of the Music Department, is of the kind that undoubtedly will produce some lively composers for the church: and Mr. Barrett-Ayres has also been responsible for establishing a musical tradition in the Abbey of Iona (where services are held for the Iona Community during the three summer months of the year) which preserves what is authentically Presbyterian without giving ground to musical philistinism of any sort. Of the recently established Dunblane Church Music Research Group we shall write a little more on our closing pages.

While these inventors are thrusting forward the church style to points from which the stagnation of the nineteenth century seems unbelievably remote, the general practitioners continue to compose in the simpler and more accessible styles. One of the minor accomplishments of modern church music is the way in which composers who pretend to little in the way of pioneer work, and who admit the derivativeness of their music, can yet write in a manner that has freshness and integrity. Seniors like Arthur Milner are still publishing first-class music. Up to his death, Alec Rowley was composing industriously—though perhaps not always wisely. Desmond Ratcliffe, Arthur Pritchard, Arthur Wills and Robert Ashfield continue to write without flagging; Donald Cashmore shows a considerable invention in much of his recent work. And, again among the seniors, Bernard Naylor recently completed a set of *Nine Motets* (1962) for the Church's seasons, which make a major contribution to modern church music through the advanced use of dissonance and elliptic allusiveness. Nor should the sacred music of Lennox Berkeley be forgotten—it is perhaps the nearest thing we have to a direct comment on Britten. *Domini est terra* (1938) represents his earlier mood, and *Thou hast made me* (1960) his later; both are works of persuasive beauty. A cantata, *Batter my heart, three person'd God*, with words from a sonnet by Donne, is in process of completion as these words are written.[1]

Perhaps what we have so far said may be brought into focus if we now consider two outstanding occasions in English church music which have taken place in the last ten years: the Coronation of Queen Elizabeth II on 2nd June, 1953, and the Consecration of the new Cathedral at Coventry on 25th May, 1962.

It is something of a pity that the whole of the musical settings at the opening services of the Coventry celebrations has not been published, as the Coronation service was, in volume form: if that had been so, everybody would be able to see how remarkably the two occasions complement each other, and with what aptness they sum up the periods of history to which they belong.

The Coronation service was a summary of English church music up to its date, while the Coventry services were at least in part prophecies of future forms. And the dates are right for this. It must have been evident already to the reader that it is the fifties of the present century that really mark the musical turning-point. We must leave the final judgment on this to the musical historian of another generation; but nearly enough 1950 may be called the milestone-year. So much of what is really creative, rather than reconstructive, has happened since that date. And it was in 1952 that they began to prepare for the Coronation service. Apart from the classics of other ages, excellently represented there, the composers commissioned to write for this service (to some of whose contributions we have already referred) were Vaughan Williams, Sir William Harris, Herbert Howells, Sir George Dyson, Healey Willan, and Sir William Walton. Of these only Walton was born in the twentieth century, and his *Te Deum* was an electrifying incursion of contemporary music into a service which was primarily an exposition of traditional dignity. Every composer involved in it who wrote new work gave his quintessential best, and the aesthetic impact of the service was unforgettable. What is more—it was at the time an occasion which made one feel that English church music could rise to any occasion, and that English church music was still very much alive. What it gave no hint of (and of this of course the listener in June 1953 was quite unconscious) was the direction which church music would take in the future. Walton apart (and Walton is not here at his most violent), the sounds were traditional, not experimental.

It was a superb musical structure in the traditional style—just as Liverpool Cathedral is a superb church structure in the traditional style, with just enough sub-modernity in it to make it not positively archaistic.

At Coventry it could not have been more different. The scale of celebrations was somewhat less ambitious, and less patient of large musical adornment. This was all liturgical music, chamber music of the church. But just as that edifice makes a truculent architectural gesture in that symbolically tortured city, so the music that went with the opening celebrations made a defiant musical gesture. Now and again the stress was relieved by the singing (somewhat acoustically disorganised) of familiar hymns (and the choice of hymns in this and some subsequent celebrations there seems to have been governed by principles that are only too mournfully traditional). But the choral pieces had moments of astonishing insight.

The musical principles were strictly modern, in being closely associated with medieval liturgical music. The medieval cadence in the opening antiphons for Psalm 24, composed by the Precentor, the Reverend J. W. Poole, shows where the music had its roots.

Similarly the unaccompanied chain of short anthems sung to the
words inscribed on the walls of the cathedral, the composition of John
Hotchkis, is music that stands on contemporary ground but reaches
far back into the sixteenth century for its texture and rhetoric.

Ex.32

There was in this dedication service none of the monumental unity
and proportion that the Coronation service had. The old style and
the new were juxtaposed without any sense of incongruity. The Queen
entered the cathedral to the sounds of Parry's "I was glad", and they
later sang "Christ is made the sure foundation" to a tune by Henry
Smart. But the liturgical music had a freshness and an almost aggressive

positiveness that matched the unclerically dramatic sound of the Bishop's voice, and the unecclesiastical rhythms of the specially translated prayers. A new composition by Howells, one of his finest, marked the end of the liturgical part of the service, and an apt transition back to the traditional music with which the whole service closed after the Archbishop's sermon. The Eucharist on the following day was sung to a new, restrained, and perfectly adapted setting by another senior musician, Harold Darke. Services which followed in the ensuing week made much use of new and experimental church music, and it is much to be hoped that a forward-looking ethos has firmly established itself at Coventry. It would be heartening to know that something was likely to be done about the hymns. . . .

NOTE TO CHAPTER 5

1. First broadcast performance, 29th October 1963.

6

Organ Music

SOME organ music has already been mentioned in our discussions of these contemporary composers. It must here be recorded that one of the most significant things in twentieth century music has been the revival of interest in the organ as a musical instrument worthy of the attention of serious musicians.

In this there is a touch of irony, for in Britain the days of the massive organ are largely numbered: the age in which the organ grew to its largest and most resourceful scale are now over. Organs are expensive pieces of craftsmanship, and in Britain the days of the big organs were the days of the church's prosperity. In large organ design in Britain only the instrument in the Royal Festival Hall (1951) has really made a decisive gesture since the Second World War. But our cathedrals are all equipped now with large instruments, sometimes of a somewhat pretentious and romantic tonal design, and so at the time when good organ music is once more becoming available in great variety there is still a market for it. But organ recitals are rarely well attended, and the organist's profession remains a very precarious one, despite the raising in other ways of his status and culture.

But there is another irony beyond this. It was in England that the "King of Instruments" cult of the organ had its freest expression— before it was exported to America. The image of the organ as a source of gigantic dignity and overwhelming sensationalism in music took possession of two generations in England; perhaps it reached its most positive expression in the organ of Liverpool Cathedral, originally built in 1925: which is, however skilfully it be handled, a source of atmosphere rather than rational sound.

In England (Wales and Scotland hardly enter into this, with their very different church-structure) the building of the Royal Festival Hall organ in 1951 was a dramatic, and at the time a controversial, gesture. Here clarity of sound was sought before (and largely at the expense of) the creation of atmosphere: even the traditional organ-case was dispensed with: many who first saw it were as shocked by the unashamed display of pipes in functional rows as they were by the, to their ears, harsh and uncompromising tone of the instrument when played. But this was to accommodate to England the principle which continental organ builders had followed since the time of J. S. Bach, and for a century or two before that. It is still necessary to go to the Continent, or to those regions of America where the continental cultures are most influential, to find the best examples of "baroque" organ building in the modern style: in the U.S.A. Holtkampf and Schlicker are building some remarkably successful instruments on a considerable scale but preserving the principle of clear mutations and low wind pressures (such as, for example, the Holtkampf instrument in the Church of Christ, Lexington, Kentucky, and the Schlicker in the Chapel of St. Olaf College, Northfield, Minnesota). In Britain there is an excellent example in the rebuilt Llandaff Cathedral of the new style, and another in the Chapel of University College, Oxford.[1]

These are attempts to reproduce in modern building the effects of the classical baroque organ. It is in Europe alone that ancient examples exist. But the new interest in this tonal structure, which makes for contrapuntal clarity rather than homophonic grandeur, has influenced the writing of new music, and of course brought out a new interest in the music of the pre-Bach composers. It can also be said that the new kind of writing and the new kind of organ are parallel developments in reaction against the sentimentality whicn had accompanied the old attitude to the instrument. Both statements are true: the modern organist wants an instrument that will play the sort of music he wants to play: but if he has not got one made to measure, he makes every attempt so to play his romantic instrument that it will sound like a baroque one; and those with long memories of successive organists in one place where the organ has undergone no more than minor tonal changes will recall without difficulty the disappearance of a certain kind of playing and registration, and its replacement by one of much greater clarity, so that if they were able to hear the organist of forty years ago and the organist of today playing the same instrument they would find difficulty in believing that the instrument itself had not been replaced.

In Britain at any rate this development is of greater importance as yet than the advent of that astounding genius, Messiaen—who will be referred to at length a little later (below, pp. 130–133). Long before Messiaen's compositions of the thirties—which have recently made such a sensation here—were known to any but specialists, organ music was showing a quite new kind of purposefulness in Britain.

The repertory of the ordinary organist in 1910 could be fairly safely guessed at as a few popular pieces of Bach, the Mendelssohn sonatas, the Rheinberger sonatas (and is there one of these, for all their academic rectitude, all of whose movements one can now play without a blush?), some Widor, if he was agile enough, a few pieces by Samuel Sebastian Wesley, and a ream of stuff from the underworld of romantic France and England. Once again Parry and Stanford came to the rescue —Parry with his chorale preludes (1912 and 1916), his Fantasia and Fugue in G (1913) and his *Wanderer* Fantasy; Stanford with several pieces in prelude-and-fugue form and several books of short pieces many of which (as for example the *Prelude in Form of a Chaconne* from Op. 88) have proved to have plenty of staying power.[2] Basil Harwood and Charles Wood added to the conservative post-romantic repertory, and most effectively. Sir William Harris joined in, with a number of short pieces (to which additions are still being made, and welcome!), and a large organ Sonata.

The organist whose technique was short of FRCO standard and whose environment was hostile to music of a very progressive kind has been admirably catered for by Eric Thiman, Lloyd Webber and (a composer of somewhat less wisdom), Alec Rowley. Percy Whitlock achieved great popularity in his Five Pieces of 1930, and his *Plymouth Suite*, which provided excellent recital music. Sir George Dyson (the Prelude from his *Prelude and Postlude*, 1956, is a particularly charming example of late post-romantic organ music), Armstrong Gibbs and Heathcote Statham have given of their best to the instrument. Of Howells's important contribution we have already written; and we have drawn attention also to the significant use that some of the later choral composers are making of the organ as an accompanying instrument. In the latest decade of the twentieth century music of this middle-of-the-road style continues to come from the presses, modestly inventive, sound and liturgically adequate; Desmond Ratcliffe, Arthur Pritchard, Donald Cashmore, Robert Ashfield—there is no lack of good composers of accessible music. Henry Coleman, C. S. Lang, and Arthur Wills continue to write well for the instrument. Of the more conspicuous composers, Vaughan Williams himself contributed to the literature a set of three *Chorale Preludes* (1920), of which the middle one, *Rhosymedre*, is the best known, the gentlest, and associated with the least suggestive of hymn tunes. The other two, *Bryn Calfaria* and *Hyfrydol* are more demanding, more dramatic, and more characteristic; this set he followed in 1921 with the very remarkable *Prelude and Fugue in C minor* (1921, revised 1930), a work of considerable difficulty and of majestic eloquence. Holst did not, and Britten has not yet, shown interest in the organ as a solo instrument. Geoffrey Bush has had two pieces published, both of typical energy and zest.

The most inventive organ music either of Britain or of the Continent seems to have come, Messiaen apart, from the fifties. In Britain Francis Jackson has lately written a number of unusually brilliant and stimulating short works; Arthur and Anthony Milner have both made highly creative contributions, and in the work of both, as in their choral music, the affinity with Howells is clear—especially perhaps in the "courtly" idiom implied in the titles and content of Arthur Milner's "Galliard for a Festive Occasion" and "Sarabande for a Solemn Occasion". Brian Brockless contributes one of the very few English organ pieces to be composed on a twelve-tone row (*Prelude, Toccata and Chaconne*, 1959). John Cook (formerly an English organist, now in the U.S.A.) shows an advanced-romantic style in several good recital pieces. Heathcote Statham is perhaps the most reliably interesting, in his astringent approach to organ composition, of the composers of the "old guard". In all these one does see the effect of the new approach —a leaning towards counterpoint and a clean score, and to sonorousness strictly governed by rationality.

The continental organ composers have served their generations well during the past sixty years, whether they have remained in their own countries or, as fairly often, carried their cultures to the U.S.A. What is significant about the last ten years or so is that British organists have become aware of this fact. The house of Novello, in publishing its "International Series of Contemporary Organ Music" has taken the lead in making much remarkable organ music available that does not come from the British church culture. To this series we owe so far, for example, the *Five Little Preludes and Fugues* of Karel B. Jirak, a Czech-born composer who now lives in the U.S.A., the *Phrygian Toccata* of Richard Tynsky, also Czech, but living in his native country, and a series of pieces by the Belgian-born Camil van Hulse, of which the *Biblical Sketches* (Op. 107: 1958) and the *Seven Preludes and Fugues* (Op. 106: 1961) are especially remarkable. Ivan Langstroth, American-born but writing in a strongly contemporary-continental idiom, is also represented in this series in his *Theme with Variations*, (Op. 43: 1961), and elsewhere by other interesting compositions. All these make tonal experiments of a kind that are still too little heard in organ recitals, let alone in the church context.

Of French organ music we shall have more to say when we discuss Langlais and Messiaen: but the pioneer of revival has been Marcel Dupré, who has founded a school of composition and performance that has had great influence within and outside his own country, and that has, in fact, provided a good deal of inspiration for latter-day English organ composers. Flor Peeters, the eminent Dutch organist, has evolved a style in which the truth within the idiom of J. S. Bach is, as it were, "demythologised" and presented in a modern context: the same is true of that dry and astringent German composer, Ernst Pepping. On the larger scale, the repertory now contains such inventive and profound works as the Sonatas of Hindemith; and attention is increasingly being drawn to such as Krenek's Organ Sonata and Carl Nielsen's *Commotio*, both of which have received extended treatment in the *Musical Times* of early 1963.[3] In the hands of such as these, the organ is gradually being separated from the image which represented it in 1900: which image can be most aptly described in that expressive modern epithet, "square". The organ was formerly a musical expression of the conventional "shockableness" of the church—so much was taboo, so much was out of place. Gravity, relieved only by dulcet romantic adornment, was the rule: the end-product, unspeakable vulgarity.

It is not in the least out of place, but on the contrary a good illustration of the changing ethos of organistship, that at the highest "establishment" level a gesture has recently been made about the use of the wedding march from Mendelssohn's *Midsummer Night's Dream* at weddings as an outgoing voluntary. When the Duke of Kent was married in York Minster in 1961, a suggestion was made by the organist of the Minster (Francis Jackson) that instead of Mendelssohn's march, the last movement of Widor's Fifth Symphony should be played. This was instantly accepted. Giving later his reasons for the suggestion, Dr. Jackson said, in sum, "(*a*) why have a march at a wedding? (*b*) there is enough good organ music now to make it unnecessary to play an unsuitable arrangement of an orchestral piece, and (*c*) the sentimentality and levity which gather round the Mendelssohn piece when played out of context are wholly out of place in church[4]. The Widor turned out to be so attractive, and festive, and suitable, that it was used again at the wedding of Princess Alexandra in April 1963.

What that situation, and its happy outcome, exposes is a slice of musical history. Resourceful organists in the thirties were still filling the gaps in the repertory by playing transcriptions of well known orchestral works. In public this is never done now. In the thirties the organ and the organist were still regarded as primarily purveyors of anonymous atmosphere rather than as sources of music in their own right. Perhaps the Widor will soon become hackneyed; perhaps it will become fashionable, and will be attempted at weddings by organists who cannot play it. But its suggestion, and acceptance, indicate a new approach to church ceremonies, which is the consequence of a new confidence on the part of organists, and a new appreciation of the authority of music. It is only in those places where the old idea still prevails: where the organist is a hack whose remuneration is grudged and whose status in the church is simply not thought about: that at weddings the Wagner and Mendelssohn wedding marches persist. They are, it is not surprising to hear, much more heard in Scotland than in England nowadays. But Scotland (subject to what we write in our concluding pages) has everything yet to learn about the place of music in worship.

NOTES TO CHAPTER 6

1. Any who have not the chance of hearing this organ may be referred to a recent record of early organ music made on it by its organist, Mr. John Webster (12 in. L.P. Delyse E.C.B. 3160).

2. On the organ music of Stanford see a recent comment in two articles by Gavin Brown in the *Organists' Quarterly Record*, April and July 1962; on Parry, see S. de B. Taylor in the same journal, April and July 1961.

3. Krenek, in *Musical Times*, January 1963, pp. 54–55; Nielsen in *M.T.*, March 1963, pp. 208–209. The whole series of articles of which these are two is most informative.

4. Francis Jackson's lecture in which these comments were made was reprinted in the *Organists' Quarterly Record* for October 1961. It is, I find, only proper to record that this royal wedding was not the first occasion on which Widor's *Toccata* was used as a wedding-march. The idea had occured some years before to Mr. Herrick Bunney, organist of St. Giles, Edinburgh, who used it at a wedding before 1960.

Developments Overseas

The United States and Canada

THE twentieth century revival of music in the churches of the United States has followed a pattern which is at many points congruent with that of the European countries. An assessment of church music in the U.S.A. is, however, even more difficult than in Britain, because of the many religious and cultural streams which are mingled in the evolving culture of the American nation.

In some ways, and inevitably, American church composers have taken their cue from their European colleagues; in other ways they preserve the qualities of their racial cultures; in yet other ways they are exploring new lines of work. But what introduces a very important difference between the U.S.A. and Britain (and to some extent, all Europe) is the different pattern which we find if we combine in one picture the economic growth, the religious development and the musical progress of the U.S.A. and of ourselves. In Britain, musical revival and even revolution has accompanied a dramatic withdrawal of economic patronage; the prosperous ages of Britain were the ages of church music's shame. In the U.S.A. the astounding success of the churches has come at a time when musical expansion can be based on a much livelier consciousness of musical values. Taking the picture as a whole, it ought to be true that the enormous amount of church music now pouring from the American presses is of a better quality than the correspondingly enormous amount that was printed over here fifty to a hundred years ago. There is, equally, every possibility of over-writing and over-publication, of platitudinous degeneracy, if the American composers and publishers do not discipline themselves to learn from the errors of their European cousins.

At the beginning of the century American church music was ruled largely by the concepts of Lowell Mason amplified by the exuberances of such composers as Horatio Parker. American sentimentality tended on the whole to be more boisterous and less lachrymose than that of Britain. Success, meteoric social development, was behind the growth of American churches, and Protestant unimaginative rectitude governed their ethos. During the present century the balance of Protestants against Catholics has been redressed a good deal in favour of Catholics, and the immigration of a great deal of outstanding musical talent from central Europe, largely in consequence of the Second World War and what preceded it in the German political *bloc*, has raised musical standards on every level. Between the wars, the U.S.A. was already providing some of the leading symphony orchestras; now it provides far more of them, and along with them chamber-music groups of international standing, artistes of incomparable technique, and schools of music whose name is legion.

Economic expansion has yielded many advantages even to church music. It has provided fine modern churches with large organs, massive congregations and enthusiastic choirs. To meet this demand, the publishers are now working at high pressure. Moreover, the universities are operating courses in sacred music which qualify for academic credit—a thing absolutely unheard of in Britain. At Union Theological Seminary, New York, there is a School of Sacred music in which are gathered, for the study, teaching and promotion of sacred music, men and women of the highest scholarly standing. Summer courses in sacred music are attended by enthusiastic crowds; highly efficient church organists are appearing in greater numbers than before. In a word, church music has, in its own right, "status", in a sense in which it has never had it in Britain.

Of course, success brings large numbers, and large numbers make for immobility of taste; and the average American Protestant church is still singing dreadful congregational music, however enlightened the editors of its hymnal may have been. There is a tendency still to adorn choir-anthems with decorations to be played on the chimes, without which no American church organ in the East reckons that it can claim self-respect. There is, and it is widely admitted in the U.S.A., a vast and amiable vulgarity about much that goes on in the practice of church music.

There is, on the other hand, a virtuoso-cult in church that can easily, if steps are not taken to integrate it with liturgy and theology, transform the churches into concert-halls for the connoisseurs. In many of the larger foundations in the East, two or three anthems will be heard in a service: in one very famous church of cathedral-like proportions and academic associations the programme on one July Sunday in 1962 included Byrd's *Ave Verum*, a complex aria from a Bach cantata, and Brahms's "How lovely are thy dwellings", sung with masterly and enthusiastic skill by a first class choir, accompanied by an organist who would give a good run to the best of English players: but if anybody asked why these things were sung, together and at that time, an answer would be hard to find. There is a story, which sounds credible, that in a large and well-appointed American church an excellent rendering was given of Palestrina's *Tu es Petrus* on the Sunday which was particularly set aside for the commemoration of the Reformation.

It must not be forgotten, of course, that the musical culture of the United States extends only to part of the country: the Eastern seaboard and the large centres of population. There are large areas where church music is rustic and simple: and there is considerable resistance in cultured areas, especially in the South, to progressive music by the interests of very conservative theology. But where music is making progress, it is making it with all the energy and enterprise which one naturally associates with the American economy.

The most productive quarry for contemporary American church music seems to be the style which was at its most vital in Britain in the twenties and thirties. It is significant that the music of Dr. Eric Thiman, for example, has a much larger interdenominational currency in America than in Britain; and his style of simple, extravert writing has commended itself to many American church composers and choirs. There is often a touch of modality and diatonic optimism that one here found in Martin Shaw. It might fairly be said that the music of many successful composers in America today—Austin Lovelace, for example, Evan Copley, Philip Dietterich—is derived from a Nicholson-Thiman-Shaw style. In this middle-of-the-road stream of church music, which is at present having such success, it is rare to find either the melodic bombast of the earlier generation or any excessive introverted chromaticism. Now and again the voice of Vaughan Williams is heard as in the dramatic parallel fifths of Robert Baker's "O Lord God, to whom vengeance belongeth", and there are obvious affinities between Leo Sowerby's work and that of Charles Wood.

The hymn-anthem (here we anticipate a reference which will be made below, p.105) has had a great vogue in the U.S.A., and for much the same reason that made it so popular in Britain during the thirties—a consciousness of the possibilities of hymn tunes for musical suggestion, and of the need for making known good tunes that congregations do not have in their ordinary repertory.

For more advanced styles the reader will find the work of Seth Bingham, for example his *Four Marian Litanies* (1955), and that of Joseph Goodman, especially his *Missa Brevis* (1959) well worth studying. Goodman's "When the Lord drew nigh" (1954) is a very remarkable example of up-to-date sixteenth century style polyphony. From this kind of work it is evident that church music is very much at the stage where new scholarship concerning old styles is having its influence.

At present there is no native movement in America towards that "pop" style of church music with which we shall later deal, and which has attracted so much attention in Britain. So far as the music of Geoffrey Beaumont has been heard there it seems to have made little impression. No doubt this is because of the very different connotations that "pop" and, even more "jazz" has in a multi-racial society, and because of the existence in America of a social pattern that does not lead to such frantic conscience-searching, on the part of middle class religious people, as is fashionable among us here.

The pattern of things in organ music corresponds very much with that in choral music. There is a great deal of pedagogy that emerges from the zest of Americans for instruction: the Abingdon Press published in 1962 a book of 55 *Hymn Intonations* by Harald Rohlig which does on a smaller scale the same thing as the Swiss *Intonationen* we mention below (p. 95). Chorale-preludes abound as freely as hymn-anthems; and the response of the organ composers to the large resources of the typical church organ there, and to the demand for fresh music, is well exemplified in such pieces as Robert Powell's *Four Psalm Preludes*, John Dierks's *Six Sacred Compositions for Organ*, and R. Evan Copley's *Toccata for Organ*, three volumes of organ music in very different styles, all published in 1962.

The vitality of American church music is abundant, and the prospects are of a considerable surge forward in an environment where the professional musician is highly regarded and where scholarship is enjoying an increasing status. On the whole, instrumental music seems to be a little ahead of choral music, and choral music a very long way ahead of congregational music. The audience for which the organ music is being composed is clearly enthusiastic for new sensations: the congregation that sings the hymn tunes is equally obstinate in its entrenched aesthetic interests. But where there is such vitality, there is every chance of lively conversation which may produce before long a new integration of the many styles that meet in American church music of today. Certainly the impetus of the movement away from casualness and sentimentality is at present enormous, and rightly channelled this could produce a musical tradition in the American churches that transcends anything known in Europe. At present it is entirely unsafe to judge what are the chances of any such happy outcome of the present condition of strenuous musical activism.

NOTE: On Church Music in America, see L. Ellinwood, *History of American Church Music* (New York, Morehouse-Gorham Co., 1953) and W. Douglas (rev. L. Ellinwood), *Church Music in History and Prac ice* (London, Faber, 1963).

The situation in Canada is at present far less well developed. The central church music figure there is Healey Willan, an Englishman who at an early stage migrated to Toronto, and who has there established a high reputation as an administrator, recitalist and composer. The only piece of music in the 1953 Coronation service that came from outside England was his "O Lord, our Governour". As a composer his output has been neither large nor distinguished for much originality of style; but he has focused attention on the improvement of professional standards in church. Canada has not the teeming population or the complex racial pattern of the U.S.A., and the very large influence of the United Church of Canada (which includes what we call Methodists, Congregationalists and, principally, Presbyterians) has ensured that an attitude to music comparable with that traditional in Scotland shall prevail in a large part of the country. Much is being done to raise standards by widening the vocabulary of church music, and by bringing to church people's notice the greatest music of other ages. Schools of church music are far from unknown, and the congregational equipment of both the United Church (the Baptists uses the same hymnal with small modifications) and of the Episcopal Church is, in their hymnals, adequate for the expression of the right values. But from that small and successful country little has yet come in the way of a significant musical contribution, and the tendency in most churches is to be content with a traditional Victorian style of music adorned now and again with something in the sub-modern tradition. The best that is happening at present is in that revival of interest in music's history which must always go before the establishment of a new musical régime.

Der Kapellmeister

Developments on the Continent have followed, *mutatis mutandis*, much the same lines as those in Britain. All continental countries, Protestant or Catholic, passed through a phase in church music in which the operatic and sentimental idioms were fashionable and the classics largely forgotten; and in all such places a return either to the classics or to fold music has been apparent. Something of this has already been seen in our discussion of major continental church works. There is, however, another line of development which appears especially in Protestant Germany and Switzerland, and which emerges partly in the work of such musicians as Ernst Pepping, Hugo Distler, Micheelsen and, most interestingly, Heinz Werner Zimmermann.

The centre of German Protestantism is, of course, Lutheran doctrine and practice, and its music centre is correspondingly the Lutheran chorale. Just as the classic chorale was the backbone of the church compositions of Bach and his predecessors, so now, after a romantic interlude, there is a return to church music based on the chorale. A good deal of this manifests the special qualities of what has been called *Kapellmeistermusik*—it is somewhat dry, pedantic and emotionally cautious. But Distler and his contemporaries have encouraged especially a new manner of singing, and arranging, chorales which has depended not on the use of a large organ for accompaniment, but rather on the use of a small group of instruments supported by a small organ as *continuo*. A certain amount of this music has been recorded, and some reference to these records will be found in the Bibliographical Index. In free composition these composers have largely based their settings on chorales, providing elaborations which are often, like Micheelsen's *Nunc Dimittis* and some of Distler's motets, of great beauty and energy.

Heinz Werner Zimmermann, however, has gone a good deal further. He has developed a *Kapellmeister* style which owes something to the jazz-technique, and which emerges as something entirely unlike the "pop" technique of that English school with which our last section will have to deal.

He is best approached through his short motets, of which three are conveniently recorded on a *Cantate* disc. Of these *Das Vaterunser* is the most impressive. It is a setting of the Lord's Prayer for seven-part choir (of which one part, the second tenor, is reserved for the singing of the chorale, *Christe du lamm Gottes*), accompanied by a pizzicato double bass, and a bowed 'cello supporting the chorale tune. The double bass plays an independent bass part in absolutely regular beat against the complex syncopated polyphony of the voice parts. Its beat is continuous and relentless, being interrupted only twice—on the last page of the piece. *Lobet ihr Knechte* and *Uns ist ein Kind' geboren* are treated in the same way, except that as recorded they support the chorale with a single brass instrument. All these pieces were composed in 1956.

Gelobet sei der Herr täglich (1959) is a later example, employing a four-part choir with double bass, one of the vocal parts being reserved for the chorale *Wie tief Kreuz Trübsal oder Pein. Herr, mache mich zum*

Werkzeug deines Friedens (1959) is a setting of the German version of a prayer of St. Francis of Assisi known in English as "Lord, make us instruments of thy peace" (and set to music by Martin Shaw in his anthem of that title as one of his last works in 1957). This has no chorale, but uses a six-part choir and double bass. His most ambitious work in this style is the *Psalmkonzert* (1958), a work in five movements, and on the sleeve-note of the record of this work Zimmermann says that he is using a "jazz" technique because jazz is the only kind of contemporary music that can still express joy. Here he varies the disposition of the choir from movement to movement, and while the double bass keeps going throughout the work, in its first and second movements he introduces three trumpets and a vibraphone (the second movement being for solo voice). In the fourth movement the trumpets are heard and a vibraphone part is allowed for in the score, but no notes are written for it. After the fourth movement the first is sung over again: but on this repetition a children's choir is heard singing the chorale *Nun danket*, which is not heard the first time it is sung.

The effect is most dramatic. Hearing the record with the score in one's hand one notices that a considerable latitude is allowed for the trumpeters and the vibraphonist, who make alterations and additions to the written notes in the fourth movement, somewhat tentatively applying the principles of "swing" to the interpretation. Zimmermann explains in the score of *Psalmkonzert* why he is particularly pleased with the clear tone of the vibraphone: and his use of it against the vivid voice parts and the trumpet fanfares is extremely skilful. But the music differs radically from the "pop" style of the English school in being, so far as its harmony and counterpoint go, strictly orthodox and *Kapellmeister* in its preservation of the decencies of choral music. It is clear that Zimmermann's approach to "jazz" is wholly different from that of Beaumont and Williamson, who, as we shall see, write music which, while making concessions to popular idioms, makes none to traditional church-polyphony. It was possible for a record reviewing magazine to mistake Zimmermann's *Vaterunser* for *Kapellmeistermusik*; it could not possibly be taken for "pop". Therefore Zimmermann, coming as he does from the central tradition of orthodox music, stands by himself in the way he uses the "jazz" idiom.

Ernst Pepping is one of the more prolific of German church composers in the most orthodox style, and he has, in his dry and almost satiric way, produced some very characteristic music in the "anti-*romantisch*" manner. A good example is his *Te Deum*, for unaccompanied choir (1956)—a work notable rather for its cerebral than for its emotional content, but within that field, something of a *tour de force.*

In much of the *Kapellmeister* tradition there seems, indeed, to be more than a touch of fear of the emotional. This, when one remembers the special problems inherent in the psychology of German Protestantism, is not surprising. The advanced Lutheran in music is far more uncompromising than his English opposite number when it comes to the admission of the *romantisch* into church. The result is music which largely relies for its inspiration on the forms and subject-matter of the predecessors of Bach.

At one point, in Protestant Switzerland, this has had a surprising and possibly suggestive consequence. A large book of *Intonationen zu den Melodien im Gesangbuch der evangelisch-reformierten Kirchen der deutschen Schweiz*, published in Bern in 1955, is worth the attention of any who are interested in the byways of modern church music. This is a book of "chorale-preludes", using that expression in the strictest sense. Whereas "chorale-preludes" are now normally thought of as pieces of music in their own right, because of the amazing sufficiency of Bach's works in that form, a chorale-prelude is so called because its original intention was to provide an instrumental introduction to the congregational singing of a hymn. In other words, the familiar "organist's play-over" that one hears in church nowadays in Britain is more like a chorale-prelude than some of the complex pieces which nowadays bear that name. The interrelation between the speed of the chorale in a Bach prelude and the customary speed of congregational singing in his time must not be too strongly pressed, because some of his "preludes" are really organ-arrangements of instrumental fantasias on chorale tunes originally incorporated in cantatas: but essentially a chorale-prelude is a *prelude.* Now this book of *Internationen* provides for every tune in the hymnal in use in the Evangelical Protestant church of Switzerland several brief "preludes" for the organist: of each set, one at least is very easy to play, and arranged on two manuals only. But the book is commended by the President of the German-Swiss organists' guild in the name of its central council, and the intention is that it should be used instead of conventional play-overs or unbridled improvisations throughout the local congregations of that church. Some examples from classical organ composers like Pacheleel are included, but mainly these short contrapuntal introductions are the work of contemporary church musicians. Here are two of the three *intonationen* prescribed for the tune known as CHRISTUS DER IST MEIN LEBEN (*English Hymnal,* 360):

Ex. 33 A

Ex. 33 B

Those examples illustrate not only the ingenuity of the composers but the strictly disciplined contrapuntal writing that the neo-archism of this culture wanted to insist on. This is anti-*romantisch* in a decisive way.

8

Hymns and Psalms

THE story of hymns and psalms—the people's music—in the twentieth century is one that has often been told already; and of the music of hymns up to the fifties I have myself written in *The Music of Christian Hymnody* (1957). Only a brief survey is therefore required here; but in twentieth century church music the remarkable history of hymn-singing holds a key position. What the editors of hymnals have decided to teach people to sing, and what in fact the people have shown themselves willing to sing, are questions of especially lively import in the twentieth century, and especially in England.

It is now just over a century since *Hymns Ancient and Modern* set a new standard, and a new fashion, in hymn books. There for the first time in a widely circulated hymn book, tunes and words were printed together. There also for the first time in a widely circulated hymn book the principle of selection from a large repertory rather than inclusiveness was promoted. There thirdly a hymnal appropriate especially to the Anglican liturgy was compiled. With small exceptions, the rule up to then had been that hymns were in one volume, which the congregation sang from, and tunes in another, which the precentor and the organist (later, the choir) would use. The more hymns, the better was also an accepted principle. *Hymns Ancient and Modern* in its first edition (1861) had 273 hymns: the *New Congregational Hymnal* of 1859 has 1,281. And whereas hymnals formerly were largely evangelical compendia of devotional lyrics, *Hymns Ancient and Modern* set out to be a companion to the liturgy.

For our purposes it is only necessary to note that in that book a principle of criticism was asserted for the first time, and that for the rest of the nineteenth century it was a book whose principles no other Anglican book could ignore.

It was just before the beginning of the twentieth century, in 1899, that Robert Bridges published his *Yattendon Hymnal*—the first major gesture against what he held to be (and what are now agreed to be) defective standards in hymnody. But it must be quite clearly understood that the introduction of this radical criticism, which was dispersed on a far wider scale by Vaughan Williams's *English Hymnal*,[1] was not an introduction of criticism as such. It was only a redirecting of criticism. Where *Hymns Ancient and Modern* had selected those hymns which would be suitable in a book designed to be a companion to the Book of Common Prayer, the *Yattendon Hymnal* and to a great extent the *English Hymnal* (1906) selected those which were not only liturgically suitable but in their own right good literature and good music.

And the difference between these two seminal Anglican hymnaries was this: that whereas the Church of England knew that it could not ignore the principles of the first *Hymns Ancient and Modern*, all Protestant denominations in Britain since 1906 have, in turn, shown that they could not ignore the more radical principles of the *English Hymnal*.

Musically the popularising of a revised standard of good taste was Vaughan Williams's work. He completed the music of the *English Hymnal* long before he was a recognised composer of high standing: long indeed before he showed in his music what he would be capable of. It is only with a great exercising of the imagination that one can see in the four tunes he personally contributed to that book (DOWN AMPNEY, 152, RANDOLPH, 524, SALVE FESTA DIES, 624, and SINE NOMINE, 641) any foreshadowing of the musical revolution he was about to initiate in the larger field. Of these four tunes, two are models of what a hymn tune should be, and one might fairly be called something of a disaster. What needs emphasising is that Vaughan Williams did not bring to the *English Hymnal* the musical idiom for which he is now universally revered, and which has had so radical an effect on all composers who followed him; on the contrary, it was the researches which he pursued into the psalmody of Geneva and the folk songs of Britain and the classics of early English hymnody that inspired him to write music that did true honour to the real English tradition. Not all of this research was done on behalf of the *English Hymnal*; Dearmer, its editor in chief, selected Vaughan Williams because he knew that his interest would make it a truly "English" hymnal. But we should not have had the *Tallis Fantasia* or *Dives and Lazarus* or the *Household Music* had it not been for his work on the *English Hymnal*: and had it not been for this perhaps we should not have had the *Oxford Book of Carols*, or those remarkable compositions in *Songs of Praise* (1926, 1931) in which Vaughan Williams did bring the fruits of his maturity to hymn writing.

Here it is the same story that we have now told so many times:

G

backwards first, then forwards. It was a matter of educating church-goers towards a wider vocabulary, in which the religious emotion of stiff solemnity might be lessened in favour of a new eagerness and vitality. *English Hymnal* enlarged the vocabulary by reintroducing to currency much that had been lost—tunes from the Genevan psalters of 1542–62, tunes adapted from English folksongs, tunes from 17th–18th century Catholic revival in France, tunes from the Puritan psalters in their original forms and rhythms, tunes by Tallis, Gibbons and Lawes, and tunes already familiar in corrupt versions often restored to their original versions: this not to mention Bach arrangements of German chorales, some of whose appropriateness for congregational singing has been one of the policy-points of the *English Hymnal* most frequently brought into question. The musical work was carried on in *Songs of Praise*, edited again by Dearmer, but bringing in Martin Shaw along-side Vaughan Williams, in which a very large number of new hymn tunes were experimentally introduced. Among the more remarkable of these are Vaughan Williams's own MANTEGNA (126), MARATHON (302) and GUILDFORD (316); Arnold Bax's WONDER (107); Harold Darke's CORNHILL (41) and Patrick Hadley's PEMBROKE (311). The very beautiful tune LOVE UNKNOWN (127) by John Ireland, often attributed to *Songs of Praise*, actually appeared first in the 1919 edition of the *Public School Hymn Book*. But it was these experiments of a highly progressive sort which gave *Songs of Praise* its character. From that book were later derived many books which were used in schools, and on the whole the most experimental material in *Songs of Praise* was excluded from these smaller summaries of the book. But of all the tunes mentioned above, only that of Ireland has achieved anything like common currency. That is why we mention them. It was felt by these editors, principally by Vaughan Williams, that the time had come for the introduction of a new kind of hymn tune to anybody who would sing it. Holst very ably abetted him. It was very largely because this book contained so many tunes which have not "caught on" because in the nature of things congregations have been shy of them, that it engendered a fresh approach to what was more familiar, and promoted so many other new tunes that were more accessible—such as many of Martin Shaw's, and W. H. Harris's ALBERTA (554). No holds were barred, so far as these editors were concerned. No experiment with chromaticism, or modality, or free rhythm was too bold to be tried. But the very presence of these impracticable oddities—in their own right, superb music very often—made musicians look at a hymnal for the first time with respect.

Meanwhile *Hymns Ancient and Modern* went through new editions. In 1904 a complete revision was made, and this proved too pedagogic to be attractive and perhaps hardly radical enough to compel attention. In 1916 Sir Sydney Nicholson edited a Supplement which was incorporated with the edition of 1889 in a new full edition of 1922. In 1939 preparations for a further revision were made in an interim *Shortened Hymns Ancient and Modern*, and in 1950 the total revision then anticipated took place. In the 1950 edition there are a number of contemporary tunes, of which the most impressive are W. H. Harris's NORTH PETHERTON (235), Heathcote Statham's ARNCLIFFE (381) and Leonard Blake's REMISSION (324). But the principle here remained "what they will sing" rather than "what we must try to get them to sing". There is no tune in the book which one could call "experimental", although there are many contemporary ones which are beautiful and suggestive.

The effective of *English Hymnal* on the later editions of *Hymns Ancient and Modern*, its chief competitor for the attention of Anglicans (who have never had an officially authorised hymn book) was as small as it could be. Copyright restrictions have traditionally excluded each from the use of the other's property. This has not been in effect a bad thing: it has meant that musically *English Hymnal* gave expression to the radical revival while *Hymns Ancient and Modern*, in all its editions, carried on the tradition of conservative reconstruction. Vaughan Williams and Holst are in *English Hymnal*: Wood, Parry and Harwood appear more in *Ancient and Modern*.

Perhaps the radical revival would not have had so great an effect as it has had if there had not been also a revival of interest in congregational singing amongst Anglicans. And this was not chiefly the work of Vaughan Williams himself, but rather of musicians of a very different stamp—Walford Davies, principally, and Hugh Allen. Martin Shaw became the bridge between the practical pedagogy of these and the musical radicalism of Vaughan Williams. Walford Davies's personal case is interesting in that he came to the Church of England from a nonconformist background on the borders of Wales: and it was largely due to him that an interest among congregations in the quality and content of their singing was aroused. He used broadcasting from its inception with very great effect towards this end. Allen was, in effect, the inventor of that very popular religious pastime, the "Hymn Festival"—for as early as 1912 he was gathering congregations together in the Sheldonian Theatre in Oxford and making them sing hymns for the fun of it from specially printed sheets. It is fitting that as a composer Sir Hugh Allen should now be known only by two hymn tunes, one of which, MIDIAN (*B.B.C. Hymn Book*, 339) is one of the most remarkable and successful "bold experiments" ever made in the form. But out of this dual movement in university and church has grown a custom which has for many years provided the B.B.C. with its most popular sound-broadcasting programme, "Sunday Half Hour"—a programme more recently adapted for television in "Songs of Praise". The Hymn Festival Movement in America (it is thus referred to in the American Hymn Society, which now largely promotes it) is another offshoot from the same source. Of course, the indiscriminate singing of hymns can be a self-indulgence of a peculiarly squalid sort; but nowadays we can say two things in favour of the pioneer work of Walford Davies and Allen: one is that "Sunday Half Hour" and similar programmes have effectively replaced in our dispersed society the godly custom of singing hymns round the parlour piano on Sunday nights; the other is that it is much easier now than it was to get congregations interested in new hymn tunes through planned programmes designed partly with a teaching purpose.

Nonconformist hymnals one by one have shown the influence of the new musical criticism of the *English Hymnal*. Generally the tendency has been to widen the vocabulary and to include at least a few tunes, and collocations of tune with words, to which *English Hymnal* gave currency. This can be seen to a large extent in the Presbyterian *Church Hymnary* (1927), to a somewhat less extent in the *Methodist Hymn Book* (1933); the Congregationalists and Baptists paid a minimal attention to the *English Hymnal's* criticisms in the first books they produced after 1906 (*Congregational Hymnary*, 1916, *Baptist Church Hymnal*, 1933), but in their later and now current books they absorbed a great deal of the Vaughan Williams principle (*Congregational Praise*, 1951, *Baptist Hymn Book*, 1962).

In Canada and America the same forces have been at work, the *Hymnal* (1938) of the Episcopal church in Canada has a great deal of *English Hymnal* in it, and the *Hymnary* (1930) of the United Church of Canada shows the influence of *English Hymnal* as it was mediated by the Scottish *Church Hymnary*. The books of the U.S.A. published since 1940 have shown parallel developments: an interest in native American hymnody from the eighteenth and early nineteenth centuries corresponding to the interest of Vaughan Williams in early English tunes, and a direct taking-over of many of the *English Hymnal* principles: although here it is noticeable that the Americans frequently take their *English Hymnal* through *Songs of Praise*, a book in which they have consistently shown greater interest than the English editors have done.

There has then been, in consequence of fifty years' *English Hymnal* influence, a marked widening of the vocabulary of hymnody, an extension of the repertory, and a critical approach to hymn singing which have greatly improved English worship in the eyes of musicians. In one practice Englishmen remain obstinately and unhappily rooted: that of supplying congregations with books containing only the words of hymns. Economics are usually adduced as the cause of this, but in German circles the issue of any hymn book without the melody-line added to the words is unheard-of, and in many American churches every member of the congregation is supplied with a full music edition. This has retarded the progress of hymn-singing in Britain to a considerable degree, in a time when so many people have as a matter of course learned to read at any rate one vocal line of music at school. The cause of this may partly be also the love of Englishmen for singing in harmony, or what they take to be harmony, and the habit of Englishmen of believing that no male person ought to be asked to sing any note higher than tenor D. Part of Vaughan Williams's campaign was based on the assumption that all congregational singing should be in unison: but it would have gained much more force if English congregations had to a larger extent taken advantage of the melody-editions of his books upon which he insisted, and if their publishers had forsworn words-only editions. As it is, however, much has been done.

There are signs, however, that two eras are coming to an end simultaneously. On the one hand, the day of the large denominational hymn book may soon be over: economics from one side and the effects of the ecumenical movement from the other may well bring about the issue of a general hymnal with denominational supplements. On the other, the publication of the *English Hymnal Service Book* in 1962—a book which elects about 300 hymns from the existing *English Hymnal* and in very many cases sets them to tunes which show a complete repudiation of the principles for which Vaughan Williams stood—seems to mark the end of the acceptance of radical criticism. Again, the advent of the new style of "popular" hymn, together with the questioning of all the traditional idioms, may bring with it an approach to hymn singing which will render all existing hymn books outdated. That is the subject of our last main section: but meanwhile we can record that Vaughan Williams did succeed in a long lifetime in making English hymnody fit for musicians to notice. Had he not done so, and had nobody done so, hymnody might by now have been relegated altogether to the aesthetically irresponsible religious underworld.

Here are a few twentieth century English hymn tunes which repay the musician's attention:

English Hymnal (1906 edition)

SHEEN, by Gustav Holst (310), for "From glory to glory advancing"—an extremely ingenious setting of an extended metre.

LASST UNS ERFREUEN—originally from a seventeenth century German Catholic source, but largely in this form the composition of Vaughan Williams (519), for "Ye watchers and ye holy ones".

MONKS GATE—adapted from a folk song by Vaughan Williams (402), for "He who would valiant be".

Oxford Hymn Book (1908)

SOUTH SHIELDS, by Bishop T. B. Strong (65), to "In the bleak midwinter".

RAGLETH HILL, by Basil Harwood, the musical editor—an example of fantastic over-complication but of sedulous musicianship (242), to "Lord it belongs not to my care".

The New Office Hymn Book (1908)

TRIUMPHE! PLAUDANT MARIA, by Vaughan Williams (125, ii).

ALMA CHORUS, by Vaughan Williams (Appendix 17).

These two tunes of Vaughan Williams are otherwise unknown and commonly elude his biographers; neither they nor the rest of this book are of much musical interest.

Hymns Ancient and Modern (edition of 1904)

COSMOS, by Sir Sydney Nicholson (329)—a very early composition of a future editor.

ALVERSTONE, by C. V. Stanford (337), to "Praise to the Holiest" —an example of Stanford's rebellious attitude to conventional hymnody: compare his AIREDALE at no. 498. (Also at 205 in Revised edition).

INTERCESSION, by C. H. H. Parry (129), to "O word of pity" (also at 115 in 1950 edition).

Songs of Praise (1926, 1931: numbers in 1931 edition)

ENNISKERRY, by Ina Boyle (240), to "Service and strength".

CUMNOR, by Vaughan Williams (213), to "Servants of God".

ALBERTA, by W. H. Harris (554), to "Lead kindly light".

CHILSWELL, by Gustav Holst (498), to "Gird on thy sword".

EXON, by Thomas Armstrong (469), to "Close by the heedless worker's side".

MARCHING, by Martin Shaw (678), now a very popular tune to "Through the night of doubt and sorrow".

COBBOLD—attributed to "S.M.W.V.R." but presumably a joint composition of Martin Shaw and Vaughan Williams (Appendix i, p. 850), to "Sing, brothers sing".

The Public School Hymn Book (1919)

WOLVERCOTE, by W. H. Ferguson (first marked "Anonymous") (189), to "O Jesus, I have promised"—an early and good example of the "public school" hymn tune—broad melody, warm harmony, and unisonal texture.

The Methodist Hymn Book (1933)

GRAINGER, by G. F. Brockless (489), to "Workman of God"—an experiment in modality.

GOD OF MY LIFE, by F. L. Wiseman (429), to "God of my life"—perhaps the first tune for a congregation to be written in 5/4 time.

NEARER MY GOD TO THEE, by T. C. Gregory (468, ii), without exception the most remarkable essay in melodic atonality in a hymn book in common use.

Hymns Ancient and Modern (Shortened edition, 1939)

FENITON, by Sir Sydney Nicholson (717), to "Not a thought of earthly things" (also at 392 in 1950 edition).

The Public School Hymn Book (1949)

BURRINGTON, by C. S. Lang (500), to "Rise up, O men of God;" —one of the farthest developments of the "public school style" mentioned above: many other examples from this composer are in this book.

Hymns Ancient and Modern (1950)

See references in text above: also

BARNET, by R. H. Jesson (223, i), to "When morning gilds the skies"—composed by a choirboy of fifteen, clearly under the influence of Nicholson.

ELTON, by John Dykes Bower (534), to "Who dreads, yet undismayed".

Hymnal for Scotland (1950: being the English Hymnal of 1933 reprinted with a Scottish Supplement)

MARGARET, by Vaughan Williams (748 in Supplement), his last example.

B.B.C. Hymn Book (1951). Note especially tunes by the three music editors, W. K. Stanton, G. Thalben-Ball and Cyril V. Taylor

SHERSTON, by W. K. Stanton (287), to "Ye servants of God"—containing the boldest modulation in the literature.

HAMBLEDEN, by W. K. Stanton (314), to "Thee will I love"—a finer example, featuring a massive diatonic clash in the seventh phrase.

JESMIAN, by George Thalben-Ball (63), to "Brightest and best", in which, as in most of his tunes, the composer shows himself a good pupil of Walford Davies.

ARTHOG, by G. Thalben-Ball (256), to "Angel voices"—a particularly well-knit musical argument.

ABBOTS LEIGH, by Cyril Taylor (176), to "Glorious things"—easily the most successful "new tune" since Vaughan Williams's "For all the saints" in gaining general popularity.

RIPPONDEN, by Norman Cocker (243), to "For those we love".

Congregational Praise (1951)
BEEDING, by Eric Thiman (505, i), to "Christian, seek not yet repose".

TRAVELLER, by Eric Thiman (495, i), to "Come, O thou Traveller".

LANCING, by A. Brent Smith (193, i), to "When morning gilds"—a pre-Beaumont example of "pop" writing.

TEILO SANT, by J. P. B. Dobbs, (21 i) to "Eternal light".

Sunday School Praise (1958)
EDMONTON, by R. E. Perrin (264), to "It is finished".

Among Roman Catholics in the twentieth century there has been a realisation that hymns are something more than popular religious songs offered by way of concession to public taste, and a remarkable feature of the 1940 *Westminster Hymnal* was the influence which the Genevan Psalters were allowed to exert in the style of its newer compositions, largely through the advocacy of Sir Richard Terry. As a rule, however, the popular hymn-vocabulary in the Roman Catholic church remains very limited, since in the nature of things hymns are far less used in that Communion than in the others. Propaganda in churches and schools and through broadcasting in favour of better music is, however, having a discernible effect.

The end of this story, however, must be read in our concluding section: and that may portend the beginning of another.

On the continent of Europe hymnody has been subjected to a scrutiny hardly less searching than it has received in Britain and America. Sources for this are the latest hymnals of the Protestant bodies; and not infrequently the Dissenting bodies show more invention than the established ones: for example, in Germany the Church of the Palatinate, in its hymnal, *Evangelisches Kirchengesangbuch* (Speyer, 1954), and in Holland the Dutch Remonstrant Church in its *Oude en nieuwe Zangen* (Bussum, 1954). In Sweden a considerable reformation of hymnody has taken place under the inspiration of the eminent theologian, Bishop Aulen, who is also a composer and the head of the Music Academy in Stockholm. And in the U.S.A. Winfred Douglas was the chief inspiration of the movement towards better hymn-music in the Episcopal church; he has had many followers in the Protestant denominations, with the result that a great improvement has been notable in such recent books the *Hymnal* (1940) of the Episcopal Church in the U.S.A. of which he was himself editor in chief, the *Hymnbook* (1955) of the Presbyterian group of churches, the *Pilgrim Hymnal* (1958), and the *Service Book and Hymnal* (1958) of the United Lutheran Church.

Along with the great interest in hymns has arisen in both countries a fashion for composing "hymn-anthems"—which correspond, as has already been said, to the "chorale-preludes" in the organist's repertoire. These are essentially hymn tunes set with varied organ part, varied choral treatment, descant, fa-burden, and any other composer's device that will turn three or four verses of the same tune into an attractive anthem. One of the earliest practitioners of this art was Charles Wood, whose great interest in the old psalm-tunes caused him to write several very skilful hymn-anthems which used them as subjects: examples are "How dazzling fair" and "God omnipotent reigneth", both posthumously published in 1929, and both founded on Genevan tunes. Stanford's "O for a closer walk" is another early example. Henry G. Ley's "The strife is o'er" and "Lo round the throne" are two of many which he founded on German tunes. W. H. Harris's "O what their joy and their glory must be" is a highly complex example of the form. Bairstow's "The day draws on" uses a French Church Melody and his "Blessed city", already referred to, makes subtle and dramatic use of the plainsong tune URBS BEATA. Hymn-anthems should, of course, be distinguished both from anthems which use the words of hymns but give them a continuous and original setting, and from anthems in hymn-anthem form but using a tune by their own composer: of this last form Eric Thiman wrote what is perhaps the earliest in "Sing Alleluia forth", and followed it up with many others. The essence of the hymn-anthem properly so called is that it uses an existing tune, and treats it partita-wise, offering variations and musical comment. The great advantage of most hymn-anthems is that they are easy to sing; but they are also disastrously easy to write, and in consequence when the form falls into the wrong hands its music value is rather less than the value of the original hymn tune. Some of the most tedious music in the literature is in this form.

Much of the music at present being published for church choirs in America is in hymn-anthem form. There is much concern there, as we have seen, for the publicising of good but not always familiar hymn tunes, and the American choral and organistic set-up encourages the writing of such pieces which give plenty of opportunity for the organist to carry the main burden of musical accomplishment. Again, there is a good deal of cheap and vulgar material among this literature, but there are many examples which are simple and effective. Now a few are based on early and half-forgotten American tunes, and to that extent are very welcome: such are Samuel Walter's "How firm a foundation", Gardner Read's "Vital Spark of heavenly flame", and van Iderstine's "Garden Hymn" and "Wondrous Love". Austin Lovelace's "Dear Lord and Father" makes effective use of an old Irish melody. Healey Willan's "Christ whose glory" is a workmanlike comment on the familiar tune RATISBON. So the U.S.A. has its Charles Woods and its Bairstows, and at their best they are serving the choirs well.

One of Britain's more remarkable recent essays in this form is a whole cantata, Raymond Warren's *The Strife is O'er* (1960), based, Bach-like, on a single hymn tune: five of its eight movements (the rest being recitatives) make direct reference to the tune which W. H. Monk adapted from a phrase in Palestrina; it is perhaps in Monk's form an indifferent tune, but by the time Mr. Warren has done with it it proves itself an effective subject for this kind of extended treatment.

Another characteristically twentieth century development is the increased, and still increasing, interest in singing carols. As is more fully explained in my book, *The English Carol*, this movement has its roots in the early nineteenth century: but a scholarly approach to it was introduced by G. R. Woodward in his *Cowley Carol Book*, to whose musical arrangements Charles Wood made a large contribution: and the idea of carols as appropriate to seasons other than Christmas was made common currency in the *Oxford Book of Carols*. The demand for Christmas carols has, however, built itself into the commercial life of both this country and the United State: as a result, carols of every possible complexion, from the exquisite to the abysmal, are available for any who want them, and carol books of varying degrees of completeness and literacy are increasing in number year by year. The only significant thing to be said in this book about carols must be left until near its end (p. 184); some Christmas seasonal pieces by the composers who have already entered into the story have been or will be mentioned in their place. For the rest, I beg to refer the reader to my other book.

In the matter of psalm-singing, however, this century has made one contribution which may turn out to be of far-reaching effect—the psalmody of Joseph Gélineau. The problem of singing the psalms congregationally has proved intractable ever since plainsong was abandoned by the Protestants. Protestants have normally translated or paraphrased the psalms in metre and sung them as hymns, and the most consistent form of this practice is still to be found in Scotland. The Anglican communion has consistently compromised on the Anglican chant, which is harmonised and stylised development from plainsong. By the beginning of the present century the music of psalmody in both forms was very largely settled. Metrical psalms had their classic tunes, and there remained little to add to the enormous repertory of Anglican chants, some magnificent musical epigrams, some grotesque, which had accumulated since William Byrd wrote his setting of Psalm 114. In Anglican chanting what the twentieth century has concentrated on is performance and interpretation. Sir Walford Davies was a pioneer in "speech rhythm", and his tradition has been preserved and made nationally familiar through the work of his Temple Church successor and pupil, Dr. Thalben-Ball, in the broadcast services of the B.B.C. The Royal School of Church Music spends much time in propagating this principle, and it is axiomatic that the choir of a cathedral, collegiate church or good parish church will understand its principles. The difference between the manner in which Anglican chants are now sung, when a good choir sings them, and that in which they were sung in 1900 is so enormous that one needs to hear one of those rare and precious old acoustic records of a parish church choir of Edwardian days to be convinced of it.

Dr. Thalben Ball has himself done as much as anybody in our time to make the Anglican chant more flexible and sensitive: and to this end he has composed many chants in unusual and asymmetrical forms for the *Choral Psalter* (1940) and later for the *Broadcast Psalter* (1950). But unhappily once the principle of speech-rhythm was established, many editors sought to adapt it to their own notions: and today there is a disconcerting diversity of psalters available, of which the *Parish Psalter* (1930) and the *Oxford Psalter* (1929) are only two celebrated examples. In nonconformity a pedagogic urging of the claims of speech rhythm has silenced the old angular style of singing without very successfully inculcating a new congregational rhythmical style; so that the psalms are nowadays much less sung in Dissent than they were. Never was there such exquisite psalm-singing as one can now count on in the cathedrals: but the congregation at large has to some extent lost by this.

The claims of plainsong have, of course, been increasingly pressed by its admirers: but the unhappy fact is that plainsong still has a political connotation in church circles, and the sound of it causes the low-churchmen still to bristle. It does require a highly skilled accompanist (if it be accompanied) if its subtle beauty is to be made evident to a congregation, and too often where it is used the accompanist is content to play in four parts, with no modal sense and no breadth of invention, with results that are much more tedious than the unaccompanied singing would have been.

At the time when what was obviously needed was a demythologised plainsong, that is precisely what Pere Gélineau provided. Gélineau, a French priest-musician, is now famous for the new French translation of the Psalms which he made, following strictly the rhythm of the Hebrew, and which was published in full in 1956. Before that date he had begun to make musical settings for some of these translations; and these he devised in different rhythmical shapes, and sometimes in adaptable shapes, so that the rhythms of the psalm, or different rhythm within the same psalm, would be faithfully reflected.

His principle was extremely simple. Instead of using, plainsong-wise, a melody inflected only at the end of the phrase, he constructed a melody whose change of note (or accented repetition of note) would occur with the strong beat of the verbal rhythm. Syllables falling between these beats are then arranged to form a four-beat bar. This runs directly against the "speech rhythm" of Anglican chanting, which abhors the minim-two-crotchets rhythm and loves the triplet and the quintuplet. Its regularity of bar and stress opposes the genius of Anglican chanting which draws out or compresses "bars" to follow the rhythm of the English translation.

A Gélineau chant often goes to two "verses" at a time, so it may well be in four sections, or in six. Given the principle, all that is needed is a genius for musical epigram equal to that which the best composers of Anglican chant possessed. This also Gélineau supplied. The effectiveness of his tunes is quite astonishing. They follow no set rules of tonality, in that they may be (they normally are) modal and diatonic, but they

may equally take a thoroughly romantic turn, as does his tune for
Psalm 22 (23), or they may use chromatic touches, as does his tune for
Psalm 136 (137). Records have already been issued which show how
these tunes may be treated congregationally: they are in use at the
Taizé Community in France (a community of Protestant lay brothers
vowed to work and missionary service founded in the fifties); they
have been used by a congregation of 3,000 at Strasbourg (see below
on Langlais, p. 134); they have been recorded by children's choirs and
by the pop-singer Cy Grant with a guitar accompaniment. They have
been sung, now and again, even in the High Kirk of St. Giles,
Edinburgh (they were first sung there in March 1961).

   An example of Gélineau's psalmody follows, with an extract from
the authorised English translation that follows precisely the rhythms
of Gélineau and of the Hebrew:

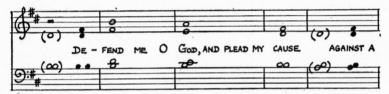

The psalms are designed to be used with antiphons, and in English
use these are partly composed by Gélineau and partly by other composers, notably Dom Gregory Murray, who has been personally
responsible for much of the initial publicity that this method of singing

has achieved. During the past five or six years Gélineau has become in Britain almost as well known, and almost as favoured a talking-point, as Geoffrey Beaumont. What he certainly has done so far is to introduce the psalms in a quite new way to his Catholic co-religionists. And without doubt he has found a method of psalm-singing which has neither the verbal distortions of metrical psalmody not its ponderous tedium, nor the demand for extremely careful singing that the Anglican chant makes, nor yet the "Catholic" associations and methodological demands of plainsong: for Gélineau supplies all his own harmonies, and all the organist needs to do is to play the succession of chords in strict time: the rest is up to the singers, and none of his tunes takes more than a couple of minutes to learn.

(NOTE: All the words and music of the Gélineau Psalms at present available can be obtained on inquiry to The Grail, 58 Sloane Street, London, S.W.1.)

A complete 'Gélineau' English translation of the Psalter was published by Collins Ltd., in Fontana Books in September 1963.

PART THREE

TAKING DOWN THE WEST WALL

Is music ahead of the other arts? There is only one answer—No! So far from being ahead, it is mournfully, miserably, cretinously laggard! This is normal. It has always been so; but never never has the gap been so scandalous as it is now. This is why we must support with all our energy those—a ridiculously small company: three or four in the whole world—who are trying to regain a little of the lost ground.

OLIVIER MESSIAEN, 1937[1]

9

The Terrors of "Modern Music"

QUITE recently Mr. Deryck Cooke, writing in *The Listener*,[2] put the following question: "Can one name even one up-to-date English composer of importance anyway? Britten is certainly, to quote another writer, 'anachronistic' . . . Yet Britten is the towering English genius of our time!" "Anachronistic" is explained here as implying that Britten's harmony "hardly out-dates Stravinsky's neo-classical period". A better claim is advanced in the same article for Mr. Humphrey Searle, our most distinguished exponent of serial techniques in music.

Up-to-date.

It is the general assumption that church music is in any case dispensed from the necessity of being "up-to-date"; and therefore church music can be looked at with a sort of mystified indulgence, or an irritable contempt, by musicians who are concerned with the pressing forward of the new kinds of music.

What we have to say here is this: that while everybody knows that the tempo of invention in music has accelerated, and appears to be accelerating at something more than the geometrically progressive speed of gravity, in our own time, in the field of church music (in the widest sense, anyhow), there has been plenty of indication that the gap in achievement between sacred and secular is rapidly closing.

But since to many people the most "contemporary" of modern music is still a mystery, and something of a repellent mystery at that, we must offer a few notes and recollections concerning the principles that seem to govern this strange revolution.

The Parisian music-critic, M. Fred. Goldbeck, wrote a most interesting essay which is translated in *Twentieth Century Music*[3] under the title "Twentieth Century Composers and Tradition". Urging the reader to read the whole essay when he has the chance, we here offer a summary and a few quotations from it.

"The substance of music", says M. Goldbeck, "is tradition". It is not notes or sounds. It is tradition. Music is a function of memory—and of memory in a number of modes. That is to say, the appreciation of a piece of music depends not only in your being able to connect, by memory, one note with another, and one phrase with another, and a subject with its varied repetition: it depends also on your familiarity with all the music that went before it. That is how music operates *now*. It was not always so.

> For a very long time now, and until the end of the nineteenth century, the music of everyday life with which musicians were mainly concerned (excluding, of course, the special domain of church music) was new and contemporary, with perhaps a sprinkling of music belonging to a very recent past. The music of Louis XIV [1638–1715] and his contemporaries was the music of Lully [1632–87] and his contemporaries. For a professional musician like Frederick II [1712–86] the latest sonata of C. P. E. Bach [1714–88] was the music that mattered, and that of John Sebastian [1685–1750] a curiosity that one would have to hurry to get to know before it became quite demode. "Contemporary music" was a sort of pleonasm a hundred years ago. It was what everybody played. . . . The composer in those days was a person who belonged essentially to the present.
>
> That the situation today is very different is obvious. I would not even mention it were it not for a fact that never ceases to amaze me, and that is that no one has taken the trouble to notice that it is here that the key to the "modern" outlook is to be found. It is here (and not in any isolated phenomena such as dissonant, serial, electronic or any other systems) that we must look for the kind of Copernican change that has affected music. *Before*, music gravitated round the square we call the present and the avenues leading directly therefrom. *Today*, music of the present gravitates round the whole history and tradition of music.

M. Goldbeck here implies that the great change in approaches to music is connected with the revolution in Western Society that the sudden new facility of communication, and the consequent dispersal of scholarship and knowledge, has brought about. The modern Western listener has, as it were, been quickly raised, as if by a funicular, to a great height from which he can without effort see an enormous expanse of history. Being there, he begins to think in terms of the assumption that this is natural and that everybody has always been there. But before music was in this sense everyman's business—and before musicology similarly became everyman's business (so that he can hardly avoid hearing an enormous amount of music of many periods, furnished for him by people who dig it out of the recent or remote or even very remote past) the manner of listening was something which a modern listener can scarcely imagine. Consider the implications of a later amplifying sentence in M. Goldbeck:

The composer of those days if he were a Gluck, hoped that in composing an *Orpheus* he would do better than his contemporaries, and replace the old-fashioned *Orpheus* of a preceding generation. He had nothing to fear from competition with Monteverdi, of whom very probably he had never heard.

Quite so. And in church music we may remark that, since until very lately the provincial, domestic ethos preserved itself there when it was passing away outside the church, when Stainer wrote his *Crucifixion* he really did not expect competition with the *St. Matthew Passion*; nor did the local vicar, in writing his hymn tune, suspect that a hymnologist in 1950 would compare it with another tune in the same metre by William Croft.

M. Goldbeck then introduces Debussy as "a musician who by reason of his originality and the freshness of his imagination could have dispensed more easily than all the others with tradition", but who instead "brought us back to Rameau, to the polyphonic masters of the Renaissance, to modal music and all the most forgotten traditions, real or forgotten, of monody".

The rest of his argument is exciting but we will not go on with it here except to quote one more remark: that "the *avant-garde* aestheticians often hold extremely conservative views as to what constitutes *avant-gardisme*". That makes the point which must here be stressed especially because it has a special bearing on church music.

Modern music, so-called, began with a new consciousness of ancient music. And it continues with it: and it explores music of what were up to recent times unknown and unexplored foreign cultures—so we get Messiaen's experiments with hindu-rhythms, just as we get sociological comment on Western society based on the findings of anthropologists who have studied marriage-customs in Bengal. Music partakes of the sudden shrinking of space and telescoping of history which is the framework of "modern knowledge". And Vaughan Williams's gestures in English church music are the best example one could find of this process—a new-sounding music based on forgotten folksong, and on a new appreciation of Byrd and Josquin and "Sumer is icumen in".

As M. Goldbeck rightly says, this leads to a lot of pastiche, neo-classicism, neo-archaism, and neo-prehistorism. A good deal of this pastiche music is music of a *Gebrauchs* kind—music which had its uses but which need not be remembered; its uses being not so much social as historical. It bridged a gap temporarily while a proper structure was being built. A good deal of the quietly experimental church music of the twenties and thirties was no doubt of this sort. But it was required, after the foreshortening and telescoping process had been recognised by the musicians, that they should discover what they, and only they, could say to their age.

The most important factor—for our present purposes at least—in the new creative thinking has gathered round a philosophical question concerning the elements of time, and of inspiration.

In an American symposium, *Problems of Modern Music*[4] the distinguished American composer Roger Sessions contributes an essay on "The Problems and Issues Facing the Composer Today".

In the course of this he states clearly that the "problem" is to find a new language that is free of what he calls "cliche". The modern musician's criticism of what we still call conventional music is thus stated:

> The characteristic pitfall of the nineteenth century was undoubtedly that of literary association and the manner of over-emphasis—sentimental, violent, or pretentious—just as that of the eighteenth was a certain type of elegant and formal conventionality. Our own particular brand of emptiness is perhaps beginning to emerge in a variety of clichés, derived both from so-called neo-Classicism and from serialism in its earlier as well as its later phases. In each case we are dealing with a manner that has become generalised through lack of substance, and not with ideas in any positive sense.

The modern musician has found the root of cliché[5] in the cadence,[6] and this he has first attacked. (We have seen already that of this at least twentieth century church music provides plenty of examples. It was Vaughan Williams's starting point.) Secondly, rhythm has come under criticism—and here again, church music provides abundant evidence of a simple and accessible kind. But from there the musicians have proceeded to "total organisation"[7]; and this has had two main branches of effect. On the one hand, the whole matter of the sacredness of "inspiration" is brought into question, so that music becomes a matter of devising, then applying, formulae of a near-mathematical kind. On the other hand, experiments are being made with sources of tone which are infinitely controllable, and whose relation to composer and performer is entirely different from that in which the traditional instrumentalist stands: so that instead of a fiddler or a trombonist, the composer uses electronic tones, scientifically producible and controllable, to convey his message. On this Mr. Sessions writes as follows:

> Is music simply a matter of tones and rhythmic patterns, or in the final analysis the organisation of time in terms of *human* gesture and movement?[8]

The use of serial technique quite obviously implies a radical question about the element of chance in musical inspiration; and the use of electronic instruments implies a similar question about chance in the instrumentalist's performance. Mr. Sessions, however, goes on—

> The element that "total organisation" leaves out of account is not chance at all. It is the organic nature of movement as such, of the fresh and auto-nomous energy with which the performer invests each musical phrase, every time he sings or plays it. . . . It is more than the element of "surprise"; it is rather that if the expression of movement is to become effective, we require not only the evidence of movement from one point to the next, but a sense of the motivating energy behind it. . . .
>
> The danger of dehumanisation is a real and patent one, and the individual can, and certainly should, resist any dehumanising tendency with all his strength. But this cannot, and must not, blind us to the claims of whatever is genuinely new and vital in the arts (p. 33). What is necessary, if the pitfalls are to be avoided, is that composers . . . should always retain the courage of their own artistic vision, that teachers should emphasise the supremacy of real musical imagination, and that listeners . . . should, by holding them-selves open to whatever genuine and even unexpected experience music can bring, learn to discriminate between what is authentic and what is fictitious (p. 25).

In the same symposium, Ernst Krenek in "The Extent and Limits of Serial Technique", provides a valuable amplification of this—the more so for the general reader because it includes extensive reference to a work of his own which is the only piece of electronic music written on a Christian theme easily available on record to English readers.[9]

His description of his aim—specifically mentioning his oratorio for voices and electronic effects, *Spiritus Intelligentiae Sanctus*,[10] is to produce what is "Premeditated but unpredictable". He is able to show precisely how he organises his material—answering a question which had you put to Beethoven he would have thrown all his books at you—and then says—

> It may be stated that whatever occurs in this piece at any given point is premeditated and therefore technically *predictable*. However, while the preparation and the layout of the material as well as the operations performed therein are the consequences of serial premeditation, the audible results of these procedures were not visualised as the purpose of the procedures. *Seen from this angle, the results are incidental.* They are also practically unpredictable because the simultaneous progress of highly complex rhythmic patterns at various relative speeds together with the corresponding transpositions of

equally complex pitch patterns creates situations that defy precise visualisation.[12]

Now hear what he says about traditional "inspiration".

> Generally and traditionally, "inspiration" is held in great respect as the most distinguished source of the creative process in art. It should be remembered that inspiration by definition is closely related to chance, for it is the very thing that cannot be controlled, manufactured, or premeditated in any way. It is what falls into the mind . . . unsolicited, unprepared, unrehearsed, coming from nowhere. . . . Actually the composer has come to distrust his inspiration because it is not really as innocent as it was supposed to be, but rather conditioned by a tremendous body of recollection, tradition, training and experience. In order to avoid the dictations of such ghosts, he prefers to set up an impersonal mechanism which will furnish, according to premeditated patterns, unpredictable situations.
>
> Ligeti[13] characterises this state of affairs very well. "We stand in front of a row of slot-machines, and we can choose freely into which one we want to drop our coin, but at the same time we are forced to choose one of them. One constructs his own prison according to his wishes and is afterwards equally freely active within those walls—that is: not entirely free, but not totally constrained either. Thus *automation does not function as the opposite of free decision*: rather free selection and mechanisation are united in the process of selecting the mechanism". In other words, the creative act takes place in an area in which it has so far been entirely unsuspected, namely in setting up the serial statements (selecting the slot-machine). What happens afterwards is predetermined by the selection of the mechanism, but not *premeditated* except as an unconscious result of the predetermined operations. The unexpected happens by necessity. The surprise is built in.[14]

And thus Krenek quotes in the end from Pierre Boulez, one of the most notable of modern French *avant-garde* composers, who wrote "There is no creation except in the unforseeable becoming necessary".

Philosophically, these are deep waters. Only just round the next headland, as it were, is the church's ancient debate with itself on the subject of predestination. But, since we must not write here more than is necessary to our main subject, we must be content with these quotations and demonstrations from the practitioners of a branch of music which to most readers remains virtually an unknown field. What is most necessary is to grasp the *reason* why these composers believe in this kind of music. Having passed clean through the stage where history suddenly opened itself up, and memory in musician and listener became suddenly (suddenly is not too strong a word, taking the historical view) so greatly extended in its range, these composers

seek for a new speech to communicate to a new age. They therefore
ask the question about music at its deepest and most functional level—
and bring up answers of many varied kinds. These musicians are more
articulate, more self-critical, more anxious to please (though not to
please large numbers of people) than any musicians have ever been.
But they self-consciously turn away from any cultivation of effect for
effect's sake. Where a "conventional" musician reckoned it part of his
duty to estimate with accuracy the effect of what he was writing—the
measure of its difficulty and rewardingness for player or singer, the
measure of its impact on the hearer—these musicians leave all that to
take care of itself. "Surprise" is not eliminated, only re-located. The
amount of deliberate contrivance that lies behind the apparently
spontaneous effects of any musician between Berlioz and Britten is no
secret, although it is conventionally a secret from the immediate
hearer: for art, we say, must conceal art. But there is nothing more
spontaneous in the conventionals than there is in the *avant-gardes*;
rather, like the modern organ-builder, they are at no pains to conceal
the mechanism. And they regard it as beyond their proper business to
estimate effects.

Therefore their music, whatever the strangeness that a conventional
listener hears in it, has many virtues, or at least many defences against
temptation, that are denied to Dyson and Bairstow. They are miles
away from the danger of "creating atmosphere"—which is one of
those activities in which if the mechanism shows through, what you
have is practically an indecent sight. Well, say the moderns, we make
no secret of the mechanism, and so we cannot manipulate your emo-
tions. This ought to be a matter for enormous congratulation on the
part of people who are bemused and sated with the nineteenth century
ecclesiastical devices for creating musical atmosphere.

In other words, there is an agnosticism here where in the other kind
of music there is an assurance: and an explicitness where elsewhere
there was reticence. It all reminds one of the current trend in religious
thought. The combined impact on the alert in the churches of the
revolutionary concepts of Rudolf Bultmann, Dietrich Bonhoeffer and
Paul Tillich, as they have been popularised in the book, *Honest to God*, by
John Robinson, Bishop of Woolwich[15] appears to many to be a removal
of foundations and an affront to faith. It may well appear, when the
controversies have become somewhat more recollected, that they are a
re-deploying of agnosticism: the challenging of certain assurances, the
enthroning of certain neglected truths. The whole complex of revolution is the direct consequence of a social development of the West, and

whenever it appears it is associated with a re-examination of the remote past and a new consciousness of spatially distant cultures.

But that the modern musician is far from diffident is surely evident from an essay of Pierre Boulez, recently published under the title *L'Esthétique et la Fétichisme*[16]. The passionate and satirical contention of this essay is that modern musicians are a serious fraternity of artists, scientists and craftsmen. Well, if they seek, in its own right and for its own sake, no element of surprise or shock as they play and sing to us, any secret hope they may have that they will surprise their listeners is surely being amply gratified at present. What is of concern here, however, is that there is no divorce whatever between this music and the church. A small quantity of it has already appeared. More will. But never at any point do these musicians "write down" to the church. Never do they write without sincerity or integrity, or with patronage or pedagogic indulgence, for the church. In the reason for this there is no particular virtue; it simply happens that you cannot do such things with this kind of music. You can only write it. You cannot write it in this way or that. There is excellent reason for guessing that this music may turn out to be the best conversation that the musicians have yet had with the church, just because there is a certain kind of bad manners which, by definition, its composers cannot affect, and which, by convention, has been the greatest temptation to church musicians of the conventional sort.

NOTES TO CHAPTER 9

1. C. Samuel (ed.), *Panorama de l'Art Musical Contemporain* (Paris, Editions Gallimard, 1962) p. 313.
2. *The Listener*, 4th April, 1963, pp. 610, 613.
3. R. H. Myers (ed.), *Twentieth Century Music* (Calder, 1960) pp. 21–28.
4. P. H. Lang (ed.), *Problems of Modern Music* (New York, W. W. Norton Co., Norton Library paperback N. 115).
5. ib., pp. 24–25.
6. ib., pp. 26–27.
7. ib., p. 31.
8. ib., p. 32.
9. E. Krenek in *Problems of Modern Music*, pp. 72–76.
10. E. Krenek, *Spiritus intelligentiae Sanctus—Pfingstoratorio*, D.G.G./L.P. 16134.
11. *Problems of Modern Music*, p. 81.
12. ib., p. 83.

13. Gyorgy Ligeti, "Analysis of Boulez", *Structures* for two pianos in *Die Reihe* (Vienna) no. 4, p. 38.

14. *Problems*, pp. 90–91.

15. John Robinson (Bishop of Woolwich) *Honest to God* (London, S.C.M. Press, 1963).

16. P. Boulez, "l'Esthétique et la Fétichisme", *Panorama*, pp. 401–415.

From Romantic to Electronic

A GREAT deal of the most *avant-garde* music has come from the continent of Europe, and the largest scale works of church association in the new idioms are still the work of French and German composers. This therefore is the point at which we shall survey briefly the field of twentieth century church music from the Continent. It must begin with music of a more traditional kind, but it will move quite shortly into the farther reaches of contemporary music.

It soon becomes evident that almost every country has its Vaughan Williams: at any rate, most countries which had not, by 1900, a Viennese-type professional tradition in music of good standing had one. This was, as has been indicated already, the beginning of the break-up of the Viennese musical empire, and the pattern becomes clear as soon as one looks about in Europe. Czecho-Slovakia throws up first Dvořák (1843–1901) then Leos Janacek (1854–1928), both of whom looked to German orthodoxy for their technique but to the folksong of their countries for their subject-matter. Hungary produces Zoltan Kodaly and Bela Bartok, great musical folklorists of their own nations. Scandinavia produces Ludwig Matthias Lindeman (1812–87)—hardly a Vaughan Williams in his devotion to conventional ecclesiastical techniques, but none the less a folksong collector of eminence and the founder of a continuing interest in it in Norway. Brazil—to go far afield for a moment—produces Villa-Lobos. Spain has its Falla (1876–1946) and Turina (1882–1949), who founded a new "national" style having reference to national origins if not to folksong specifically. Thus the "fringe" cultures of music in the nineteenth century become the new centres of a dispersed musical interest after the political disruptions of the twentieth. It is the same with Britain.

Germany, on the other hand, becomes the home of violent and serious forward-looking musical dissent. There it is a head-on collision between the old style and the new, and the result is Schoenberg, the centre of the whole twelve-tone movement in music.

France is a special case: for France has had a continuing musical tradition of great strength, but of such a kind as to become in the nineteenth century a continuing dissent against Viennese values. The great moment for the reawakening of France's music—apart from the historic appearance of Debussy, of which we have already taken account—was the gathering together of those eccentrics (as they were thought) who called themselves "Les Six"—having first been thus labelled by the critic Henri Collet. These were Milhaud, Durey, Auric, Honegger, Tailleferre and Poulenc: and Poulenc has a distinguished place in our story. These were the forerunners of that contemporary French music which is now so vital in the work of such as Boulez: and theirs was as much a national and temperamental reaction against Teutonic values as anything else.

But if we recall Goldbeck's pinpointing of Debussy as the founder of modern music in his re-assessment of ancient music, then we find that France fits into the pattern perfectly well, and only the Teutonic culture lies outside it: which is entirely to be expected. In all these other countries, it was first a staring into the soil rather than a staring at the sky which revitalised music. But note that probably nowhere does this come through in the music itself so obviously as it did in Britain. It is not, on the whole, in these European countries, so much a matter of putting folksongs bodily into music, as Vaughan Williams quite often did; nor even of writing tunes which had a noticeably folky sound—as again Vaughan Williams often did in his more unbuttoned moments: it was much more surely, a recapture of nerve and confidence consequent on the study of the national music, and, perhaps primarily in the case of Janacek, the national literature.

In some ways Britain is too much like Germany to be a good example of what really produced Continental modern music; the Teutonic strain in Britain still makes for literal-mindedness, self-consciousness and a tendency to argue "not this, therefore that", and thus to produce rather over-emphasised national music when it is being national at all. The same strain keeps one stream of British music firmly wedded to Brahms. But how much more like Brahms Elgar is than Dvořák! Both owe so much, and yet if Dvořák says things in a Brahms-like way, he never says Brahms-like things: and Elgar does—and so do that long line of English church musicians to whom nobody in Europe corresponds at all.

Janacek comes near, and perhaps just over, the frontier of our country in his impressive cantata, *Věčné Evangelium* ("The Eternal Gospel", 1914). This is a spacious setting of words adapted from the poetry of Joachim of Flora (d. 1259), the strange medieval off-beat Abbot and man of letters who propagated a millennial teaching about the immediate coming of a new age of the Holy Spirit. The poem here speaks of universal love, and the work was written in the shadow of the Balkan War and on the eve of the First World War. When he wrote it Janacek was sixty; but he was to wait some years yet for any kind of international recognition. That is typical of the situation at the time. The musical world was full of Brahms and naturalised aliens like Rachmaninov: and although there is to the modern ear nothing in the least startling in the idiom of *Věčné Evangelium*, not a bar of it sounds like the music that gained acclamation in the more crowded concert halls of 1914.

This is even more true of his last large work, the *M'ša Glagolskaja* ("Festival Mass", 1928). In his last years he gained recognition as a composer, and this opulent score is full of confidence and joy. Here, as in his operas, one finds the highest employment of his characteristic gift of "integrating the brusque cadences of his tongue with a broad melodic line"[1]. The broad melodic line still consists of short folk-like phrases, but the total conception has a massive unity and assurance which make it one of the greatest of all post-romantic scores.

More unambiguous contributions were made to church music by a successor of Janacek, Bohuslav Martinů. Does Martinů play Holst to Janacek's Vaughan Williams? Perhaps only in his clearer score, in the fact that he did special service in music for fighting soldiers, and in his singular aptitude for making much of modest resources. This is especially to be seen in that extraordinary work, the *Polni Mše* ("Military Mass"), composed during the Second World War and published in 1947. This is a work which nobody should miss the chance of hearing: and it is accessible in Britain on a record. It is scored for male voice chorus, flute and piccolo, two clarinets, piano, harmonium and a good deal of percussion. That is, it is scored for what you could raise in the N.A.A.F.I. if there were a few competent bandsmen available. The piano in performance has to sound like the N.A.A.F.I. piano, and it is a capital mistake (which is unhappily made on the record) to play the harmonium part on a full-scale church organ. Virtuosity is nowhere called for: just military competence and alertness.

It is not really a "Mass", for it sets very few of the words of the Catholic service. It is a Mass about as much as Brahms's *Requiem* is technically a Requiem. Apart from what are hardly more than references to the liturgical words, it takes phrases from the Psalms, and for the rest it uses poetry of an appropriately patriotic and nostalgic kind. In the following example the words come from one of these poems.

The passage is typical of the astonishing power of this work for evoking great matters with simple musical effects. Here is the stanza from which the words in the example come:

From foreign shores, Lord, I call;
I pray to thee from distant lands;
I search with songs for thee throughout the heaven;
Yet will you know? How will you see
That it is I who in anguish call thee,
I, son prodigal of my native land,
No stranger, only I imploring thee?
How can you know me in this field,
    So distant from my home?
O my good Lord, keep me alive;
When crushed by war, I shall reel.
Just for my life, O Lord, I beg and pray,
So that thy hands may lead me home again.
Who knows, if death will find us brave and strong?
Did not even your own son weep bitter tears of fear?
O my Lord, from this dark Mount of Olives hear us calling
With hearts sad unto death:
Eli, Eli, do not forsake me!

His last composition, *The Prophecy of Isaiah* (1959) is a setting of words from the 24th and 21st chapters of Isaiah, dedicated to the people of Israel, and scored for soprano solo, male voice chorus, piano, viola, trumpet and timpani. He wrote the work to the words of the English King James Version; in the published score it appears in English, Hebrew and German. It is not clear whether the work was or was not finished at his death, but its two parts make a complete whole in themselves. It is a masterpiece of restrained yet passionate declamation.

Of the great Hungarians, Bartok contributed nothing but some brief arrangements of carols and folk-music to the literature of the church; but the contribution of Kodaly has been notable. His three major church works have been the *Psalmus Hungaricus*, Op. 13: (1923), the *Te Deum* (1936) and the *Missa Brevis* (1951). Of these the first two were state-commissioned works: the *Psalmus Hungaricus* to celebrate the uniting of the two cities of Buda and Pesth, and the *Te Deum* for the 250th anniversary of the recovery of the city of Buda from Ottoman rule. But all three are in the highest tradition of modern dramatic Christian music, scored for full orchestra and chorus. The music is characteristic—rich, flexible and passionate. Perhaps the *Missa* is the greatest of the three, but a generation earlier the *Psalmus* made music

Ex. 35

which Edwin Evans described as "one of the most impressive choral works of modern times."[2] Among his smaller works, *Jesus and the Traders* (1936) is one of the most remarkable short works for unaccompanied choir of its age.

A contemporary of Kodaly's on the other side of the world was Villa-Lobos, who amongst a large amount of highly individual music based on research into Indian themes in the heart of South America composed one work for the church—his *Mass of Saint Sebastian* (1937). This work is something of a *tour-de-force*, being composed for three voices a capella (men's voices, or women's or boy's: or, as the title page indicates, with all three doubled at the octave). Villa-Lobos was a highly successful composer, much given to facile vulgarity and to presentation of colossal musical occasions: in 1931 he gathered a choir of 12,000 singers at São Paulo and four years later he promoted a concert in which 30,000 singers were supported by 1,000 instrumentalists, In 1940 he capped this with a choir of 40,000 in the Vasco da Gama Stadium in São Paulo. The recent critic[3] who furnishes this unnerving information judges that the best of Villa-Lobos is in his genuinely "folky" music, and the worst in his imitations of classical styles. It is remarkable that the comprehensive source from which his article comes omits to mention this quite charming little score, whose modesty and intensity are matched only by its inventiveness. It concedes to "classicism" a good deal of fugal writing, but it has many moments of unusual contemporary grace, as in the "Pleni sunt caeli" from the Sanctus, where he inverts the theme of the "Sanctus" over a rhythmically contrapuntal accompaniment to give great spaciousness, within his limited vocal resources, to the interpretation of "heaven and earth are full of thy glory": (Example 36)

Returning to Europe, we must now deal with three French composers whose contribution is perhaps the most important of all at the present time. François Poulenc's death in 1963 was one of those events which made one feel that a light had gone out. His music is still very little known in this country, apart from a few popular piano pieces. But he is easily the most accessible of "Les Six" to the ordinary listener. A master like his musical friends, of the satirical, he succeeded in bringing to church music just that astringent touch which it needed for its revival. There was little church music of the least consequence being written in France when his *Mass in G* came out in 1937; and certainly none that sounded in the least like this: (Example 37)

It was as if church music there was imprisoned until it gained the release of satire, wit and lightness of touch. Lennox Berkeley in his

Ex.36

Ex.37

memoir of the composer at the time of his death wrote "there are
many passages in his religious music that are strangely haunting—
moments that reveal a touching tenderness and simplicity of heart, and
that remain in the memory".[4] The works of his that any listener should
get to know include *Litanies de la Vierge Noire* (1936), *Stabat Mater*
(1951) and his scintillating *Gloria* (1961) commissioned by and dedicated to the distinguished conductor Koussevitzky. His organ concerto

(1938) is only now becoming known in this country, but it is a work of resounding high spirits and profound poetry. Poulenc's is as much as anybody's of our age the music of "holy worldliness"—of sacred laughter. If he "reacted against romanticism and impressionism" with frivolous results in his early years (Lennox Berkeley's judgment), in his maturity he brought to church music a gift that made him eminently suited to qualify for St. Francis of Assisi's description of a *ioculator dei*—a merry man of God.

When we come to Olivier Messiaen, however, we come to a new point of departure. Messiaen is quite unique among modern composers in several ways. For one thing, he looked farther back, and also farther forward, than any of his contemporaries apart from the electronic experimenters. He found a peculiar fascination, not in folk song but in the song of the birds—which he has used especially in his secular works—*Le Reveil des Oiseaux*, *Cataloge d'Oiseaux*, and *Oiseux Exotiques*; and his experiments in hindu rhythms extend into his church music, especially the staggering *Livre d'Orgue* (1951), in the fifth section of which he wrote as follows:

> This contains, over a melody of independent rhythmic construction played on the full organ and with four-part double pedal, six hindu rhythms, three answering three as rhythmic "personalities", one group progressively augmenting, another progressively diminishing, another again remaining unchanged, and none of the rhythms sounding together at any given moment. This gives a series of very complex combinations, which I have had to indicate above each note for the player. . . . In the final section, entitled "64 durations", I have thrust to its utmost limits the human perception of durations of great and of minimal length—and, more difficult yet, perception of very short and very long durations at the same time.[5]

And that provides a very fair introduction to what one is up against when one seeks to handle this quite astonishing composer.

For another thing, however, Messiaen has always regarded himself as a "theological" composer. Not as a "mystic"—a word he dislikes when applied to himself. He dislikes it because it misses his main point—which is the severe rationality and strict organisation which he applies to his music. For no modern composer is church music less of a "sideline". But—and here is a third point of uniqueness—his church music is very largely written not for voices but for the organ. If there is one instrument (we have already seen this) whose literature is almost entirely *Gebrauchs* to a depressing degree (Bach apart), it is the organ. Noting could be less *Gebrauchs* than Messiaen's music. It is organ music because it must be organ music, not because this is the only instrument on which one can conveniently provide incidental music in church. And it is organ music for the altogether astonishing reason—but in his hands a cogent reason—that the organ has certain peculiar rhythmic qualities that are denied to other conventional instruments.

This is the rebirth—one might almost say the only authentic birth —of organ music. For consider: the organ is by its nature very largely a machine. It is the one instrument which flourished throughout the period of orthodox music that posed questions about predestination such as we saw the modern music-technologists posing. It is a machine. Once the note is pressed, machinery takes over, and the pipe opens. You cannot control your tone by pressure on the key. You can control it only (1) by your choice of stops and (2) by your use of *duration*. Here alone, the note sounds at unvarying volume and timbre for precisely as long as the key is pressed. Human breath or pressure does not enter into the matter. And all through the literature of the organ this has been regarded as a necessary limitation. Messiaen uses it as a liberation. Even the finest of organ music of the conventional kind— Bach's—can be played as effectively on a pedal-harpsichord. Yes—the harpsichord takes timbre and volume out of the performer's hands: but it has no control of duration; the sound begins to die as soon as the note is struck on the string. Bach makes no special use of the organ's capacity for duration in itself. Other composers make use of certain positive qualities in the organ—its capacity for romantic expressiveness, a resonant building's property of echo (from the old pre-Bach Toccatas onwards); the special clarity of counterpoint which a baroque organ shares with a good harpsichord. But not this purely mechanical property of duration: that is what Messiaen discovered. And since he uses all the other properties of the organ as well, he, a true son of the technical age, can be said to have discovered for the first time how the organ can fulfil itself.

Take for example the obsessive and repetitive din—it is difficult to call it anything else—of his early organ piece, *Apparition de l'Eglise Eternelle* (1932). Without some kind of context, this piece is virtually impossible to listen to. But its whole point is precisely continuous *noise*—noise that does not vary in a human fashion but just goes on and on, relieved only by an equally obsessive rhythmic figure in the pedals, and by the originality—a terrifying originality—of the juxtapositions of chords that alone give the piece a movement. It might be worth recording that your present writer first heard this piece on a record; and that when he bought the score he was obliged to play the record through at once, because he fully believed that the whole of what was played was not written in the score. The effect on hearing is of immense duration, of accumulated *longueur*; the score runs three pages. And this piece just could not be played on any other instrument whatever: the piano (with however many hands you bring in) runs out of tone: any group of wind players would run out of breath at this high degree of volume. This is an early study in simple duration—and the ear that does not know what to expect inevitably registers the impression that it is a study not only in duration of sound but in the listener's endurance.

But neither here nor anywhere else can we believe that Messiaen misjudged anything. This must be precisely what he meant. The trouble with most organ music is that one feels that it is as near to what the composer meant as the instrument will allow him to come.

Messiaen has written at length about his own music. In *Technique de mon Langage Musical* (1944) he explained at length the rhythmical and serial principles upon which he worked.[6] These are complex in their working-out, yet the principles themselves are simple and severely logical. Incidentally he shows more than once how his use of chords is anticipated in Debussy and Ravel,[7] and how much it owes to a study of the harmonics inherent in single fundamental notes. But it is rhythm that is at the basis of his stylistic novelties, and while one can only invite the reader who is interested in these matters to go to Messiaen's own literature for a full explanation, the following example, from one of his better known organ works, "Les Bergers" from the massive suite, *La Nativité du Seigneur*, shows in a simple way a characteristic rhythmic pattern in his work: (Example 38)

The two-note phrase at the beginning of the melody here, and the following three-note phrase, are simple examples of Messiaen's principle of "added value"—the amplification of familiar rhythms by adding an unexpected note of half-value. This principle he deduces directly from his study of hindu rhythms.[8]

Round this framework of exact and logical thought, Messiaen builds up strange and variegated structures of imagination, and these he relates, in his organ music, to Christian concepts. In the opening paragraphs of *Technique* he writes that music has no nobler end than the expression of religious sentiments "exalted by the theology and the truths of our Catholic faith". The end-products of this process are sometimes attractive at once to the unsophisticated ear—especially "Les Bergers", and the final (E major) section of "Dieu parmi nous", from *La Nativité*. In *L'Ascension* (1934) there is also some haunting

Ex.38

music that makes its effect at once. His short motet for solo voice and organ, "O sacrum convivium" (1935) is likewise most attractive. But the height and depth of his imagination are fully to be seen in the *Messe de la Pentecote* (1950) for organ, and the range of his inventiveness can be found at its most disconcerting in the curious music and the invented nonsense-language of *Cinq Rechants* (1949). Messiaen has aroused furious opposition in some, and passionate partisanship in others; but his place in church music is adequately summed up in the following judgment from a French critic:

> Messiaen's miracle is to have thrown a bridge between the spirit of French music and the rigours of technical research: to have proved the compatibility of the element of "inspiration" and that of "technique". The first (inspiration) was suspect in the eyes of the new generation, and the second was rejected with horror by those who held to a certain tradition— that which owes its being to Gounod rather than to Debussy. But in the work of Olivier Messiaen, whose attractive qualities nobody can deny, the two are inseparable.[9]

Jean Langlais is an almost exact contemporary of Messiaen, like him a distinguished organist, and as a composer, while short of the giant stature of Messiaen, still one of the leaders in French church music. He lacks also Messiaen's standing in secular music. But there are three points at which he has already established himself as a major contributor on the church field. His organ music, first, is uncommonly free-ranging, exploiting especially the expressive qualities of the baroque instrument. In his *Three Characteristic Pieces* (1957) and his *Triptyque* (1958), works of considerable difficulty for the player, the score is very clean, two-part writing is virtually the rule, the exceptions to which produce a special dramatic effect, and the idiom is contemporary without attempting Messiaen-like radicalism. Echoes of Messiaen appear here and there, but these are impressionistic effects rather than structural principles. His *American Suite* (1961) is an astonishing compendium of organistic effects, well suited to the mammoth romantic instruments to be found in that country, and exploring very freely the frontier between sacred and secular. The eight pieces are given titles including names of places, ranging from "New York on a Sunday Morning" to "St. Buffalo Bill's Grave", and the Vox Humana and the Chimes receive duly respectful attention. This suite is recital music for the virtuoso, and profundity is incidental.

But in his own organ-loft Langlais can rise to moments of remarkable inspiration, and his *Missa in Simplicitate* (1953), a liturgical setting of the text of the Mass for solo voice and organ, is a memorable example of this. Here one sees Langlais' devotion to plainsong, and the fruit of his close study of it. The voice-part is a series of expressive phrases, often bursting into *melismas* of passionate exuberance, making contemporary, as it were, that primitive energy which is the true secret of plainsong. The organ accompaniment is largely confined to sustained chords, sounded at every degree of intensity from pianissimo to fortissimo, and supporting by subtle harmonic suggestion the flexible melodic line.

A motif that runs through the entire piece and provides the intonation for the Gloria and the Credo provides also the only movement in the organ-part:

Ex.39 A

GLO - RI - A   IN EX-CEL-SIS DE - - - O

Here is a typical melisma, being the "Amen" of the Gloria, to be sung with full voice, *Allegro* and supported by abundant organ tone:

Ex.40

The inherent modesty of this music shows what Langlais can do when nothing but the need of the liturgy is in view. He can be forgiven a good deal of French-organist high spirits in his organ works for the sake of so exquisite an evocation as this.

The third matter in which Langlais has made his mark is in the unexpected—it might seem in this chapter incongruous—realm of hymnody. The continental contribution to hymnody, apart from what we have noted in chapter 8 is, of course, negligible. But a special occasion called forth from Langlais what is perhaps the finest modern hymn tune in the literature. The occasion was the "Bible and Liturgy" Conference in Strasbourg in July 1957, at which a large gathering of Catholic theologians met for study, and in the course of which a novel form of "Vigils" service was held on the Saturday, in preparation for Sunday's High Mass. In this service, after the reading of lessons from the Old Testament, the Epistles and the Gospel (all in French, the Gospel being also read in Latin), and the preaching of the Sermon, the open Bible was displayed before the people with the words, "Voici la parole qui nous sauve: vénérons la! Ce que nous oreilles ont entendu, que nôtres coeurs l'acceuille et le garde.* At once a canticle was sung, whose words were specially written for the occasion, and the tune was the composition of Langlais. The tune and the first two

verses of the words follow. This service, which was recorded (see bibliography) is remarkable also for its extensive use of liturgical psalmody by Josef Gélineau.

Switzerland has chiefly contributed to church music at the Kapell-meister level (see above, p. 93) ; but one major work, of oratorio scale, has emerged from that country in recent years. It is Frank Martin's *Golgotha* (1949). This is a Passion Cantata in two parts, running an hour and a half in performance, scored for full orchestra, piano and organ, with four soloists and choir. The text is partly from the Gospels and partly from St. Augustine's Meditations, chapters 15 and 18. Its style is Teutonic-dissonant rather than either modal, romantic or *avant-garde*. Martin in secular work has gone much further in the

* Here is the Word that saves us. Let us venerate it! What we have heard with our ears let our hearts gather and keep.

direction of serial music, and his other large church-score, *La Mystère de la Nativité* (1959) shows somewhat more willingness to ally his experimental techniques with a religious text. Both are works of great eloquence and uninhibited dramatic feeling.

The same can be said of a distinguished contribution from Poland —Szymanowski's *Stabat Mater* (1928), a setting of verses from the well known medieval Latin hymn for chorus and orchestra. Szymanowski was a contemporary of Stravinsky, who on a much smaller scale experimented in many musical forms, allowing himself to be influenced by composers as diverse as Debussy and Richard Strauss as well as by the earlier work of Stravinsky himself. The *Stabat Mater* is a study in dissonant chromaticism, on the whole conservative in its main principles, ambitious in its technical scope within a 20-minute production, and dealing with remarkable skill with the problem of introducing variety into the setting of so monochromatic a text as this. It is easy to listen to, and in its way highly moving.

Music in the strictly serial style has, in the nature of things, made little impact on the church, apart from the occasional organistic experiment (to one or two of which we shall refer a little later on). The hymn tunes of Vincent Persichetti, the distinguished American authority on modern musical techniques, sometimes move in this direction, but naturally some concessions are here made to the needs of ordinary ears. The Viennese masters—Schoenberg himself, Berg and Webern, took no part in the development of church music. (Well: church music is still liable to be in C major). But it is worth pausing a moment to mention Wolfgang Fortner's *Die Schöpfung* (The Creation). This was composed in 1955, and is a setting of a remarkable poem, paraphrasing Genesis 1, by the American negro poet James Weldon Johnson, beginning

> And God stepped out on space,
> And he looked around and said,
> I'm lonely—
> I'll make me a world.

(This poem was read at the Service of the Arts, which was part of the consecration-celebrations at Coventry Cathedral, and held on 8th June, 1962: it is printed in the order of service published on that occasion.) Fortner had the poem translated into German, and set it not romantically, but to music of strict serial development. It ends with an "Amen" which combines a "rhythmic series" taken from the medieval musician Philippe de Vitry with an independent tone-row. The result is at first strange to the ear; one wonders how the highly evocative poem inspired the musician to such music. The answer is— and by now it should be expected—that this is a study in juxtaposition, not in integration. The music is sent on its way, and runs simultaneously with the poem, and what effect may be produced by the juxtaposition is, apart from the initial choice of themes, neither contrived nor immediately intended by the composer. Listened to with that in mind, it throws up all manner of suggestion which a "romantic" setting would have excluded.

Whether one stage would be better than another at which to con- sider that cosmopolitan giant, Stravinsky, may be debatable. It seems right to mention him at this point because in all his output, with all its variety of style—comic, classical, dramatic and weighty by turns —the serial technique has its place, and it finds its way into some of his religious music. Stravinsky is on record[10] as saying "we commit fewer musical sins in church", and as stating a conviction that church music is, or can easily be, as high and beneficient form of music as any. "Religious music," he said, "without religion is almost always vulgar. It can also be dull. There is dull church music from Hucbald to Haydn, but not vulgar church music." (Of course there is vulgar church music now, but it is not really of or for the church); and again, "without the Church, 'left to our own devices', we are poorer by many musical forms." Asked whether one must be a believer to compose music in specifically church forms, Stravinsky replied, "Certainly, and not merely a believer in 'symbolic figures', but in the Person of the Lord, the Person of the Devil and the Miracles of the Church."

Stravinsky has consistently shown a lively interest in writing music not only to religious texts (such as the *Symphony of Psalms*, 1930), but for the church's liturgical use, such as his *Mass* (1948) and his *Threni* (1958), of which he said that he had hoped to hear both used liturgically, but had been disappointed of his hope. In the *Canta* of 1952 he used serial technique for the first time, and he uses it more extensively and consistently in a more recent religious work, *A Sermon, A Narrative and a Prayer* (1961). In this last work, still little known, the English text of passages from the Epistles, of the Death of Stephen in *The Acts*, and of a prayer by Thomas Dekkar (d. 1632) are partly sung, partly spoken, against a serial design scored for full orchestra. And while it is impossible, as it is impossible with all such music at present, to make any kind of judgment about its quality, and although it must always be clear that the kind of judgment that one makes about all post-romantic music is made in a language which does not apply to this, at least one can say with reasonable safety that the contrived emotionalism and portentous moralising that overtook romantic music when the Church used it are absent from scores such as this. Some may think that everything else is absent too—and yet—this is why we introduce Stravinsky just here—can it possibly be true of Stravinsky? Here is a composer who more than any other proved himself a master not only of organisation but of invention in every kind of contemporary style before he embarked, at 69, on serial music. He had never said, as Boulez no doubt would, that serial music is the only way for a modern musician to speak: he has never abandoned older styles with Schoenbergian heroics. More than anybody else he can lead a listener across the bridge that spans the gulf between totally organised music and inspirational music. One can never be quite sure, and nothing could be more out of character than to attribute a Teutonic explicitness, purposefulness and self-conscious logicality to Stravinsky: but on the whole it looks as if it were safe to say that if Stravinsky can turn to this at 69, there is more in it than the dream of a handful of crazy young men. That, anyhow, is the best way to approach this problem for any reader who is still shy of the new approaches.

This brings us back to Krenek himself, whose Whitsun Cantata, *Spiritus Intelligentiae Sanctus*, we have already referred to in passing. Here is electronic music applied to a religious concept, and all we can here say is—listen to it if a chance presents itself. At first it appears to be the very reverse of *intelligentia*—but after several hearings memory takes over, and the pattern begins to make itself visible. Either this is a naif representation of chaos, and as such a caricature, or it is a portent of what we are to look for in the music of the future. For my own part I see no reason why the church should be afraid of this for its unfamiliarity; and if it represents an invasion of the religious field by a music closely allied with technology and reason, the influence of such music could be wholly salutary. But we cannot here make more than the most speculative sort of judgment.

NOTES TO CHAPTER 10

1. C. Samuel (ed.), *Panorama de l'Art Musical Contemporain* (Paris, Editions Gallimard, 1962) pp. 80–81.

2. O. Thompson (ed.), *International Cyclopaedia of Music and Musicians* (U.S.A. 1938, London, Dent, 1942) p. 943.

3. Lennox Berkeley on Poulenc, *Musical Times*, March 1963, p. 205.

4. *Panorama*, p. 683.

5. *Panorama*, p. 311–12.

6. O. Messiaen, *Technique de mon Langage musical* (Paris, Leduc, 1944): English translation, *Technique of my Musical Language*, tr. Satterfield, Leduc, 1956.

7. Musical examples of above work, pp. 39–40.

8. *Technique*, p. 14–17.

9. *Panorama*, p. 312.

10. The quotations in this paragraph are all taken from *Stravinsky in Conversation with Robert Craft* (Pelican Books, A. 517, 1962) pp. 136–38; the book was originally published in the U.S.A. in 1959 as *Conversations with Igor Stravinsky*, and by Faber & Faber (London) under that title in 1959.

II

Some English Experiments

Our previous study of British church music brought us near the edge of *avant-gardisme*; and indeed some of what was mentioned in our first section sounds *avant-garde* enough to the comfortable ears of ordinary churchmen. But it is probably fair to judge that there are as yet few musicians who have attempted to bring into the English churches the fruits of their contacts with the serialist culture in music. We will here mention four only.

Michael Tippett is the most experienced disciple of Schoenberg to make any contribution to church music. *A Child of our Time* is probably just the other side of the church-music boundary, although its religious passion is quite unambiguous. But his *Magnificat and Nunc Dimittis*, composed for St. John's College, Cambridge in 1961, is a *tour de force*. The Magnificat opens with, and is adorned at subsequent points by, a prodigious fanfare specially written with the trompette real on the St. John's organ in mind, but of course playable on any unenclosed high-pressure organ reed stop. The Nunc dimittis demands a virtuoso choir-boy for a continuous solo over an almost unrelieved alternation of the organ chord.

Ex.42 A

with the vocal three-part chord, sung to the repeated word "Lord":

Ex.42 B

at various pitches. The total effect is electrifying, and profoundly moving, for the work, short though it is, combines a passionate rhetoric with an inevitability of musical argument which impress the hearer even before he has begun to follow the argument through its various stages.

It is natural that composers in this idiom should find it a taxing discipline to write for the church. It is surprising that any of them have the patience to do so. But they will find publication only if there seems to be some prior probability that their work is performable by any church choir. To achieve some sort of practicability within the routine of even a choir of high musical capacity, and some remote chance of appreciation by those who overhear the choir's music, places a discipline upon such composers which it is gratifying to find that they do not all reject as irksome.

Peter Maxwell Davies, an English schoolmaster, and the youngest composer to be mentioned in this book, is another who has proved that it can be done. Like Messiaen, he not only writes music for religious use, but projects religious ideas into music of wider connotation—for example, in his wind sextet, *Alma Redemptoris Mater*. His music shows much medieval influence, skilfully combined with an avantgarde approach to tonality. His carol, "Ave Maria—Hail Blessed Flower", was published in *The Musical Times* in 1961, supported by an editorial assurance that the policy of that journal was from that time to be the encouragement of such music, and it caused a considerable sensation. Controversy continued for some months between those who found it inexpressibly ugly, and those who saw in it a major musical break-through. Compared with some of his work it is almost conservative: there is profounder music in his carol-sequence, *O magnum mysterium* (1961), and perhaps more effective music as well. He has had the advantage of being able to judge his music's effectiveness on a school choir—he was appointed Director of Music at Cirencester Grammar School in 1959—and his success has already been a good deal more than local. Again like Messiaen, he has allowed a close study of Indian music to affect his composition; and at the time of writing he is working out a style which will combine a contemporary intellectual integrity with the clarity that will come through to children.

The influence of Webern is at its strongest, in English church music, in the extraordinary *Monody for Corpus Christi*, by Harrison Birtwistle. This is a suite of three pieces—a setting of the old Corpus Christi carol, "The fawcon hath borne my love away", an instrumental interlude, and a setting of the Wedderburn carol, "O my dear heart". A solo soprano is accompanied by, or more properly takes equal part with, a flute, a violin and a horn. This is "new German" music, as it were, untranslated, with the free rhythm, the precipitous melodic inter-changes between one line and another, and the defiance of tonality that Webern brought to so impressive an artistic level. It is at present, somewhat significantly, published only in an edition that provides a German translation of the English text. It is a gesture: one cannot at present judge in any way of its success, and such a judgment is anyhow irrelevant to the rationalist scheme of the serialists.

A different line, however, is being taken by Malcolm Williamson, a still young Australian-born composer who has lately made a considerable impression in Britain by producing in quick succession a good number of pieces in two distinct idioms. He has made a decisive gesture in the "pop" idiom, which we shall comment on in our last section. But he has published a good deal also in an advanced "square" idiom (if we may thus anticipate language proper to our section on "pop" church music.) This music appears partly for voices and partly for organ. Williamson is said to have taught himself to play the organ in order to study at first hand the work of Messiaen. His most notable published work to date is *Vision of Christ Phoenix*, which was written for the consecration of Coventry Cathedral (1962). This is a work of astonishing violence and power, using every resource of a large organ and an able player, presenting variations on the theme of the "Coventry carol". That so gentle a theme could produce so wrathful and colourful a set of variations may appear the height of improbable incongruity until it is remembered that the Coventry carol mentions Herod with some directness: and it is at that point that the terror of the bombing of Coventry in 1940, represented in the opening passage of this work, makes contact with the old carol. Williamson's *Organ Symphony*, first broadcast in January 1963 and awaiting publication, is a much more ambitious work, running to a playing time of over thirty-five minutes and six movements. Here a good deal of Messiaen's violence and energy is mixed with a number of experiments in "pop"-rhythms which, as it were, bring the penultimate section of the Poulenc organ concerto up to date. This work has many moments of great impressiveness and tenderness, and may prove to be one of the major organ works of the century—but again, we dare not be more positive than that.

Three vocal works of Williamson's are worth studying. The *Symphony for Voices* (1962) is not a church work, but is an accessible example of his extended vocal style. It has a monodic "Invocation" which shows his interest in pure melody: and its overtones are Christian in an astringently "holy-worldly" sense. Musically it experiments with homophony and monody rather than with counterpoint or atonality. Its third movement, entitled "Jesus", is written in parallel octaves throughout. Dance-rhythms of many kinds are exploited, and the impression is that the composer is less concerned to present homogeneous stylistic gesture than to set, in the manner of the traditional composers, a series of suggestive poems in a manner that the singers will enjoy.

Planctus (1962) a monody for two groups of unison men's voices, is a more radical experiment. Its text is a passage of Latin from Abelard, and its context the contemplation of death. Basses open with a long recitative; tenors take over, overlapping by only one note with the basses, and that at the octave; the basses return, and in the end both voices sing together, but always at intervals of two octaves, or one, or at the unison. This is the final sentence of this tiny two-page score:

Ex. 43

Tenors.

Do QUI-E-TEM FIDI-BUS   VEL-LEM, UT ET PLANCTI-BUS

Basses.

SIC POSSEM ET FLE - - TI-BUS: LAE-SIS PULSU MA-NI-BUS

RAU-CIS PLANC-TU VOCI-BUS DE - - FI-CIT   ET - SPIRITUS

Wrestling Jacob (1962) an anthem somewhat more conventional—although still showing great musical ingenuity—sets three verses of Charles Wesley's famous hymn, "Come, O thou Traveller" to music of singular ingenuity. Its rhythms owe something, surely, to Messiaen's "added values". It has a very light and suggestive organ accompaniment, and its treatment of tonality is unusual, even for these days, in employing the same keynote throughout, but three different modes in the three verses, the final verse settling down happily in F sharp major.

K

Ex. 44

Williamson, then, is another composer of whom we can as yet make only a subjunctive judgment. But when we add to his music that has just been mentioned here the important contribution he has made in the new popular field, we cannot call him insignificant. He shares with Messiaen, his acknowledged master, a profound religious concern: but his translation of Messiaen into English has produced results very different from those which the French genius looked for. He has, surely, not yet lost his ability to surprise us.

Finally, we may mention two compositions which are, at the time of writing, brand-new. One is *Sing we Merrily* (1963) by Frederick

Rimmer, a composer in the faculty of Glasgow university whose experiments in the contemporary idiom have already commanded attention in the secular field. This is an anthem written largely in serial style for organ and choir, and provides another example of the singular aptness of this harsh yet often convincing music to Old Testament texts. It is worth careful study: and it is especially interesting to compare it with Sydney Campbell's equally excellent setting, in more traditional dissonant style, of the same words (1960).

The other new composition is Dr. Geoffrey Bush's *Two Latin Hymns*, simple *a capella* pieces which show an emotional depth and a central serenity surrounded with jubilation that make them singularly well fitted for contemporary eucharistic use. If we quote a few bars from the close of the first, "O Salutaris" they will show how the needs of the occasion have been met in the use of a thoroughly contemporary musical style. (Example 44)

PART FOUR

GOING IN AND OUT

When I hear a Beethoven Symphony, I don't feel anything. When I
hear our kind of music I feel something away down deep, like oatmeal.
(A young lady in America, who was
involved in the "payola" investigations
of 1960: quoted in *Life* magazine,
16th May, 1960, p. 119.)

12

The Vexation of "Pop"

ON Christmas Day 1955, some of us thought we had Church music pretty well where we wanted it—"taped". We could talk and write about its development from Palestrina to Vaughan Williams: or, if we wished to appear learned, from the cantillations of the Jewish Synagogue of a century or two B.C. to the latest Britten.

I remember very well how in the last week of that year I received for review a proof-copy of Geoffrey Beaumont's *20th Century Folk Mass*, and was required to give an opinion on it as best I could from that score in photostatically reversed print. If anybody cares to refer to what I wrote he will find it in the British Weekly files (30th December, 1955). Within a few months the Folk Mass had become the talk of the country. It was even mentioned on a B.B.C. Brains Trust. "Pop" had invaded the sacred field of church music: and, as it now appears eight years later, it had come to stay.

"Pop" music of the secular sort has received plenty of attention from music critics. It is easier to write of it as a social phenomenon than to criticise it with any closeness, because genuine "pop" is strangely ephemeral, and what is known to millions as I write this will very probably be forgotten and unobtainable in score by the time this page is printed. So we have to begin by treading the now well-worn path of sociology.

Writing of the "pop" idiom in another field of art—painting—Mr. Lawrence Alloway recently quoted a well-known "pop" painter to the following effect:

> I think of my purpose as a search for what is epic in everyday objects and everyday attitudes.[1]

A little later in the same article its author writes that genuine "pop" art is "The appeal to common sources within a fine art context".[2]

These are useful comments, although at first sight it might seem odd to describe much of what is called "pop" music in such exalted terms.

The sense of oddity arises from the difference between the "pop"
painting which Mr. Alloway is describing and the "pop" music which
sells to Englishmen and Americans by the million copies. And the
difference is this: that the "pop" painting is a self-conscious gesture by
painters, which Mr. Alloway says began in 1949, while "pop" music
is, in a sense, a much more ancient, and much more instinctive affair:
indeed, its practitioners are not given to the kind of articulation of their
own motives that we hear in the quotations above.

But what we are here going to find is that the new movement of
"pop" church music is a sophisticated, articulate and self-conscious
movement. I am, indeed, going to describe its most impressive practi-
tioner as an artist writing "in dialect". Therefore this approach seems
here to be the right one.

As an example of this articulacy and self-consciousness, here is what
Geoffrey Beaumont[3] writes in the Preface to his *Folk Mass*.

> This setting was composed at the request of an East London Vicar who
> said he was "deeply concerned that nothing has been written since the
> Elizabethans, which can properly be called a Folk Mass", and that church
> music is utterly foreign to the majority of people. The theory behind this
> setting is that the music used at the Holy Eucharist in apostolic days was the
> normal music of the day, and only became "church music" when it arrived
> with definite church associations in Western Europe, where it developed
> itself into the plainsong we know.
>
> In the title, the word "Folk" is used literally to mean the normal everyday
> popular kind of music.

Here at once we have a heavy emphasis on one of the two elements
of the aphorism from which we started—"the appeal to common
sources within a fine art context". "The majority of people", "normal
music", "normal everyday popular music"—these phrases represent
the search for a "common" contact in church music. Nothing is here
said about "fine art", and Father Beaumont has often been heard to
say that he does not regard himself as a musician in any professional
sense—only as an amateur who devotes his talents to finding this
contact between the church and "normal" people.

Now it is impossible to fail in sympathy towards the pastoral zeal
which lies behind this adventure of Father Beaumont's; but it was
probably unwise of him, or of his adviser whom he quotes, to be
dogmatic about the kind of music that was sung at the Eucharist in
apostolic times. It is far from certain that any music was sung at all
at that celebration in the first generation after Christ. If the famous

description of an early Eucharist in Dom Gregory Dix's *The Shape of the Liturgy*[4] is true—that is, of a purely domestic rite, held in the largest room of somebody's house without any kind of vestments or liturgical appointments is a true one, then we need not suppose that at the Eucharist any music was used at all. On the other hand the author of *Ephesians* encourages Christians to speak to one another and comfort one another "in psalms, hymns and spiritual songs" (Eph. 5, 19), and this indicates that when Christians gathered (the purpose of the gathering being altogether undefined) they were accustomed to sing. "Psalms" may be just what they appear to be—the Old Testament psalms which ex-Jewish Christians would have known well; "hymns" and "spiritual songs" may be new compositions of praise to Christ, with a touch of the "ecstatic" or "improvised" implied in the word used for "spiritual": but what immediately precedes that passage shows that its author was particularly concerned that Christians should sing thus and not "give way to drunkenness and the dissipation that goes with it" (Eph. 5, 18, *N.E.B.*). In other words, his advice here is part of a considerable argument which shows the difference between the way Christians are to follow and that which "the world" follows. The parallel passage in *Colossians* (3, 16), where the same three kinds of singing are mentioned, places the exhortation to sing in the context of a passage about gratitude, saying more positively that the Christian's mind must always be turned towards Christ. Both passages, one negatively and the other positively, emphasize the "separation" of Christians.

Nothing—this is the point here, and it is pivotal to the whole of our argument on this subject—was further from the apostolic mind than that Christians should make any concessions whatever to the "normal" and "everyday" standards of the non-Christian world. We know no more about Christian singing from the apostolic writings than we can gather from the passage above—except for a word from St. Paul in I Corinthians 14, 26 which does not bear on this part of the subject; but what we can be assured of is that although the idea of bringing the popular music of secular life into the church may nowadays be an admirable one, it was not an apostolic one.

Still less was it a likely notion to be entertained by the church of the fourth and fifth centuries, when the Fathers of the Church consistently wrote of church music as a thing that must be consciously separated from pagan standards.[5] But apart from all this, the comparison between musical outlooks in the early church and today will not stand much weight. Music in ancient times was closely associated with dancing and with pagan religion. The idea of a "popular music" as such was foreign to those times. It is quite likely that a modern era would find difficulty in distinguishing between a piece of music written for "sacred" purposes and one written for secular ones, because the spectrum of values covered by ancient music appears to a modern ear so narrowly restricted. It was, indeed, so narrow that it was possible for Plato to make his celebrated remarks in his *Republic* about the moral implications of certain musical modes without appearing to anybody of his age to be talking nonsense. We have to contrast with this the opulent variety of the music that is nowadays available to everybody, with its many instrumental colours, harmonic textures, and emotional associations.

Yet again—the modern idea of "pop" has social overtones which were unknown to people in the first Christian century. It not only did not occur to early church leaders—it could never have occurred to them—that the use of "popular" music could be a means of evangelising the kind of people who enjoyed it. They simply did not think, in that way, of "kinds of people". There were Christians and there were pagans, and the duty of Christians was to set a good example, remain loyal to their faith, convert the pagans and baptise them. Even the idea of arguing with the pagans and "out-thinking" them came some generations later than the apostolic church. The idea of taking what was supposed to be essentially and inalienably pagan and by using it in church, drawing the pagans in, waited thousands of years to be put into practice.

The real difficulty in understanding what is happening now comes when one is unwilling to recognise how modern, in a Christian context, is this honouring of the "normal" and "everyday" in the non-Christian culture that surrounds the church. It is really a natural symptom of the post-Christian society in which Western Europe and the United States now live. I here propose to maintain that at bottom it is not only natural but appropriate, right and wise. But it would not have been thought so anywhere before about 1914.

We can insist on this even against any who wish to say that the secular elements in the medieval carols, or the use of folk-song by Martin Luther as the basis for his Reformation hymns, or the use of music obviously derived from the style of the "Beggar's Opera" by the Wesleys, are examples of the same tendency at an earlier date. The carols, whose magnificent juxtapositions of sacred and secular ideas shock and delight the modern singer (like "Tomorrow shall be my dancing-day") are a gesture against the false separation of certain natural ideas from the Christian Faith, but they appear after two centuries of pseudo-puritan superstition, much more impressive to us than they would have appeared to those who first sang them. Luther's "pop-songs" can be called so only if one remembers that what he was using was music associated with aristocratic rather than with artisan circles (for if his music has a connection with the Minnesinger and Meistersinger,[6] then that is what we have to say about it). Similarly, the Wesley hymns were "pop" only in as much as they used music derived from the bourgeois culture of their day, and the upper-class culture, rather than in traditional church styles. But not only John Gay, but Pergolesi and Handel were really going to the same quarry for their materials. The poverty-stricken drunks of Redruth and Wednesbury were not providing this music for the Wesleys.

But the affluent and vociferous youngsters of the 1960's are providing this idiom for the Church now. That is the difference, and we must make no difficulties about admitting it.

It is difficult, maybe dangerous, to generalise about "pop" music today. The more one looks at it, the more slippery and elusive it shows itself to be. It is not "jazz"; the distinctions of jazz are in its deep-seated racial responses, and in its ecstatic use of improvisation. Jazz is a form of music which can command and hold close attention. Its lovers and votaries take it with a seriousness as analytic and as dedicated as any lover of the classics gives to Beethoven. Those who try to shrug this off as an affectation or a form of self-deceit, and to dismiss jazz as something essentially trivial, have been sufficiently exposed and convicted of false arrogance by many serious writers.

Yet "pop" has something in common with jazz.*

Neither, however, is "pop" the same as what used sixty years ago to be called "music hall". Take a music-hall classic like "Daisy, Daisy": the effect it made on an audience was gained through its catchy tune and the talent of a good straight singer, within a context of innocent, shameless and usually rowdy goodwill. It was essentially rhetoric of the old fashioned kind that demands a captive audience, and that looks for a noisy round of applause. It produced a tune which people whistled in the streets. It spoke with a kind of earthy authority about earthy things like love and mothers-in-law and conviviality. The contrast between this and modern "pop" could hardly be

* Any reader who is reading this chapter without having read the earlier part of the book should note that another approach to jazz in church music is discussed on p. 92 above, where the work of Heinz Werner Zimmermann is under review.

greater. The modern "pop" song is boosted into the public consciousness by a powerful commercial thrust; it is sung not to a music-hall
audience but to the hidden audience watching television or listening
to a record. Its singer is an idol surrounded by a mystique which the
late Marie Lloyd would have found quite incomprehensible. Its words
are, as often as not, the words of wild ecstasy or quasi-mystical, half
religious aspiration—or so they sound when sung: sometimes they
make little sense when read. The technique of singing them is not
that of the lusty hall-filling deep-chested comic tenor or contralto,
but that induced by the factitious intimacy of the microphone. Its
emotional content is fantastically exaggerated in the vocal modulations
of its singer. Everything about it, in production, is magnified to a
prodigious degree, and its trajectory reaches the mind and affection of
a listener who is far more captive than was the audience in the music-
hall: for he or she is a listener who must show no emotion, who must
follow the deadpan convention of contemporary youth, who must be
a stranger to praise or criticism, but only worship dumbly the personality of the performer.

And yet "pop" is not entirely unaffected by the music-hall tradition.
Is the "pop" song nowadays, then, what it was in the thirties?

Here we come nearer to the style we are thinking of: and yet the
difference is not inconsiderable. In the twenties and thirties of this
century popular music began to sort itself out into two streams—the
music of the big "musicals" of stage and later cinema, from Noël
Coward through Jerome Kern and Cole Porter to Hammerstein,
and the earlier forms of sheet-music-ephemera which any reader now
in middle age will remember from his youth. The "Big musical"
provided broad and sumptuous tunes, with romantic words that
fitted more or less into the plot and were often touched with satire.
The "ephemera" are now a possible subject of study (which here we
shall not attempt) because after the passing of a generation it is still
possible to hear a few of them otherwise than in broadcasts of a nostalgic or "period" kind. That age saw the birth of the "pop" singer and
instrumentalist; it saw the enthronement and, within twenty years
the abdication, of the theatre organist. And the changes which came
over "pop" music during that period 1920–50 were all associated with
the sudden and successful mechanisation of musical entertainment.
The gramophone had been invented in 1896 and the cinematograph
in 1897, but it was in the inter-war period that they achieved their
spectacular success. The B.B.C. came in 1922 and the dissemination
of culture at all levels increased in acceleration as if from arithmetical to

geometrical progression. All this was a process which in its latest phases has been responsible for a very natural evolution of "pop" from "Night and Day" to "Telstar".

But one thing must not be overlooked: this is the breaking down of the intimate connection that used to exist between "pop" and dancing. It was in the ballroom and the dance-hall of the twenties and thirties that "pop" found its centre. This was its ideal milieu: for "pop" is seldom music which will bear much close attention, and to use it for dancing is to put to its best use a music which is more successful as a background than as a means of communication.

There is a vast difference between the climate in which the "pop" of the thirties flourished and that in which it now lives: for now it is not primarily thought of as dance music. It can be so used, and is so used: but it is now the object of a cult. Juke Box Jury and the arbiters of the "Top Twenty" (who are in the end the buying public) attend to it with a strange judicial detachment; it is not now the handmaid of dancing. It is not anybody's handmaid. It is the ruler of a culture. Compared with the eminence, opulence and cultic exaltation of such an artist as Liberace, Charlie Kunz was a pigmy. That he was probably a better pianist is neither here nor there. They thought highly of Mr. Bing Crosby in the thirties, and of Mr. Frank Sinatra in the forties: but the English product in Mr. Adam Faith and Mr. Cliff Richard, not to mention that archetype of "pop" stardom, Mr. Presley from the U.S.A., receives more unanimous adulation than was ever accorded to those senior stars; and a precipitous descent from premature honour is already a well known and tragic possibility for such as these, on a scale which the Hollywood of the thirties, wild though its ascents and descents were, hardly dreamed of. It remains to be judged whether the talents of our present-day "pop" idols will prove as genuinely many-sided as those of Messrs. Crosby and Sinatra turned out to be when they took to film acting.

All this goes with the vast social change of the fifties, of which again the thirties had scarcely a premonition. The affluence of the young has made them a new and receptive market for commercially promoted music. The contemporary tendency away from sociable sport and entertainment (among the modern undergraduates football recedes and fell-walking comes in) takes the dance out of "pop"; gives it with a more passive ethos. Indeed, it is not strange that the public attention to "pop" music has had to be artifically induced by the "Top Twenty" cult. The music is no more capable of receiving concentrated and alert *musical* attention than were the corresponding songs of a generation ago. Commercial attention is the only kind it will wear. The artificiality of the social life of the newly affluent young—where stewardship is still a long way from catching up with wealth—provides also a context in which the appearance of the "payola" scandals in the U.S.A. in 1960 is no matter for surprise.[7]

"Pop", then, is in its own right a new phenomenon, corresponding with the new society of the West which arose after the Second World War. Yet it shows some of the characteristics of all the other related forms of music that went before it and that to some extent still surround it.

With jazz it has this in common: that it depends far more than does "square" music (so to call what is usually miscalled "classical") upon the performer's interpretation. We shall have to return to this point. Here we will only say that whereas the music your music master at school teaches you must be played or sung with strict obedience to the notes and expression-marks as written in your copy, "pop", like "jazz" is not only legitimately but necessarily decorated with interpretative gimmicks at each performance. To put it otherwise you may interpret your Beethoven sonata or Britten song-cycle, but you must be interpreting Britten or Beethoven; and although this was not always the case, it is nowadays regarded as the act of a very vulgar fellow to arrange a Tchaikovsky slow movement for the organ, or a nineteenth century ballad like "Alice, where art Thou?" as a piano solo. But every "pop" number appears in a new arrangement, with new decorative notes and interludes, for new instrumental ensembles, at every performance. Jazz, of course, goes much further and provides for the actual improvising of whole sections—cadenza-wise—by whatever instrumentalist is to the fore at any moment. But in neither jazz nor "pop" is there anything like the fundamentalism that is deemed appropriate to the performance of the "square".

And "pop" has this in common with "music-hall", that while it is not the poor man's music, it is the music of the man who had he lived in 1900 would have been poor: it has its own way of compelling the attention of him who is not accustomed to mental concentration. The methods are different. Marie Lloyd did it by sheer power of personal presence. The "pop"-promoter does it by cashing in on a social revolution: and if his results are more corrupt than Miss Lloyd's, this is because he does not feel it is his business to criticise a social order which allows people to associate mental effort with snobbery, and to exalt its evasion into a cult.

"Pop" is again the lineal descendent of the last generation's dance-numbers; but it is not primarily danced to. It does, however, share the reliance of those dance-numbers on "production", and on the personal skill of a musical ensemble, and their detachment from musical literalism. And with the music of the "big musical" it sometimes shares a thundering good tune and a sense of sociologically "leading from strength"—for the big musical overawes its audience by its sense of power and wealth in its production, and "pop" carries authority through the adventitious power of commercial enterprise, and through the disc-jockey's overbearing charm.

That "pop" has its great moments, who can seriously doubt? It is out of the question to judge yet which "pop" numbers will achieve anything like immortality, or even whether any of those which have appeared in the last ten or twelve years will show themselves to have the quality of Duke Ellington's "Mood Indigo", or of Cole Porter's "You're the Top", or of the best things in "My Fair Lady", "West Side Story" or "Oklahoma". But it seems reasonably safe to predict a life longer than the butterfly's for "The Little Drummer Boy", as sung by Michael Flanders and the Michael Sammes singers.[8] If one compares the sound this ensemble makes with the hardly literate score of the piece which one buys in a music-shop, the whole principle of "production" and local interpretation in pop music is demonstrated in an instant.

A good comment on this was recently made in the *Spectator* by Mr. Clifford Hanley.

> The ideal pop song . . . ought to sound as if it had always existed (in the same way that the Venus de Milo existed inside the lump of stone). You can apply this test to the perennial pops like "St. Louis Blues", "Night and Day", "Margie", "Some of these days" and all the rest. They give a positive reaction. So do some recent essays—"What kind of a Fool am I?" is a splendid example. It sounds familiar, old and *right*.
>
> Okay, they didn't sound right until they had been plugged silly. But no amount of plugging will make a song that hasn't got the stuff in it.[9]

In other words—some "pop" has staying power, "pop" though it is. And it is important to hold on tight to the principle that the "stuff" in it must be there before "production", let alone "plugging" can bring, the song into public favour and keep it there, if only because the listener is nowadays bemused by the variety and ingenuity of the "production" that any pop-song gets. Good "production" can make a bad song sound good: but it probably cannot give it staying-power, because the essence of "production" is in improvisation, which is by definition not a function of permanency at all.

There is one aspect of "pop" which cannot here be overlooked, although it is an extension rather than a species of the "pop" genus of music. This is the quite remarkable success of a new (again) kind of sophisticated "pop", perhaps the invention of Messrs. Michael Flanders and Donald Swann. There have been entertainers of this kind before: but the success of their revue, "At the Drop of a Hat", which when it appeared at the Edinburgh Festival of 1959 was still something to which you went late at night after the big show, has been a major event in popular music.

The real significance of Flanders and Swann seems to be that they appeal primarily to the bourgeois who are reasonably at home with "square" music, but that theirs is the first act of this kind to which a "square" has felt able to listen with a perfectly clear conscience. They can hold an audience for over two hours, just the two of them, with their amusing songs and sophisticated patter; and the audiences they hold, and the people who buy their records, include people in the highest educational and cultural brackets: they go from the middle right to the top. There are technical reasons for this. Their under-stated yet consummate artistry appeals to the man who winces at the overbearing demonstrativeness of "pop". The subject-matter of their songs is always witty and occasionally satirical without ever being profound or, on the other hand, vulgar. The piano-playing of Swann is something to which an attentive musician can listen again and again for its sheer virtuosity. And the ethos of the whole performance, which keeps the erotic at arm's length and makes its points through amusing and occasionally devastating social comment, removes from the timorous bourgeois all those fears of contamination which make him shy of "pop" and all that it stands for. Yet the music is strictly "pop" of an old-fashioned kind. It is music-hall, almost pure. It goes down excellently in pantomime—and what is more to the point, it would have done so when pantomimes were worth a man's while to go and see. It all adds up to a show that has achieved equal success in London and on Broadway, a piece of heroic and excellent art which achieves a perfection of what St. Thomas Aquinas called "proportion and consonance", and therefore provides an ideal relaxation for the confused mind of the contemporary citizen. But it is not stuff for teenagers. It is not really a unifying social agent. It is not intended to be any kind of social gesture. It simply does for our time what Gilbert and Sullivan did for theirs—and does it with staggering economy and skill. It was worth mentioning here because the name of Mr. Swann will have to be mentioned again in the course of this survey.[10]

But "pop" properly so called keeps to its side of the social line, and in this it is certainly related to jazz. An apt statement of this point is contained in the following passage from a recent novel, in which the narrator is a young middle-class man on the point of rebellion against what I have just called timorous bourgeois culture. Fairly early in the story he tells this young man says, of jazz:

> For those amongst you who do not care, or haven't bothered to care about Jazz, all I can say is that you're missing a great deal out of life. I suppose the highbrow stuff is satisfying to a degree, but the thing is, you know what's coming next. In Jazz, most of it's improvised, dig? And you never know what's up the musician's sleeve. He takes you into his own world, and through the sounds that he blows, tells you all about himself, and when you can manage to get on to his plane, there's hardly a kick to beat it.[11]

That is what you are dealing with when you begin, as a visitor from the bourgeois side, to play with jazz, and with that part of "pop" which overlaps the jazz country. It brings us right back to the philosophical crisis we were mentioning earlier (chapter 10). But the question is now stated in a more personal and piercing way. It is of the essence of bourgeois culture (against which this kind of manifesto shows a great hatred and contempt) that it is cautious about personal contacts; it is the central point in the bourgeois resistance to "pop" that its impact is as offensive as that of an unknown fellow-passenger in the train who turns garrulous or of a fellow in the A.B.C. café whom you can hear drinking his soup. This is not in itself a condemnation of bourgeois culture. Personalities need care, respect and the concession of privacy in any community, and the beatniks have their own way of insisting on this. But the class barrier between the cultures is largely built of this kind of fabric. The bourgeois is capable of deep and loyal friendship if he is approached in the right way. Adam Faith does not so approach him. He rants at him. This the bourgeois will not have. All authors are bourgeois: they have to be, because you cannot communicate unless you have a good deal of this respect for personality built into your system. Therefore I, who write this, am of these, and not of the others. It would be absurd not to admit it, and not to try to hide my sense of the value of the bourgeois culture. The subject matter of this section seems to demand a franker and more personal approach to the reader than a more solemn and remote matter of discourse would demand. So I use it. And I will at any rate ask the reader, who also will be of the same class, to go thus far with

me and with Father Beaumont, namely, to recognise that the bourgeois barrier may at any moment prove to be keeping out of the
bourgeois enclave not a corrupt *eros*, but *agape*. When this happens,
it is a serious matter: Father Beaumont means this when he writes
his *Folk Mass*.

And now we must look at this, and at some other music of the
kind, in somewhat greater detail.

NOTES TO CHAPTER 12

1. *The Listener*, 27th December, 1962, p. 1085 col. 2.

2. ib., p. 1087, col. 1.

3. There is now slight confusion about the name of Geoffrey Beaumont:
since he published his *Folk Mass* under that name he has joined the Mirfield
Community, where he is known as Father Gerard: hence he is sometimes
referred to as "Gerard Beaumont". In musical reference it seems better to
retain his secular name.

4. Gregory Dix, *The Shape of the Liturgy* (Dacre Press, 1948) pp. 142 ff.

5. E. Routley, *The Church and Music* (Duckworth, 1950), pp. 45–55, 230–37.

6. E. Routley, *The Music of Christian Hymnody* (Independent Press, 1957)
pp. 10–11 and references there.

7. M. Weinberg, *TV in America, or The Morality of Hard Cash* (New York,
Ballantine Books no. S 622, 1962).

8. *The Little Drummer Boy*, by Harry Simeone and Henry Onorati; score
from Bregman, Vocco and Conn, Ltd., London, 1958. Recorded Parlophone
45 r.p.m. 45 R 4528.

9. Clifford Hanley, "Europe goes Pop" in *The Spectator*, 1st March, 1963,
p. 265.

10. Michael Flanders and Donald Swann, *At the Drop of a Hat*, Parlophone
12 in. L.P. P.M.C. 1033.

11. Terry Taylor, *Barons Court All Change* (McGibbon & Kee, 1961) p. 28.

13

"Church Light Music"

G EOFFREY BEAUMONT's *Folk Mass*, published in 1956, is a
setting in "popular" style, of the liturgy of the Eucharist as
it is celebrated in the Church of England.

The whole of the congregational part is sung "by dictation": with
few exceptions, each phrase is sung by a Cantor and immediately
and literally repeated by the congregation. In the Creed, certain long
phrases are sung by the Cantor, and only their last bar or two is
repeated by the people. The priest's part is expected to be sung to
Marbecke's familiar music.

The composer makes it easy for a congregation to learn the whole
setting, or even to sing it without rehearsal, by the use of this device
of dictation, and also by the economical use of musical themes. The
Creed is set to its own tune throughout, but dictation makes it easy
to sing. The tune itself is founded for the most part on the first six
notes of the diatonic scale, occasionally rising to the upper tonic. The
first and third parts of the Gloria are set to a tune in a similar style,
just as easy to pick up at a moment's notice. The Introit (Psalm 150)
has its own tune, with appropriate instrumental "breaks". "Our
Father" is set to a quite different tune using the tonality of D minor
with a frequently sharpened fourth.

But these major liturgical pieces are bound together by the use of
a good deal of occasional material that appears more than once in its
course. The second part of the Gloria ("O Lord the only begotten
Son") shares its music with the Agnus Dei: the "Propers", Gradual
and Offertory Sentence are all sung to the same music; and there is a
marching tune which is used to "For thou only art holy" in the
Gloria, to the Sanctus, to the Doxology in the Lord's Prayer, and to
the Amen after the Blessing.

That is the general scheme. The musical texture of the work is
entirely determined by the resources available for accompaniment. As
printed in the score, it seems to be using "popular styles" of two broad
kinds in its melodies. Here is the opening melody of the Creed (after
an introduction "I believe in one God" sung to the traditional plainsong phrase):

Ex.45

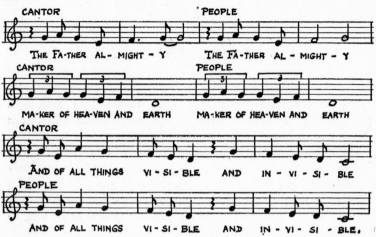

As a melody it is "popular" chiefly in being easy to sing. In itself it does not suggest anything in particular. It is only when its decisive rhythm is taken into account, and when the accompaniment is added, that it begins to sound like "pop". And once we add the harmony we see where it combines the worst weakness of "pop" with its attractive features. For the bass, as in so much "pop", is remarkably dull and repetitive.

Ex.46

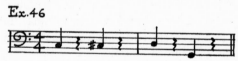

Of the 169 bars in the movement, fifty-six are occupied with twenty-eight repetitions of the bass figure quoted in the above example. This figure is the only one which contains any kind of temporary modulation: modulations of a more permanent sort are achieved by the device of shifting the whole scheme up into D flat: and then later into D—from which in the end it is quite irresponsibly thrust back into C. Thus keys are used in the unfertile way which is one of the more mournful qualities of "pop". The result is the kind of boredom that you feel when you have been trying to listen to somebody who talks a great deal but without argument and logic—it is a rattling of the ear-drums rather than speech, and it is a terrible thing for him who tries to listen. The answer to this criticism is that this music is not meant to be listened to with that kind of ear. That entirely acceptable answer we will store away for a little: it will appear again in a form that will bear comment.

The music for the 150th Psalm is much better "pop". It is easier, for one thing, for a new listener to accept it because it is setting Old Testament words that come from a semi-barbaric background. The 150th Psalm should never be sung demurely, whatever else you do with it. And here the "jazz" improvisation has its chance. A very fair example of "jazz" (distinct from "pop") in church use is provided by one of the two available records of this work—that where it is accompanied by an orchestra. After the words "Praise him in the sound of the trumpet" a two-bar "break" is indicated in the score. The score itself writes this:

Ex.47

and on the record the trumpeter and orchestra play, roughly, this:

Ex.48

On the other record, where the accompaniment is on a Hammond organ, the organist plays what is written in the score. For demonstration purposes (and these were the purposes of that record) the result is interesting: but it is obvious that without the instrumental "breaks" the music loses an essential part of its character.

But when the Mass has been sung through—as anybody who tries it out on a young people's group knows—the one tune that stays in everybody's mind is this one:

Ex.49

which is the "Sanctus" motif. And this is very nearly the same tune that Eric Coates used some years earlier in his music for the film "The Dam Busters". The coincidence has never been explained, and I for one am content to regard it as the same kind of coincidence that links the tune to "Holy Holy Holy", (Heber's hymn), the theme to "And he shall reign for ever and ever" in the Hallelujah Chorus, and the sixteenth-century German chorale *Wachet Auf.* It is just one of those archetypal commonplaces of music on which any composer may light at any moment.

It is, of course, "big musical" stuff rather than "pop"; and there is no doubt, whatever the theorists may insist on, that the public still goes for the big fat tune. It was an excellent psychological stroke to make this the most frequently recurring theme in the Folk Mass. It may sound ineffably "corny" to the sophisticated ear, but it is "everyman's music" much more exactly then anything else in the work.

The style of the *Folk Mass* is, in fact "big musical" rather than "pop" as we now understand it; for it is the "musical" that so shamelessly and cheerfully mixes its styles. Whatever will do for the situation that the plot throws up here or there is what is used, never mind where it comes from. This kind of revue-music was, some time before, Father Beaumont's special contribution to the life of Cambridge University, and the *Folk Mass* is a revival of it. But of course, just because the "big musical" gets away with its mixture of styles because of the enormous impetus it gets from everything else that makes it a "big musical"—glamour, romance, sumptuous filming or staging, multi-million-dollar production, stage-personalities, Todd-AO, and all the rest of it, the homely setting of a church hall with its youth-group stamping on the bare boards rather seldom provides enough impetus to take the music of the *Folk Mass* along with it. So, in practical experience, young people of the kind it wished to evangelise have sometimes found it unsatisfying; and those who have manifested the greatest interest in it have been intellectual Christians who thought it a useful vehicle of evangelism. It still gets a good hearing in the Student Christian Movement; but it is more rarely that one meets anybody from the section of society that is truly pop-addicted who has much time for it. Performed in church it has shocked and terrified the conservatives; but we cannot take comfort for long in congratulating ourselves on the great necessity of shocking and terrifying the con-servatives. It has not filled the churches with pop-worshippers, or done anything to transfer their worship away from the pop-idols.

No, it is not here that the *Folk Mass* has its significance. It is signifi-cant because it started something, and awakened the minds of church musicians to a quite new situation and a series of quite new questions. It is quite enough praise for any innovator in church music if we can say that he did as much as this. For whatever we do now, we have to begin by saying, "Well, what is *wrong* with the *Folk Mass*?"

One of the immediate effects of its publication has been to bring into existence a group of composers and authors who are known as the *20th Century Church Light Music Group*. This has produced a good deal of church music in a style imitative of Beaumont. Two of its more considerable works are the *Mass of Five Melodies* by Patrick Appleford, and the *Festival Te Deum*, by John Alldis. Appleford's Mass has a preface comparable to Beaumont's. He refers to it in this preface as a "Folk Mass", and says that it was written "in response to many requests for a setting in the idiom of modern light music which would not require the repetition by the people of phrases first sung by a cantor". It implies a criticism of the somewhat professional approach of Beaumont's Mass: this one is to be "singable not only by the musicians but by the whole people of God".

The composer thus set himself a more difficult task than did Beau-mont: for what he writes must be capable of being picked up without dictation. His "five melodies" are the solution to this problem. The themes (they are too short really to be called melodies) are in themselves

singable, simple and achieve the commonplace touch that the composer
was looking for. Like Beaumont's, they are such as to make any kind
of contrapuntal subtlety impossible, and the bass is uniformly dull. It
is not music to which one can attend musically, any more than was the
Folk Mass. But it is ingenious and sympathetic. One other remark in
the Preface shows Mr. Appleford's interest in trying to catch one
authentic note of "pop": Melody Four—The Theme of the Lamb—a
theme owing something to the awe-struck mood of some modern
songs. . . ." This is the "ecstatic" note in "pop" which its facile detrac-
tors can easily mistake for affectation. The melody in question is this:

Ex.50

and with the use of a little imagination it is easy to see what its composer
means.

Mr. Alldis's *Te Deum* is an attempt to set that hymn in a "pop" style.
It uses a cantor (Mr. Alldis is himself the cantor in one of the Folk
Mass recordings), and the dictation-technique. The *Te Deum* presents
problems of congregational singing which since the days of plainsong
the church has found quite insuperable. Either it has to be sung to
Anglican chants, which in turn must either provide for hearty singing
and grotesque distortion of the word-rhythm, or must set the words
intelligibly but present congregational pitfalls at every other verse (as
the admirable speech-rhythm setting of the *Oxford Psalter* does): or it
must be sung to a continuous setting which has to be laboriously learnt.
Chants can be varied, but the learning of more than two continuous
settings is beyond most congregations' patience. Mr. Alldis does at
least provide something fresh. The melody of his opening section (down
to "Holy, Holy, Holy") could easily have been written by a composer
of 1900 who believed in the four-plus-four bar technique of Henry
Smart. Indeed, there is a touch of ecclesiastical phraseology about the
whole of the melody-line which is only "unchurched" by the applica-
tion to the accompaniment of the necessary rhythmical touch and
decorative additions. The melody is no more, and no less, incongruous

than most of Sullivan's *Festival Te Deum*. It is simply "easy to sing"—
and it achieves that ease by the use of phrases in a very familiar idom,
constantly repeated. It is patient of a "pop" interpretation, but it is
undoubtedly traditional church music in disguise; and a good deal of
Victorian church music would look like this—and to be sure, look
much better than it does—if it were suitably arranged by a musician
with a modern freedom from Victorian inhibitions about four-part
harmony.

Apart from these works, the activity of the twentieth century
Church Light Music Group is mainly confined to songs and hymns.

Here Geoffrey Beaumont gave an excellent lead: for the hymn tune
has almost a common frontier with the "big musical". The first of his
compositions to arouse wide interest was in fact a hymn tune, to
"Lord, thy Word abideth", which was broadcast from Martock
parish church (Somerset) in October 1955, some months before the
publication of the *Folk Mass*: and I still think it is the best piece of
music he has written—a swinging, free-moving eight-line tune which
can be made exceedingly effective with the minimum of quasi-jazz
"production".

Ex. 51

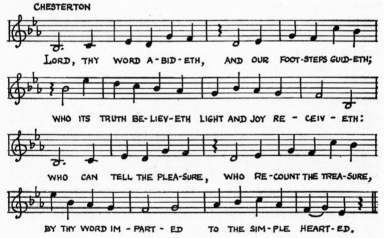

This tune later was incorporated in the recording of the Folk Mass,
together with two others "Now thank we all our God", and "There's
a wideness in God's mercy", of which the first is a rousing march, and
the second, a waltz fit to stand alongside any of the classic waltzes of

the Noël-Coward era. "Lord, thy word abideth" and "Now thank
we all our God" are the only Beaumont tunes which by 1962 had
appeared in a standard English hymn book; they appear as CHESTERTON
(250) and GRACIAS (18) in the *Baptist Hymn Book* (1962). There is no
question that Beaumont can do this exceedingly well. Other tunes of
his appear in his *Eleven Hymn Tunes* (Weinberger, 1957), and in the
two books of hymn tunes published by the Group, *Thirty 20th Century
Hymn Tunes* (Weinberger, 1960) and *More 20th Century Hymn Tunes*
(1962). Perhaps none of these is as musical as the three famous ones: but
the true quality of Beaumont's gift shows itself in the best of them
through their use of long phrases and of a purposefully moving bass.
At the same time, the extent to which these tunes depend for their
effect on "production" can be judged by comparing the Oriole or
Paxton recordings of the *Folk Mass* with the Tower recording of five
Beaumont hymn tunes: for the details, see Bibliography. The "production" in the *Folk Mass* records, especially the Oriole, is excellent:
that in the Tower record is lamentable—especially the harmony.

Other members of the Group contribute to the two books of hymns
mentioned here. I hope it is not unfair to guess that most of these seem
to lack Beaumont's free-ranging gift of "big musical" writing. They
certainly do not always distinguish between the "Oklahoma" style and
what might be called an "antique church pop" style. For example,
no. 23 in *Thirty 20th Century Hymn Tunes* seems to have everything
in common with the kind of tune one used to hear fifty years ago in
Sunday schools:

Ex.52

O Je-sus thou art standing out-side the fast closed door,

In low-ly patience wait-ing to pass the threshold o'er.

Is it not strongly reminiscent of a tune by a certain Geibel to "Stand
up, stand up for Jesus" which begins like this?:

Ex.53

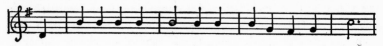

Many, indeed, of these tunes are "children's tunes", often of an attractive innocence in themselves (*e.g.* 26 in *Thirty* and 21 in *More*); with a suggestive "pop" accompaniment added. There is a strong tendency to replace a good bass by a permanent modulation—often through a major or minor third (*Thirty*: D major to B flat in no. 7; A flat to C in no. 14; A flat to C in no. 19; B flat to D in no. 27). But in some—and especially this happens in the later collection—an ecclesiastical idiom, or the idiom of the religious ballad, of three generations back makes a quite startling and dismaying reappearance. Here is a phrase from no. 28 in *More*:

Ex.54

and if one wants really to see how far it is possible to go in 1962 in the direction of the gaslight of 1885, consider no. 3 in the same book, a setting of "When I survey the wondrous cross" which, you would say "has everything", even to a throbbing repeated-chord accompaniment to pep up emotion in the last verse.

What one finds all through these two books is the concentration on unconventionality of outward manner, for which the composer always pays by being wedded to a profound and unshakable conventionality of musical thought-form. There is just one tune in the sixty that the two books contain that looks in the least eccentric—and this is by Father Cheslyn Jones (at present Principal of the theological college at Chichester) to "Love divine":

Ex.55

Unhappily he has mis-accented his first, fifth, ninth and thirteenth bars, which should go like this, and would sound much better so:

Ex.56

But he has a modal cadence and a general air in his tune that suggests that he still thinks that plainsong "has something".

This is very largely, of course, the work of ministers of the Church of England who are primarily seeking contact with an unevangelised section of the people. It is not the work of professional musicians, still less that of people who move freely and normally in the world of "pop" or "big musical". Beaumont is the one composer who shows that he could move freely there. The consequence is that it comes out as well-intentioned but imitative: and the model imitated is sometimes ecclesiastical rather than secular, so that, in such tunes as example we get in effect the imitation of an old ecclesiastical imitation of historic music hall.

It is not uninteresting—it does indeed provide an important pointer to the ethos of this music—to notice what happens when this group sets itself to the writing of religious words. Mostly their music goes to well known hymns or liturgical words. But there are six hymns at the beginning of *Thirty* which are specially written for this treatment, all by Patrick Appleford. He can write, but his idiom is usually as strictly ecclesiastical as anything in the *English Hymnal*. There is little sign in such a quatrain as this

> Lord, look down in thy compassion,
> Free thy people from their sin,
> Only by thy Cross and Passion
> May we be renewed within
>
> (*Thirty*, no. 5)

that there is much seeking for new verbal images to match the images that the music will evoke. Indeed, the words which these composers choose when they write their tunes are very often of the most undistinguished sort—like "Gracious Spirit, Holy Ghost", "Three in one and one in three", "Holy Father, cheer our way", "The King of love": all very "Ancient and Modern" and cosy, and showing no such impatience with traditional thought-forms in words that their music shows with those of music. There is one staggering love-song to Our

Lady (*More*, no. 12), by Fr. Nicholas Graham of the Community of the Resurrection, Mirfield, with a Beaumont tune, and with the refrain—

> You are
> My Star
> My Star of the sea;
> Over the ocean
> Beckon to me . . .

which brings up to date that "sacred *eros*" style of writing which in music and words is to be found rather often in the *Mirfield Mission Hymn Book* that emanated from the same Community.

In a book called *Rhythm in Religion* (Weinberger, 1960) however, we find an attempt to write new "pop" words with a religious twist, and music to conform. There are eight songs in this book, again all written by clergy. In the early fifties a custom known as "Rock 'n Roll" attracted much attention: the phrase has now passed out of the popular vocabulary and been replaced by other technical formulae; but at the time there was something to be said for writing a song on the word "Rock", which provided a contact between religions and secular imagery. This is what emerges:

Medium Rock tempo

> You've got a Rock to scare your blues away,
> You've got a Rock to turn your night to day,
> You've got a Rock that will not roll away,
> It's true—
>
> You've got a Rock, there's no denying it,
> You've got a Rock, you can rely on it,
> You've got a Rock, and I'm applying it
> To you—
>
> You may be low and feeling lost
> But you don't have to count the cost,
> You may not know just where to turn,
> Then you've one thing to learn—
>
> You've got the strongest Rock that's ever been,
> You've got a Rock and on it you can lean,
> You've got a Rock, for that's what Christ can mean
> To you . . .

This, with a very suitable tune, is pure "revivalism" of the old-fashioned kind. Once again—no criticism whatever of the traditional evangelical ways of presenting the Christian truth. There is, especially, a tendency in these songs to attribute to their singers a consciousness of aimlessness.

> "You may not know just where to turn" (no. 2)
> "I wish I knew the way to go" (no. 3)
> "Give me a lead: that's what I need" (no. 6)
> "I am weak and foolish, And I give You pain" (no. 7)

This gives the game away to a large extent. It is surely the clergy's criticism of the 'teenagers disguised as a pop-song. These devoted ministers *are* slumming, after all. There is more to be said for the objectivity of "There's a rhythm" (no. 1)—

> There's a rhythm in the way
> God has given every day
> Every morning and evening as a new creation
> Telling the glory of God—

although one might say that this is a somewhat ingenious and "S.C.M." way of talking about rhythm.

So a certain ground of radical doubt about this movement begins to mark itself out. One cannot help feeling, as one reads and sings this music, that for at any rate some of the time its authors and composers are tending to say "Actually, I don't really believe in this kind of stuff; I don't think it's good; but it seems the right thing for these people". If that criticism stands, it is a criticism of paternalism. Certainly there is nothing indigenous about this music: it is a gesture from the spiritual "haves" to the spiritual "haven'ts". Beaumont, its chief architect, could really have written a good "musical"; he is, I think, more of an artist than he himself would admit. Whether the rest of the company can be so described remains in doubt.

It is here in point to mention Mr. Donald Swann's strange incursions into this field. He has composed a setting of the *Venite* and one of the *Te Deum* (Curwen, 1958). The *Venite* is a piece of modern dance music —quite unlike what Swann is best known for, and owing much to the Beaumont approach. The *Te Deum* is more interesting musically, in that it contains a good deal of formidable discord as well as some pure "pop". It is not easy to speak as warmly of this music as one can of his revue music because there seems to be the same feeling that he is writing outside his own style in the hope of catching a mood among people for whom he normally does not write. There is much more music in both than in the 20*th Century Hymn Tunes*; and the *Venite* has an amusing whistled descant: but the listener does not get the same sense of conviction from this that he gets from Swann's *Ostrich Song*.

14

Mr. Williamson's Dialect

ALCOLM WILLIAMSON'S contributions in the field of "church pop" raise new questions and problems, partly because they contrast so startlingly with his work in other fields (mentioned above in chapter 12) and partly because it differs importantly from the music of the *20th Century Church Light Music Group* in the idiom it uses.

Williamson has become well known in the "pop" field for a series of small-scale works employing a musical diction that has much in common with the Beaumont style, and which he might not have essayed had not Beaumont made his gesture when he did. There are now available (early 1963) *Adoremus*, a Christmas cantata (1961), *Procession of Psalms, Harvest Thanksgiving*, and an anthem, *Let them give thanks* (all 1962), aside from the works which we have already referred to. He has also written a number of hymn tunes, six of which are recorded on the reverse sides of the records that carry *Procession of Psalms* and *Harvest Thanksgiving*, and all of which are published either in leaflets or in his *Hymn Tunes* (1962).

Here we have a different situation. Williamson is a musician of high and serious purpose—as we have seen. His life is primarily in music, not in some other vocation from which he makes a digression towards music. He is a first-class organist, and as a composer can handle the vocabulary of music with complete assurance. It is not necessary for him to imitate anybody, although he would no more than any other musician try to deny the influences that other composers have had on him.

Procession of Psalms and *Harvest Thanksgiving* are both short cantatas consisting of a brief sequence of texts set to continuous music of which the separate units can if necessary be isolated for occasional use. *Procession* sets the hymns "Ride on, ride on in majesty" and "All glory, laud and honour", followed by the *Benedictus qui venit* from the Mass; *Harvest Thanksgiving* sets "Come, ye thankful people, come". "The King of love my shepherd is" and a poem beginning "I met a stranger yestre'en"; but here the opening line of "Come ye thankful people", set to a choral phrase independent of the hymn tune that carries the words of the whole hymn, recurs as a kind of linking motif after the singing of the other two numbers, and the first and last verses of that hymn are sung again at the end of the work.

One can then consider these two cantatas either as compositions in their own right, or as examples of his hymn writing which can be taken along with the other hymns in the Williamson *corpus* as it so far exists.

Taken as continuous works, they are extremely evocative. The *Procession* has four contrasting sections: "Ride on" set to a slow crescendo march, each verse to the same tune but in a key half a tone higher than the preceding, so that not only is the volume greater in each verse, but the key moves up from A to D flat and the organ accompaniment becomes more weighty and complex with each verse. The music immediately shifts up one more half tone to D for "All glory": and here the tempo is a quick march, with the refrain in D and the "verse" in F, the home key being established by a surprise ending. The *Benedictus* is introduced by a two-part canonic setting of "O Saviour of the world" sung over held whole-bar chords, and reminiscent of Britten in its open texture. *Benedictus* is a quiet Andante with a slowly moving bass and conventional harmonies: it is sung three times, raised a whole tone at each repetition, and it suddenly and brutally explodes into the *Hosanna in excelsis*, the voices in syncopated octaves and the accompaniment providing a cross-rhythm in broken discords and at the end in wickedly harsh tone-clusters, where the work abruptly ends. The effect is of a series of contrasts between different approaches to the Palm Sunday events, and you are left with the animal ugliness of the crowd, after passing through the other moods of purposefulness, triumph, and awe.

Harvest takes, of course, a different line. Here all is pastoral and merry. "Come ye thankful people" is a bustling *allegro* in 7/4, pleasantly recalling the human merriment of a country harvest and the energy which it celebrates. "The king of love" is romantic—what else is right for those words? The central poem is penitential, recalling the world's need and the ministry of charity; then at the end, back to the bustle in a circular movement that adequately expresses the seasonal rhythm.

Of the two, *Procession* contains more music that has a "pop" flavour at first hearing, and the most obvious example is "All glory, laud and honour". But it is obvious that this is a different story from what the 20th *Century Church Light Music Group* tells. On the printed page, and much more in the sound as it is performed by the group that

M

renders it on the record that presumably gives an authentic performance, the "pop" element is really supplied by the manner of the
accompaniment.

Ex.57

The harmonies are little more than an extension of Stainer, but their
effect is certainly to give warmth and appeal to the whole piece. What
matters most, however, and what lifts the music out of the "Rhythm
in Religion" class, is the quite remarkably energetic bass line, and the
originality with which it uses the otherwise hackneyed device of
modulation through a major third.

Now this is just one example. Wherever else you touch him,
Williamson provides evidence that a musician is writing. There is—and
this we find for the first time in discussing music in this genre—enough
music there to occupy and hold the attention of anybody who wishes
to attend to it musically. This is true equally of the effective use of note-
clusters in "Ride on". Williamson usually manages to pack into his
"pop" music a great deal of musical wit—some fresh effect, some new
rhythm—which does not distract the attention of the incurious, but
holds the attention of the critical. This is his secret.

Take for another example the tune to "The King of love." Here
there is much that is strictly "corny"—there is another modulation

through a third, from E major to G major in verses 3 and 5. But although one need not notice it, the constant dialogue between two rhythms is fascinating. In the score it appears like this:

Ex. 58

But what the ear hears, and what certainly is really happening, is this: (Example 59)

Now consider some other of his hymn tunes. What we have noted already is written out in score, and will produce its effect if nothing but

Ex.59

THE KING OF LOVE MY   SHEP-HERD IS, WHOSE GOOD-NESS FAILETH NE-VER

I   NOTHING LACK IF   I AM HIS,   AND   I AM HIS FOR EV-ER.

the notes written is played. In the recording, true, certain additional vocal effects are introduced, with close-harmony effects and descants of a "big musical" kind. But these are not essential. Williamson has, however, written some other tunes which on paper are written down just as the Beaumont-tradition tunes are written—with a minimum of notation, in the expectation of "production-effects" in performance. None of those which have been recorded are, I think, without essential wit, but some owe more than others to Production". "Jesu, lover of my soul", for example, is given in the recording a performance which recalls all the Babylonish opulence of Gaumont-British at its most extended: double choir, cantor dictation the tune, a descant reaching, operatic heights, the whole system thrust up from E flat to A flat in the third verse, and the final line soulfully repeated, "pop"-style at the end. The effect here is derived from the power-mystique of the "big musical", and the listener is enfolded, you might say engulfed, in a mass of luxuriant sound. If he is liable to be embarrassed by this treatment, that is his bad fortune.

On the other hand, his *Easter Carol* ("Ye choirs of new Jerusalem") is a furiously strenuous setting of a medieval office-hymn in 5/8 time which surely marks the fastest timing ever recorded in hymn singing. The effect here is to leave with the singer an unforgettable image of the "Lion of Judah", of which idea the hymn makes a good deal. (One shrewd critic remarked to me on first hearing 'Jesu, lover of my soul", "How else can you properly set the word 'bosom' "? This unkind comment could possibly reveal what image presented itself to the composer of that tune: it is likely that he was unaware of the circumstances for which Charles Wesley intended his words, which are marked in his original, "In Temptation". Nothing in this music is particularly fortifying against any temptation known to the ordinary man

"Crown him with many crowns" is another fierce tune, in A minor and major (this school very rarely uses minor keys) which again as recorded owes much to production, in particular to a really impudent descant and to what one can only call some sexy pop singing by the cantor. For astonishing economy in material, one turns to "Christ whose glory fills the skies"—once again in 5/4 rhythm, and put by the performers on the record into the "Gaumont-British class" by a crooned introduction and some pretty squenchy harmony at the end of the hymn. For complete innocence and sheer beauty, Williamson has not yet improved on "Hail to the Lord, who comes".

Ex. 60

This, at any rate, goes right home when sung by anybody, production or no production.

Williamson's other two works here referred to add little to what we have encountered already. *Adoremus* is a Christmas cantata along the lines of *Harvest*. It is in three sections—*Ave Maria* in straight modern polyphony: *Adeste fideles*, one verse of the hymn sung to the traditional tune pepped up with an unvarying accompanimental figure in filled-in sevenths, and *Gloria in excelsis*, whose music is a very simple unison line accompanied alternately in syncopated dance-rhythm and in plain harmonic chords clearly calling for "production effects". The anthem "Let them give thanks" is on the borderline of "pop" and "square", using certain emphatic syncopated effects and bringing in the congregation at two points with a tune supported by harmony of the kind found in the hymn tunes.

But what emerges in the popular music of Williamson is that he is making a spirited effort to integrate "pop" with the main stream of modern music. He alone is in a position to do this. He does it con-spicuously in *Adoremus* by juxtaposing perfectly regular modern music with a jazzy interpretation of *Adeste*. He does it in *Harvest Thanksgiving* by going as far as he dare, without outraging a musician's conscience, in writing alluring and zestful music that anybody can appreciate. He does it in *Procession of Palms* by imaginatively entering into the human experience of Palm Sunday and writing accessible music that reflects this. He does it in the hymn tunes by writing, as it were, studies in various styles. But even within this popular field he is a master of many styles. And for him, as it appears, it is more important to write music which will have a popular appeal within a church liturgy than to imitate the strictly "pop" styles. This is to say that we can imagine Williamson saying, "Well, what do ordinary people like in music? They enjoy a bit of opulent harmony? Why shouldn't they? They enjoy a good big tune: so do we all. They enjoy just a taste of salt: excellent! They enjoy a decisive rhythm: they shall have it." But what one does not imagine Mr. Williamson saying is, "They like Adam Faith: I will write music as if I were writing for him, and that will catch them".

What then is a musician doing when he writes "pop" church music? What Mr. Williamson reminds me of most, I must confess, is of a good writer of English, who is at home with the standard style, writing in dialect. This music seems comparable with, for example, Mr. G. W. Target's recent novels, *The Teachers*, *The Missionaries*, and *The Shop Stewards*. There much of the writing is "straight" writing, but much of it is "dialect" writing—a special style gathered by a quick ear from the conversational habits of ordinary people, stylised, and used as a means of communication. Sometimes Mr. Williamson is writing "straight". Sometimes he writes "in dialect",—and it is perfectly possible to combine the two as they are combined in *Adoremus*, or to write the whole work in dialect, as is done in *Harvest Thanksgiving*. By the same token, one is tempted to describe the Beaumont style as "journalese"—journalese has its vivid moments and its lapses into blurred dullness, and so does the music of the *20th Century Church Light Music Group*.

At no point does one feel that Mr. Williamson's musical integrity is being compromised. With the others, one feels that musical integrity is not a matter of great concern. But again, one is faced with this: that in certain circumstances it can be right for a man who wishes to com-municate with another to set aside thoughts of his own integrity. This is a risky doctrine, and would sound like heresy to any committed artist. Possibly it risks more than a man should: possibly it is a devil's device. But in plain fact when a man of learning is talking to children he may, not only conceal ninety-nine hundredths of his learning, but actually compromise his honour as a scholar in order to be clear. Does one, when talking to the very simple, say that Jesus taught us to go the second mile and turn the other cheek, and then explain what those expressions mean? Or does one say, "It is recorded in the Gospel attributed, but not certainly, to St. Matthew, that Jesus said we must go the second mile and turn the other cheek: but those sayings may not have been spoken by him in those words, being very probably something which his later followers thought he must have said?" If one accepts critical modifications of straight statements, does one always and at every level have to give voice to them? On another level, does one say to a youngster "The three angles of a triangle add up to 180 degrees: but only if that triangle is drawn on a plane surface: and you'll never actually get a plane surface in this world?" At once one can see the dangers of admitting such compromise: but constantly one not only does it but feels it right to do it.

A preacher may be a born poet; but might not his use of poetic symbolism in his preaching be a stumbling-block to his congregation and obscure the message which he designed it to illuminate? Might not a plain style be a necessary discipline for him? Is he compromising the art of preaching if he actually gives less than he could.

Have we always the obligation, or even the right, to give all that we wish to give? Does not the right and the obligation together depend to some extent on the nature of the demand? Cannot it be that he who says "I will give all I have in this piece of music, or this poem, or this speech, is failing in one of the courtesies of conversation?

Whatever the outcome of such metaphysical debate as that, it is probably no more than fair to say that Beaumont and his followers are deliberately renouncing "musical integrity" for what they hold to be a pastoral necessity. In another way, Williamson is trying to reconcile a style conditioned by popular demand with a musicianship which leaps far ahead of popular understanding. If there is a lack of balance in Beaumont and his group, this could be because of a failure accurately to assess the relative demands of musical integrity and the need for communication. If there is such a lack of judgment, it is not for any who are more careful of integrity to throw stones; but it is quite proper to point out that music has an integrity independent of any person who uses it for communication, and that if this is corrupted, if music's language is blurred and blunted by careless use, he who does so is at fault no matter how admirable his personal intentions are.

15

A Touch of Satire

THERE is one aspect of this movement where there is an enormous gap that needs to be filled: and that, as I write (1963), is being filled by at any rate one writer. We have already noticed the way in which invention in religious verse has lagged behind invention in music. Nobody whom we have so far encountered has made any attempt to transpose religious poetry into a new key for popular singing. The one writer who has done so to any purpose—and he is as yet all but unknown in this field—is Mr. Sydney Carter. Mr. Carter is a journalist and song-writer some of whose work has found its way into the repertory of Donald Swann in the "At the Drop of a Hat" revue. Like Mr. Swann, Mr. Carter has served during the Second World War with the Friends' Ambulance Unit, and, also like Mr. Swann, developed a keen interest in folk-music, especially that of Greece, where he travelled in that service. Very little of his work has been published, although some of his secular satires are recorded.[1] But he is the first modern writer to apply to religious writing the characteristically modern technique of irony and satire. The results are very remarkable.

Consider the following poem, which he has set to the tune of an old American Shaker song.

I danced in the morning when the world was begun
And I dance in the moon and the stars and the sun
And I came down from heaven and I danced on the earth—
At Bethlehem I had my birth.

> Dance then, wherever you may be.
> "I am Lord of the Dance," said he;
> "I'll lead you all, wherever you may be,
> I will lead you all in the dance," said he.

I danced for the scribe and the pharisee,
But they would not dance and they wouldn't follow me.
I danced for the fishermen, for James and John—
They came with me and the dance went on.

I danced on the Sabbath and I cured the lame
And the holy people said it was a shame;
They whipped and they stripped and they hung me high,
And they left me there on a Cross to die.

I danced on a Friday when the sky turned black;
It's hard to dance with the devil on your back.
They buried my body and they thought I'd gone.
But I am the dance, and I still go on.
      Dance then, wherever you may be . . .

Here is folksong of a new sort—and indeed of an old sort. The words remind those who know their medieval carols of those of "Tomorrow shall be my dancing day"; but their emphasis is slightly different, and perhaps more evidently rooted in Biblical thought. For two Biblical texts spring easily to the mind on reading those lines—that concerning wisdom in Proverbs 8, which is thus translated vividly by Ronald Knox:

> The Lord made me his when first he went about his work, at the birth of time, before his creation began . . . I was there when he built the heavens, when he fenced in the waters with a vault inviolable, when he fixed the sky overhead, and levelled the fountain-springs of the deep . . . I was at his side, a master-workman, my delight increasing with each day, as I made play before him all the while; made play in this world of dust, with the sons of Adam for my playfellows.
>
> (Proverbs 8. 22, 27, 30–31.)

—and that in the Gospels where our Lord said of the careless and inattentive people around him—

> How shall I describe the people of this generation? What are they like? They are like children sitting in the market-place and shouting at each other, "We piped for you and you would not dance. We wept and wailed but you would not mourn."
>
> (St. Luke 7. 31–32 N.E.B.)

The comparison of our Redemption to a great dance is older than the medieval carol: but this particular elaboration of it is strictly twentieth century.

Among other works of Mr. Carter's is a song which has been heard on radio and television, but which is not at present printed, whose words are imaginatively put into the mouth of one of the malefactors who were crucified with Jesus. The refrain after each verse is a cry of protest against God:

> It's God they ought to crucify,
> Instead of You and me.

Now this is a new gesture. It emerges from an interest in folksong: and folksong is distinguished for its bold, brazen treatment of things that a sophisticated society holds sacred,[2] and therefore for its fertile and sometimes astonishing juxtapositions of what cultivated people regard as the sacred and the secular. Mr. Carter in these songs is using very secular language, very ordinary language, and yet timelessly ancient language. He is defying nothing natural: only the conventions that have built themselves up round religious custom, and moulded religious speech.

Carter is doing—and perhaps doing more effectively and penetratingly because he links us with history in doing it—something like what Beaumont and his school are doing in music. At least both gestures are towards a defiance of axioms which say "You cannot talk like that, or sing like that, in a religious context". And especially he is reflecting twentieth century irony.

Satire has suddenly become, as I write (again, 1963: what a year to be writing in!) the talk of the country because of the remarkable success of a television programme, "That Was The Week That Was". The first session of this series ran from December 1962 to the end of April 1963. Towards the end its inspiration flagged noticeably. But its ruthless satire has made people think that satire was invented by a B.B.C. team of entertainers. The plain fact is that "That Was The Week That Was" was nothing but the medieval "Lord of Misrule"[2] brought up to date: the pillorying of public vanities. It is probably less friendly than any Lord of Misrule. but its principle, that nothing is too sacred to stand a close and humorous look, is really an ancient one. However, the essence of this programme—and if it has disappeared when you read this, it is preserved for history on at least one gramophone record which includes some characteristic pieces[4]—is that it combines a ruthless factuality with the employment of its promoters of a gift for showing the public familiar things and people at unusual angles. Imagination enters only into the presentation: what it has been based on is plain fact—the actual career of a tycoon, the actual number of speeches made or not made in parliament by certain members, the actual attendances at and published statements of the English churches, the actual programmes presented and news announced by the B.B.C. during that week.

That is modern satire: and it can be paralleled in certain very successful revues, of which those that have gone into record include *Beyond the Fringe*[5] and those which have enjoyed great success on both sides of the Atlantic include *The Second City*. Satire has for the moment replaced romance as the entertainment of the sophisticated.

It is this juxtaposition of real things with imaginative and witty treatment that characterises, in a way, Sydney Carter's writing. The Redemption, the Cross, are as real as anything can be to a Christian believer. But one doubts now whether "When I survey the wondrous Cross" makes the Crucifixion any more real to a modern believer; at any rate, what Sidney Carter's Crucifixion song does is something very different. And the music he writes or arranges for his songs is music that Donald Swann can sing, and sing as he sings his song of the Hippopotamus or his song of the Sloth. It is modern ballad-music, yet also true folk-music. And the words are a real break-through of which I am myself moved to say that they are the answer to a question which my book, *The English Carol* (1958) left open: "Where are the carols now?" Here, if anywhere, are new carols.

One other gesture in "pop" language had been produced by these fruitful sixties—the Passion-mime written for television by the Reverend Ernest Marvin and Ewan Hooper and called *A Man Dies*. Mr. Marvin was at the time minister of a Presbyterian Church on a housing estate in Bristol whose most conspicuous ministry was to the large number of teenagers who lived near the church. He sought to produce for his youth club a presentation of the Passion which would use mime rather than speech, and would especially use modern dancing and its associated "pop" music. The music was written by two boys and a girl in the club.

This was presented on Television at Passiontide 1961 on the A.B.C. network, and created a considerable sensation. A film was made of it, and at the time of writing it is necessary to order it for private showing about ten months in advance.

And this becomes the first major gesture of folk-music coming from the *folk*. When one sees the mime, one sees the great moments of the Ministry of Jesus acted out on an upper stage, while a crowd of youngsters are dancing and jiving on the main floor. Now and again the crowd becomes part of the play, and the central figure passes through it. Very little is actually said: there are brief narrations from the Bible to focus the watcher's thought, and there is a good deal of "pop" music going on much of the time. Here, indeed, we have the other side of the "dance"—the careless, terrified dance of life which proceeds with complete neglect of what the Redeemer is doing.

The ground-bass, as it were is provided by a Gospel narrative in song which appears in sections as the mime proceeds. Here are its words and music in full.

Ex.61

GEN-TLE CHRIST   WISE AND GOOD,   WE NAILED HIM TO A CROSS OF WOOD.   THE SON OF GOD__ HE LIVED TO SAVE   IN BOR-ROWED STA-BLE AND   BOR-ROWED GRAVE.

Gentle Christ, wise and good,
We nailed him to a cross of wood;
The Son of God, he lived to save
In borrowed stable and borrowed grave.

> (This verse is sung at the beginning of each section and after each verse, in strict "burden-stanza" form.)

When a boy was twelve, if he lived in the East,
His parents went to the Passover Feast,
So Mary and Joseph took Jesus with them
And they went up together to Jerusalem.

They spent some days in the town and then
The time came round to go home again.
They started back when they suddenly found
The young boy Jesus was nowhere around.

His mother and father looked long and looked hard,
And ran him to earth in the Temple yard.
He'd been talking, and hearing the teachers all day,
And forgotten he ought to have been on his way.

They travelled back to the town where they stayed
And apprenticed the boy to the carpenter's trade.
He lived in Nazareth, so we are told,
And worked at the bench until thirty years old.

  ★ ★ ★

When he walked into the shopping street
We threw spring flowers before his feet,
Glad to get an excuse to shout,
No need to worry what you shout about.

We looked for a leader to free us from Rome,
We thought we could rule much better at home.
So we welcomed the Saviour with noises and din.
We didn't much want him to free us from sin.

  ★ ★ ★

Angry words our Lord did say,
Choked with those who would teach you to pray,
Who yell out their sins and fall to the ground,
But only when there's someone to see them around.

When they pray, they kneel down
Right in the busiest street in town.
They put their money in the plate at Church
So they can tell their friends how much.

They say, as many would say today,
"We wouldn't have treated our Saviour that way ";
But gentle Christ, wise and good,
They nailed him to a cross of wood.

  ★ ★ ★

Soldiers came at Pilate's call,
Led him into the common hall,
Took sharp thorns and made a crown,
Dressed him in a scarlet gown.

They spat at him and mocked him then,
Lashed his back again and again,
Laid the cross upon that back,
Forced him up the narrow track.

He stumbled through the city gate
Became too weak to lift the weight,

A man who passed him, black, it's said,
Carried up his cross instead.

At last they came to the hanging place,
A hill we call the Eyeless Face,
They gave him drugs to kill the pain;
He pushed the cup away again.

The soldiers hung him on the cross,
Played for his clothes at pitch and toss.
When each of them had won a share,
Sitting down they watched him there.

That is the narrative-song: there is another which runs in parallel to
it, appearing here and there in sections, beginning "Go It Alone".
There are incidental songs also, one of which begins—

What's the use? Where's the point,
  Might as well live when you can,
Knock it back—fill your head,
Not much use holding off till you're dead.

It is fierce, red-blooded, sometimes cruel stuff. It is theologically
offensive at points in that it seems to give expression to, and to engender,
a hatred against "the wrong people" which is no part of Christ's
teaching. But it exposes the scars and distortions of modern 'teenage
life: and the effect of the mime, acted and sung with the utterly
expressionless faces that its actors naturally wear, is moving and
frightening. All the time, the "dance" goes on.

Not all of this, then, is written by people of "missionary" mind. Its
author, of course, seeks to evangelise. How far he did this nobody
knows. What the mime did for its actors is entirely speculative. No
conversions are recorded. Even a TV interviewer could get nothing
much out of the principal actor when he asked him what the play had
done for him. Possibly its chief impact is, like that of Beaumont, on
those who, themselves orthodox in upbringing but alert in perception,
are shocked into a new view of what life means to housing-estate
teenagers. As with all this music, we can make no final judgment. But
its tunes are haunting, and its words, in places, devastating.

The conjecture that this kind of music finds a special welcome among
people for whom it was not specifically designed is borne out by what
took place at the Quadrennial Congress of the Student Christian Movement at Bristol, 1st–7th January, 1963. For the first time since these

quadrennial congresses began in 1954, music took a place in the proceedings which exceeded the demands of mere convention. There is always plenty of hymn singing at these congresses, of course, and at no other had this been in any way different from what would be expected at any international Christian gathering. But in 1963 the directors of the Congress music, the Reverend Ian Mackenzie and Mr. Peter Cutts, were allowed to take a very free hand in its organisation. As a result, at every plenary session—morning and evening—at least one of the hymns sung was something which the large majority of those present could not have heard before; and on several occasions it was something newly composed for the occasion. About five minutes' practice for the whole assembly was all that was permitted for each hymn. About 1,600 students were present, of whom something like a quarter came from outside Britain—so the necessity of giving ground to English conventions about church music was a good deal less prominent than it is in an ordinary church gathering. The praise-list for these sessions is worth recording in full, and this is done in Appendix I.

A wide conspectus was given of the possibilities of post–1950 church music in popular hymnody. Some of the music was of the "squarest"— like the Langlais and the two new hymn tunes just mentioned. On the other hand, Beaumont and Williamson had their showing. It is impossible for one who was present at this affair to say which "went" best. All were sung with quite surprising readiness by a congregation of reasonably alert young Christians, all of whom were provided with the melody of the new hymns in their service-sheets. But what is of historical fact is that by far the greatest impact, in terms of being talked about with enthusiasm afterwards and through the Congress, was made by—Beaumont's Psalm 150. There was not a person in the hall who came from that section of society which Beaumont had in mind when he wrote that piece: but this was the music that "went home" most effectively and produced the most immediate reaction.

This is not in the least surprising. Every new piece was in some sense a gesture of dissent against convention—even the tune to "Love divine", which was certainly the most conventional of all the new music, was an attempt to achieve a simple melodic line with supporting harmony that did not use the Stainer idiom. *At the time* all the new tunes made enough impression to get sung well. *Afterwards* it was the Beaumont that was talked about. It was the Beaumont about which people found it easiest to be articulate. This is important. Beaumont makes the clearest gesture of them all. It is more obvious what he is doing than what any of the others were doing. He is making a social proposition, where the others are making musical propositions or aesthetic ones as well as social ones. And this kind of social proposition was just the sort of thing the Congress was convened to talk about. It was *mission*: and there could not be a clearer confirmation of what we said earlier—that it is as *mission* that "church-pop" makes its primary appeal, and that it impresses those who are the senders of the mission a good deal more than those who receive it.

But the two genuine secular "pop" tunes that were used marked a new departure yet "the strife is o'er" was sung to a transposed version of "Wonderful Land", which had been in the Top Twenty some months before—an unusually evocative "pop" tune. The almost universal reaction to this, where it was articulate, was, "Well, it makes a surprisingly good hymn tune." (This and similar things I know because I was in charge of a music workshop at this same Congress.) It involved a kind of singing which was entirely inappropriate to the ordinary hymn tune, but which had already been inculcated into the singers by some of the other music, and by the interpretations of traditional music which the music-leaders gave.

The final hymn, the new words to "Telstar", was deliberately left until the last minute. It was represented on the service-sheet by a blank page. It was simply announced on Friday night that a new set of words was wanted for one of the current "Top Twenty" tunes; and of course this could not itself be chosen before the beginning of that week. "Telstar" was number ten in the English "Top Twenty" list and number one in the American that week. Its association with a reference in the Queen of England's Christmas broadcast, and with the Epiphany season made it a useful choice. Members of Congress were to be seen in the restaurants and supper-houses of Bristol feverishly composing words to this intractable tune as late at night as such gatherings were permitted by the managements, and eventually a set of words was chosen for performance, and, after much frantic telephoning to the jealous publishers of this precious Top Tenth, sung on Saturday night.

The words are unmemorable and not worth recording here. The point is that something was expected to emerge, and did emerge, from the Congress itself which contrasted sharply with the praise that had otherwise been chosen for it.

It is much more important that the Congress itself wrote the hymn than that it was set to "Telstar". And moreover, it is much more important than either of these facts, that the words were thrown away after their single occasion of use, and are not expected ever to be revived again. (Apart from anything else, anybody who wished to do so would have to go through all the copyright business over again: and that, in the case of these precious first editions, is a dismaying prospect.)

This is a new point. It says something quite fresh about "pop", and so far as I know it is Mr. Mackenzie who has first brought it to the church's attention. There is, according to this view, a place in church music for what is impermanent, as "pop" is impermanent. This is a remarkable thing to say. For we are now settled in a habit which 150 years of cheap music printing has led us to accept, that that which is written for any church occasion ought *eo ipso* to be suitable for and worthy of performance throughout the church: that if a new hymn or tune has given pleasure at the parish church of Appleby, Westmorland, it ought to be printed in a hymn book which will serve ten thousand such parish churches: and that if it is not of universal usefulness it can have no local usefulness. This is not to say (heaven forbid!) that the church should look for a way of emulating the ghastly conformism of commercial "pop"—everybody singing this new tune this week, forgetting it and singing another next week. It is rather to say that the church might well explore the possibilities of "local" music, and of material which because of its emergence from a genuine local situation could make a decisive impact once without being such as would make any impact at all on any repetition. Certainly, if this were considered seriously by a church group, the chances of getting some of the rust off the joints of that local enterprise which in folksong days was the very life of the nation's music become a little less dim than they are at present. After all, certain sections of the church have thrived, on a practice of "Local preaching"—which means the welcoming of the ministry of a preacher who because of his local knowledge and associations is acceptable in a district without claiming any kind of "ordination" which implies his ability to represent, as the ordained minister does, the great church to the local church. If local preaching, why not local music—in about the same proportion?

Not that "Telstar" is local music: but the words set to it were a local gesture. "Telstar" was at the time folksong, although by the time these words are read it will probably not be.

But it may well be that "local" rather than "pop" is the heart of the matter. There is always a place for the "universal" kind of church music —universal in the standing of its composers and in the range of its communication. "Local" music may turn out to be sometimes "pop": but not necessarily so. Where else in these pages would it have been appropriate, for example, to mention such an enterprise as the *Feast Day Melodies* (1957) composed by members of "The Grail" in Grailville, Loveland, Ohio (U.S.A.)?[6] Here are a series of settings of psalm-antiphons which can be used within or outside the Catholic liturgy. They form very short, easily-memorised songs, mostly being printed just as melodies, but occasionally appearing in two-parts. In the Preface to this collection of simple tunes we read, "Through the Grailville Music Center a number of young women over the past dozen years have been awakened to the significant relationship between music and the whole spiritual activity of man. They have been exploring the many implications of this relationship and finding practical ways of sharing their discoveries with others. . . . Work of this kind has given a new dimension to the professional activities of these young musicians."

These one-line or two-line songs are sometimes a little like plainsong, sometimes more like snatches of folksong: sometimes rhythmical, sometimes free and unmetrical. In a sense they are so short and so "natural" that one cannot call them "serious" music: a composer of any of them would not probably wish to include it among his catalogue of opus numbers. And yet it is just this absence of "seriousness", of self-consciousness, that makes these simple antiphons so fresh and so suitable for the liturgy or for the use in the home that the editors of the book suggest for them.

Perhaps we might have dealt with them when we were mentioning Gélineau: but they are not as serious, as consciously pioneering, as Gélineau. They certainly have nothing to do with the great tradition of choral music represented by the composers in our parts I–III. No, although there is not a hint of jazz in them, or of "pop" values, they are "pop" in their unpretentiousness, and perhaps they are more like the "pop" that the church will eventually return to: "pop" not in being highly emotive and decorated, but "pop" in being thrown off without much solemnity by good musicians who are not above assisting the musical hack-work of the church.

NOTES TO CHAPTER 15

1. *Transatlantic*, L.P. 106.
2. E. Routley, *The English Carol* (Jenkins, 1958) pp. 65–68.
3. ib., pp. 111–12.
4. Parlophone P.M.C. 1197.

5. Parlophone P.M.C. 1146.

6. *Feast Day Melodies* (1957), World Library of Sacred Music, 1846 West-wood Avenue, Cincinnati 14, Ohio U.S.A. "Grailville" is a community of the "Grail" Movement, which has addresses at 58 Sloane St., London, S.W.1, and at 36 George St., Edinburgh 2.

Evangelistic "Pop"

THERE is, of course one section of the churchgoing public which might well react to all these gestures in "pop" music with a sad and patronising smile. This is that section out of which religious "pop" of quite another kind has for several generations now been pouring with excellent commercial results. The interest shown in the 1960's in church music affecting the style of secular popular music must not make anybody forgetful that the church itself has had a "pop" section in its music which had had a continuous vogue at any rate since the days of Sankey, and possibly since the days of Wesley.

We argued above that there are important reservations that we must allow if we regard the hymn tunes of the Wesleys as "pop"; but in the sense that a division appeared in church music between one style used by one class of worshipper, and another used by another, this division did become explicit soon after the Wesleys' time. The Wesleyan "pop" tune used the secular operatic idiom of its day to form an attractive melody supported by a minimal bass; and although it was not the practice of the Wesleys themselves to write hymns with "choruses" in which an illiterate congregation would respond to the narrative of a soloist, their musicians often wrote into their tunes repetitions and elementary fugal sections which to some extent had the effect of refrains for the singers. The doubts which Charles and John Wesley had about this new "pop" music are well attested in their writings: but the essence of "pop" is certainly in some of them, inasmuch as the rationality of the bass is strictly subordinated to the appeal of a florid melody. (Example 62)

The point here to be made is that it was this music which first caused persons of cultivated taste to observe that there was such a thing as "good" and "bad" church music: that on principle certain kinds of music were to be regarded as inferior.

It came out in the end in *Hymns Ancient and Modern* (1861). This was the most successful of those hymnals, all privately published during the

Ex.62

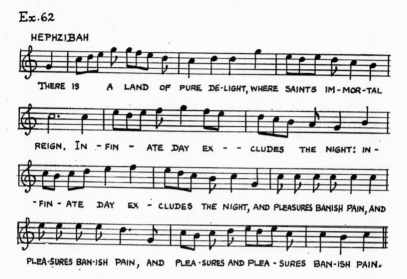

HEPHZIBAH

THERE IS A LAND OF PURE, DE-LIGHT, WHERE SAINTS IM-MOR-TAL

REIGN. IN - FIN - ATE DAY EX - - - CLUDES THE NIGHT: IN -

- FIN - ATE DAY EX - CLUDES THE NIGHT, AND PLEASURES BANISH PAIN, AND

PLEA-SURES BAN-ISH PAIN, AND PLEA-SURES AND PLEA - SURES BAN-ISH PAIN.

twenty years 1850–70, which sought to improve the taste of church-going Anglicans in the directions suggested by the authors of the Oxford Movement. What matters to note here is that the authors in these hymn books knew exactly what they meant by "improve". And within the word "improve" they concealed a complex but convinced social judgment. So that if you compare the contents of *Hymns Ancient and Modern* (1861) with, say those of *The Psalmist* (1835–43), the most successful of the early nineteenth century tune-books, you find that there is one style which *Ancient and Modern* simply will not touch: that is, the florid "Methodist" style, with its ornamental melody, static bass, occasional fugalities in the melody, and repetitions of words. *The Psalmist* is uncritically hospitable. Its Preface, to be sure, says much about the need for improving music in church: but the line there taken is that good music, and good singing, are what the church needs. It does not say that one particular style is to be proscribed. *Hymns Ancient and Modern* has no preface. Nobody says that a style is to be proscribed. It is just quietly dropped.

It is dropped because it is vulgar. Much that was accepted by *Hymns Ancient and Modern* has later been dropped because it is dull, cretinously edited, or feebly sentimental. But what appears now to show these qualities was acceptable in 1861 to people who thought the familiar tune HELMSLEY to "Lo, he comes with clouds descending" intolerably secular and demonstrative. It was not, in fact, until 1904 that *Hymns*

Ancient and Modern included that tune, although it has been wedded to the words in circles far beyond those of Methodism from the middle of the eighteenth century. The one "repeating" tune that the first edition of *Hymns Ancient and Modern* permitted was the tune to "O come, all ye faithful": but this came from a Catholic source, and the Oxford Movement's reactions to Catholic sources were somewhat different from their reactions to Methodist ones.

Hymns Ancient and Modern was a firmly bourgeois book in that it implied, but never stated, this kind of block-criticism of a whole style. This started something. Indeed, it was the beginning of what amounted to virtually a century of sociological conflict in church music. And it was within a decade that the conflict became more explicit with the arrival of the "Gospel-song" style—half music-hall, half carol, associated primarily with the evangelistic crusades of Dwight L. Moody and Ira D. Sankey.

The "Sankey" style became familiar through the very wide success of the crusades, in America first and then (from 1872) in Britain, and from the large public that received the simple songs of Sankey and his later imitators. The basis of the style is an extreme naïvety of rhythm, harmony and melody. It is "folk" music in being music which the industrial peasantry of the new age could immediately receive, join in, and take comfort from. There is no kind of sophistication in it; all the tunes are virtually the same tune, and the vocabulary they use is really a small collection of cliches whose repetition gave no kind of offence to its simple constituency. The same is true of the words, and indeed of the preaching that they expressed. Little was demanded, little was given, but that little, often and doggedly.

Moody and Sankey directed their mission towards those whom the established churches—Anglican or Dissenting—were not reaching. Two consequences followed. On the one hand, the line of division between those who approved and those who abhorred this music was drawn as cleanly as was the social line between the class which used it and the class which did not. On the other hand, wherever the "established" church (and the orthodox Dissenting churches) felt that they must make an effort to join in the work which the Salvation Army alone was doing with consistent faithfulness, they felt that the music they must use ought to be modelled on the "Sankey" pattern.

The Oxford Movement was to a large extent bourgeois: but not exclusively in the "*Hymns Ancient and Modern*" sense. There was in its followers from the first a new sense of their obligation towards the newly unchurched, which developed later into a revolt against a good deal of the bourgeois ethic in religion, on the part of such as Percy Dearmer, whose *Parson's Handbook* of about 1900 is a valiant attempt to debourgeoisise the image of the clergy and of liturgy. It is not surprising, then, that in Percy Dearmer's hymn book, *The English Hymnal* (1906), a special section of "Sankey-type" hymns was included. On the other hand it is entertaining to note that when the book was republished in 1933 with additional tunes and some typographical alterations, the legend appears over the first of these hymns (no. 567): "Not for ordinary use". In a book celebrated for the almost pedantic correctness of every note and word in it, this is perhaps the only example of tendencious imprecision.

"Not for ordinary use": that is how the orthodox—what we now call the "square"—apologise for the inclusion in a hymn book of "Hold the Fort" and "There were Ninety and nine".

Other hymnals have cautiously followed this example. The Congregationalists in 1917 had a similar section in their *Congregational Hymnary* called "Hymns with Refrains"; the Baptists and Methodists in their hymnals of this century have included a selection of "Sankey" type hymns along with the ordinary ones, making no distinction between the "pop" and the "square". Organs of special missionary effort, such as the *Fellowship Hymn Book*, largely edited by Quakers for the benefit of mission meetings, and the *Mirfield Mission Hymn Book*, prepared by the Mirfield Community especially for its downtown mission work in the West Riding, have in their own ways drawn on the Sankey heritage, or attempted (as in *Mirfield*) some new compositions designed to bring the idiom up to date. The Roman Catholics in England ever since the re-establishment of the Hierarchy in 1850 have made their special concern the welfare of the poor, and their church music has included a good deal that is written in the Sankey idiom. On the other hand, *Hymns Ancient and Modern* has rejected it with almost complete consistency—"Rescue the perishing" appeared in its 1916 Supplement, but that is as far as it went, and it was dropped in 1950. *Congregational Praise* has given it a wide berth. *Songs of Praise*, Dearmer's hymn book for schools and progressive churches, never touched it.

My purpose here is not to comment on the right use of this music, or to say more about its history.[1] I draw attention to it here because its very existence implies a quite remarkable instance of the impact of social values on church music. The "pop" of Beaumont and Williamson attracts the special attention of intellectuals: that of "Sankey" never does. It is native to its environment, and withers outside it.

Except for one quite staggering phenomenon of the early fifties of this century.

This, of course, is the Billy Graham Crusades, now of world-wide fame. Britain received these in 1954 (chiefly London) and 1955 (Glasgow), apart from smaller forays in later years. Dr. Graham's organisation had its way prepared in Britain by the united work of a number of English evangelists, claiming no particular denominational allegiance, but using with great energy and success the technique of the mass meeting: the most conspicuous of these was Mr. Tom Rees, at one of whose meetings in the Albert Hall, London, Dr. Graham was first heard in Britain in 1952.

Like Sankey, Dr. Graham brought his preaching technique from the United States. It was publicised by the most intensive and enter-prising advertising operation ever associated with a religious move-ment. And its meetings were a mixture of entertainment and uplift prepared with a skill and subtle evangelical guile such as neither country had seen before. Here was an immense sophistication of montage and build-up: a large-scale exploitation of personality, male glamour, puritan discipline and simple preaching fervour: and out of it came more "decisions" by way of response from the audience than the country had ever heard of before. Meetings up to 100,000 strong were built up, and people travelled up to 300 miles in Britain to be present at one of them.

The music used in this crusade proved to be very largely derived from the Sankey style. Some of the hymns of the nineteenth century movement were sung: some others were newly composed in a similar style. One of the most celebrated of these popular hymns, which is also much in use in broadcast religious programmes from "evangelical" sources, has the following bass line, from which the reader may care to try to identify it:

Ex. 63

The *Billy Graham Song Book* (1954, 1955) are full of this kind of music, which we still feel justified in calling by the generic term

"Sankey". Of course, there is some development of style from the authentic "Sankey" to this. Sankey himself was something of a carol-writer, a minstrel: it is said that his tunes commonly came to him on the spur of the moment, and that he sang them as solos on direct inspiration. This is wholly probable. At their best they are natural, unaffected, and quite unoriginal in the sense of owing everything to the musical tradition that surrounded him. It is most important to remember that there is no reason why music should not be like this. It does not make it bad music.

It was the unexamined assumption that music of this sort was *bad* music that caused the conflict: it was something in the way that *Ancient and Modern* shrugged it off that brought a bitterness that there need never have been. It is not true to say that music as derivative as this is bad music. What is true is that it should never claim immortality.

That is quite another matter. It is the use of this music that has brought the corruption, all along the line. This music, in fact, is the best example we have of the "easy come, easy go" variety of music—essential "pop". It has been necessary, as we saw a few pages back, for the idea of "disposable music" to be *explicitly stated* by self-conscious musicians in a church context. The true office of the "Sankey" is to be to the main stream of church music what the "pop" song is to the main stream of secular music: music that has a short life and vanishes, of which a tiny percentage turns out to have enduring qualities. In secular life the natural pressure of new "pop" drives out old "pop". The fittest survives—and what is the fittest of this week's "pop" to survive into the next generation nobody can possibly tell by examination. But the church has a disastrous squirrel-like propensity for hoarding. Everything that has been put to sacred use must be preserved: to throw it away seems to be sacrilege. So music whose proper office is to be here today and gone tomorrow (and this is *not* to call it bad music) is hoarded and subjected to constant use for which its strength is simply unequal.

This is why in "pop" there is a legitimate exaggeration, even caricature, of colour and emotion. It is vulgar. Of course it is vulgar! It is as vulgar as the exaggerated colours of an advertisement for detergent. It is designed to make an immediate impact and then go its way. To repeat it, to go on wallowing in it, is like putting up that advertisement for detergent in your drawing-room and keeping it there thirty years.

To some extent, of course, this can be said of all that Victorian church music which has become so tawdry and sentimental. But on the whole it is wiser to apply the word "sentimental" to persons than to art: it is the melancholy habit of Christians to dig themselves in at any point where pleasant sensation has associated itself with their religion: to say "That was good: let's have it again"—which of course was the mistake St. Peter made at the Transfiguration (Mark 9. 5). Music that is meant to endure, to be built into the continuing purpose of the church, needs that discipline, that understatement, that proportion and that prophetic insight that are the qualities of great art. But music for ordinary people need not always be great art. It is a crime, of course, to exclude the possibility of great art from the church's life: and the best way to exclude it is to make people think that the perpetuation of transient art is the proper business of the church.

It was therefore, surely, a mistake for the Billy Graham crusaders to build into their montage so much music which was the "pop" of two generations ago. It would have been far more encouraging, and the crusade would have kept, instead of forfeiting, the attention of many more responsible Christians, had this principle been observed, and had it produced a "pop" music of its own which was not designed to be perpetuated. The great error was in presenting the Christian faith as something whose image in music was the second-rate and second-hand. This applies to all evangelistic efforts, broadcasts, rallies and what not which deliberately use things like "The Old Rugged Cross" to give momentum to their messages. "The Old Rugged Cross" may not be in itself bad music—there is really no way of finally judging that it is bad music: but the use of it today is quite certainly bad, because it so clearly presents the qualities of transient "pop"—exaggerated emotion, over-ripe fervour, whose repeated use makes the whole process artificial and intellectually corrupt.

What now remains to do is not only to evolve a new "pop" for the church, but above all to cultivate a new understanding of the relative place in the church's life of music that is to be thrown away after use and music that is to endure. If it is all thrown away after use, some will ask, how will the good survive? We here reply that for the present at any rate less will be risked by a music that shows no concern for its own survival than by the continuance of our present habit of preserving everything that is pleasantly sacred, of giving great honour to its composers, of scrupulously guarding their copyrights, and of encouraging good amateurs to hope for an immortality that is not ours to give, when they would have been spared much disappointment had they been persuaded that to compose one tune for one Christian group to sing on one occasion, and thereby give edification, is the best ministry a musician can hope for.

For this is where the folk-music will come from: from people who are less conscious of their rights and aspirations as musicians than of the specific need for which they are moved to compose. Here is something to say. Here are people waiting to say it: let it be written, and sung, and never mind what happens to it after that. The committed musician, the musical prophet, will continue to write his great music; and if the church shows him that it will hear him, he will write for the church. The humbler minstrel can be content to leave others (and not only his friends) to judge whether his immortality will be spread over a span of generations, or whether it will be in the work of immediate charity. For there is no doctrine of immortality which restricts it to a temporal span. That men meet with reality, and indeed with God, in the momentary act of committed love is true doctrine, as the Bishop of Woolwich has recently and memorably shown.[2] For the present, this is probably the way the church can take to get itself clear of the confusion and embarrassment which too much reverence and scrupulosity have left with it. And those musicians who have asked the profound questions about predestination and purpose, of whom at an earlier point we were obliged to take notice, are perhaps the prophets to whom the church ought to attend most closely.

But this is a view from which some are dissenting. A very interesting departure from the current trend was made by Mr. Charles Cleall who in 1961 produced his *Sixty Songs from Sankey*.[3] Mr. Cleall was at the time the organist of St. Paul's, Portman Square, London, a lively Anglican church with a conservative-evangelical ethos which pursues an energetic ministry to that part of London which has come to be known as the "square mile of vice". Mr. Cleall selected some of the well known hymns of the "Sankey" tradition and reharmonised their tunes in a manner that gives them a new appeal to educated singers. (Example 64)

These hymns come out of a missionary purpose. In a long and important Preface, Mr. Cleall begins by noting that this style of song is "unfashionable in the church life of today", although they can still be regarded as "the nursery songs of the Gospel", and could have their place in the home. But "to the committed Christian they are hardly austere enough". At this point he goes on to make a point that introduces the new view: "Spiritual growth requires a music heard with voluntary rather than involuntary attention; so unmistakable 'peculiar to the Lord' that it is useless for any secular purpose; and it is the duty

Ex.64

of the church to provide it". In another place, Mr. Cleall expanded on this—and his book, *The Selection and Training of Mixed Choirs in Churches* (Independent Press, 1961) contains quite the best statement of musical faith that has appeared from the "evangelical" side of the contemporary church. It is his view that what we have called "secular pop" is primarily an exhibition of sexual paganism: "hot, trivial, unbridled—it is to this music that people inevitably turn when priestly law is absent, and discrimination blind" (p. 17). He may overstate his case passionately—the book should be read with care and gratitude—but this is where he stands. Therefore when he seeks to minister to the unevangelised of Paddington and the Edgware Road, he reharmonises Sankey.

But, he says, these are nursery-songs. And in what he next says he does not contradict, but confirms, the point which we have just made. These, he says, are songs of pre-conversion and as such they "express a consciousness of Christ in rapture, and of self in humility . . . they make no demands: the pleasure they give is unquestioned and un-questioning. . . . To seek milk, when we ought to be digesting stronger meat, is the mark of carnality; of self gratification; of a determination, like that of Peter Pan, not to grow up". These songs may be used legitimately to express an experience: but not to induce it.

This preface, like the book just mentioned, is one of the most important documents in contemporary church thinking about music. Mr. Cleall makes it clear that he is re-presenting Sankey in order to give expression, for those who sing it, to an experience which must be passed through, and passed quickly. This, then, is another approach to "throw-away" music, but this time in a different plane. It is music of permanent standing which can be used properly only at a certain stage of spiritual development. Its "pop" aspect is defined by Mr. Cleall as its "humility". The one point at which conversation with him might evoke new responses is where he seems to disregard the fact that eroticism may creep into religious music, and that a religious background is no defence against carnality. In his book he comes very near to admitting this (p. 19), but we still wonder whether the temptation to carnality will not be, in hands less firm than his, too strong for the singer.

For of course there is this to be reckoned with: that in our time we are seeing a strange revival of interest in a kind of large-scale religious "pop" to whose territory we travel through the Sankey "evangelical" country. Stainer's cantata, *The Crucifixion* (of which I have written enough in other places to leave it here without comment) was twice recorded on LP records in 1960 and 1961.[4] J. H. Maunder's *Olivet to Calvary*, first published in 1898, and, one would have thought, universally vilified among musicians over the past twenty-five years, received its first full-scale recording of any kind in 1962,[5] under the direction of one of England's leading church musicians, Dr. Eric Thiman. These are two examples of the continuing consciousness of the commercial value of a certain kind of "popular" religious music. And whereas at the times of their composition, these and other such cantatas were welcomed by Protestant christians of all kinds, liberal, evangelical and even "high church", their perpetuation nowadays is largely owed to the influence of "evangelical" religion. (A careful look at the places of performance of these recordings confirms this).

Mr. Cleall is quite evidently an enemy of this kind of music. But no amount of exhortation seems able to affect its sales-value. When it is brought into the picture, we have at last an opportunity to assess the true meaning of "pop" in its widest sense. And this is what it comes to.

On the one hand, "pop" is natural, accessible, and gives expression to the feelings of ordinary people who are without culture (secular or religious). It is a means of making contact with such people. It is transient, but this need not prevent it from having moments of greatness. It is emotionally confused, but this does not prevent its speaking now and again with clarity. Artists of standing see in it the possibility of discovering "what is epic in everyday objects and everyday attitudes".

On the other hand, the "natural" in "pop" is corruptible, and indeed often corrupt. Its unbridled quality—which musically finds expression in its tonal and melodic irresponsibility—can express and induce qualities and attitudes which are not epic but bestial. By the same token, "pop" is normally utterly uncritical of musical statements which are pretentious, unbalanced, and foolish. It exaggerates, sometimes cretinously. It permits, and encourages, fantasies of grandeur. It associates only too easily with extravagance and infantilism. It evokes the world of multi-million-dollar entertainment and of the worship of temperamental and childish "stars" of the entertainment world. It is directly connected with the monstrous tragedies which that world occasionally creates—such as the recent death of Miss Marilyn Monroe.

If therefore the church sees "pop" art as part of its mission, how is it to prevent the invasion of the church by these "pop" values which are not epic but mean?

Sooner or later we must make a judgment, even though it be an interim judgment on a situation which is constantly changing under our eyes. This shall be it.

"Pop" art in church will do what Beaumont, Cleall and all the other missionaries hope it will do if, and only if, it can be subjected to a discipline which will free it from its bondage to vile values. This is likely to be, at the artist's level, a discipline of the mind. "Pop" music with a bad bass is, by that token, intellectually degenerate. But music which employs the techniques of "pop" without insisting on its slovenliness, its pretentiousness, and its incentives to self-indulgent childishness, may be the liberation of the ecclesiastical style.

Good music, whatever its texture, its associations, or its purpose, is not music that is morally uplifting—for there is no such thing. It is music which can catch and hold the attention of a cultivated musician. It may have all the qualities that enable it to catch and hold the attention of the uncultivated—attractive melody, rhythm, harmony, ease in singing, effectiveness in performance. It need not frown at anybody. It need not be taciturn. But the goodness that is musical is that which the musician can recognise. It cannot be anything else. One must find some other word than "goodness" to describe the other qualities one may be looking for. But in any music, the listener is brought into personal encounter with its composer. If the composer writes stuff which, given all the attention of a good musician, gives back no reward, he behaves like a man who, offered the courtesy of a neighbour, turns away without a word. The true conversation of music implies an act of self-giving on the composer's part and on the listener's, equally. Suspicion, self-regard, or sloth on either side puts an end to the conversation.

There is no need to insist on dignity, solemnity, or any other secondary quality as being inseparable from the church's musical speech. The church has made the great mistake in the past of mistaking dignity and decorum for essentials, instead of seeing that they are occasional proprieties and adornments. But the church need never give house-room to anything that is deliberately slack, unkempt, or in any other way sub-human. What "pop" may be doing for the church is liberating the springs of natural joy. It will be monstrous if this good purpose is so perverted that in the end the church liberates among Christians the springs of vileness.

If this be true, then Mr. Cleall does rightly in giving his "Sankeys" a heightened intellectual content—in making them worth singing by musicians, worth attending to: and at the same time in admitting that they serve a transient purpose and that childish things should soon be put away. Mr. Beaumont does excellently when he gives us so good a tune as "Lord, thy word abideth"; he is ill-served by those who interpret his tune to "There's a wideness in God's mercy" with a slovenly bass[6] and well served by those who give it a subtle one.[7] Mr. Williamson does well when he writes into his popular music a good deal of sophisticated counterpoint, and less well when he rests on the harmonic idiom of Sullivan.[8] Mr. Marvin's television-play serves us well in producing satirical words and tunes of adequate strength for them. Mr. Carter does well when he produces more penetratingly satirical words, and melodies which it would take a genius to harmonise badly. Beaumont goes down when he constructs a whole "Creed" on a dull and repetitive bass—and so on.

The composer will bore his listener if he is irrational (as any irrational talker does), and if he has no repertory except the vocabulary and ideas of others. Stainer did not bore his generation but, since his large-scale music is constructed so largely out of the platitudes of his age, it cannot command our attention now—not for the length of time it takes to perform *The Crucifixion*. It is not enough to say that he can still hold the attention of many. If he holds the attention of the many and still commands the attention of those who move in his own world, then he writes well. How many of the composers we have here mentioned are on the right side of this division we cannot yet say. But it is the generous among them, the prodigal, those who will waste ninety per cent of what they write on the uncultivated for the sake of performing an act of "giving all that they have" who will always be the leaders. They will have their share of temporal immortality. The others may serve a generation, or a local group, but no matter how small the group or how short the generation, they will be blind leaders of the blind if their self-giving is any less than that of the great. It is not only the poor who are generous. Unhappily, they are sometimes as mean as the man in the Gospels who had one talent, with the result that they approach music-making with the attitude "I'm not much good at this: I'm not like those highbrows". Let Tom Smith, the organist of St. Jude's, Huddersfield, write his hymn tune with as much shameless self-giving abandon as Britten writes his next oratorio—he is more likely then to write what the church will hear gladly.

But "pop" church music is at present always mission-music. Perhaps it can best be seen as an attempt by "square" musicians to encourage the rebirth of an indigenous folksong.

But if this is so, the composer of church "pop" must be satisfied that the soil from which that folksong will spring is not too sour to produce a folksong that can be edifying. So his method will depend on whether he regards the "natural" and "everyday" as too far gone in error to be thus approached, or whether he regards it as fundamentally good and capable of being turned into the right path by homoeopathic persuasion.

A letter came into the offices of the London Missionary Society in March 1963 from Professor John Ferguson of Ibadan University, himself the holder of a chair in English and a capable amateur musician. It contained the following passage on the indigenous folksong of Africa and its relation to the impact of Western culture.

> Indigenous culture finds its highest expression in wood-carving and dancing. These apart, the words of the editor of *Ibadan* stand: "African music . . . still remains a folk music; an African intellectual who is conscious of Bach will feel a sense of loss until his folk music is also transformed by a cultivated genius." So in other fields. What will emerge will be a new synthesis, not the old folk-culture, nor a slavish imitation of Europe. But, for this synthesis, Nigeria must be exposed to Bach and Mozart, to Shakespeare and Brecht—must be exposed to them at their best. This is the frightening aspect of what we do. We are setting standards. We are the Old Vic, Covent Garden, the Savoy, King's College Chapel and all the rest. . . . The opportunity, the challenge, is tremendous![9]

Thus a missionary professor sees the ministry of a dramatic society of Westerns in an African context: by the exposure of the nationals to the best of Western art, helping in the creation of a new indigenous culture which will be the result of conversation, not of imitation. This is another view again. If there is a folk music in twentieth century secular society in the West today which is pagan, and the Church wishes to make contact with it, on this view the church's business is not only to show interest in the products of pagan culture but to expose that culture to the best products of the Christian tradition. Once again —let Bach be Bach and let Britten be Britten, and let Malcolm Williamson, even when he writes in dialect, be Williamson: let the "pop" gestures be a seeking for conversation not a gesture of patronage or contempt.

Somewhere between these diverse views, or somewhere in a direction towards which the resultant force of these various movements seems to lead, will be found an answer to the problem of presenting Christian truth in musical language to those who are strangers to it.

And at that point we must leave this chapter unfinished . . .

NOTES TO CHAPTER 16

1. E. Routley, *The Church and Music* (Duckworth, 1950) p. 189.

2. See note 15 to chapter 10.

3. Pilgrim Press, 1961. Recorded, Pilgrim Recordings 12 in. L.P. I.L.P. 500.

4. Leeds Philharmonic Choir: H.M.V. 12 in. L.P. ALP. 1885. St. John's College, Cambridge: Argo 12 in. L.P. RG 320.

5. Pilgrim Recordings.

6. CLM. 205, see Bibliography.

7. MG 20019, see Bibliography.

8. This is most conspicuous in *The Morning of the day of days*, an Easter Cantata (Weinberger, 1963, recorded C.L.M. 208), published after these chapters were written and showing a noticeable retrogression from the vivid style of this composer's earlier works.

9. See *The Chronicle* of the London Missionary Society, June 1963, p. 158.

Conclusion

IN a sense, of course, there can be no conclusion, for the subject of these pages has been an unfinished story. In their course much has been omitted, and such judgments as have been made are hazardous.

But perhaps the reader, before laying the book down, will glance again at the quotations with which we have introduced the four parts of the book: Vaughan Williams's moral judgment on bad taste: the wife of King David despising his enthusiasm when he danced before the Lord (and the unco-guid who wrote to the papers protesting against the Coventry ballets): Messiaen passionately declaring that only four people in the world had any interest in the progress of music: and the American youngster feeling all warm inside "like oatmeal" when she listened to Mr. Presley. The figure under which the whole story has been told is that of a church reconstructing itself, and, on showing willingness to do so, being pressed to reconstruct far more radically than it had at first proposed to do. I think that that is a fair picture of this century so far.

Its first half is full of pedagogy: its second half, of alarming creativeness: and in both aspects of music-making the church has allowed itself to be involved. I wish now to repeat what has already been said, that this is a new thing: especially the second manifestation. You can compare this age with no other: for if others have been equally energetic in music, and if in others the church has had a good share of the best music, in no other has the church involved itself so completely in the musical affairs of the secular world. The difference between this and any other age is that there are combined in it a musical vitality which no age has exceeded, a swiftness of communication which no age has approached, and a situation of peril and precariousness in church institutions which at least has not been matched since the days of Constantine the Great. It would be absurd for the church to take credit for what has happened. Churchmen may rather be thankful that the church as an institution has lost that conceded remoteness which has made it able in other ages to turn at will a deaf ear to anything it considered "profane". The church has had to get used to being in a position where it could not escape conversation with "the world": to travel, as it were, second class. Examination of the principles that made church music churchy—and made it especially churchy where the church was most firmly entrenched in bourgeois exclusiveness—has led to a discovery that half of them did not exist, and the other half were patient of much modification.

It can be for no other reason that "sacred" and "secular" are nowadays so thoroughly mixed up in church art. For no other reason has it been possible for twelve-tone composers to expect some sort of a response among Christians, and equally for churchmen to make attempts, however mishandled these have been, to communicate with the world of "pop". What we are witnessing is the first few sentences of a conversation whose end will surely be more creative than the former state of things was. The church can no longer lecture; it cannot even wait in the old-fashioned way to deliver a reserved judgment. For good or ill, it is in the world now, and is being talked to by scientists, artists and the zestful and arrogant young in tones that demand an answer. No longer monologue but rather conversation: and the theological result is, precisely, the "Religionless Christianity" cult of Bonhoeffer, Tillich and (recently) the Bishop of Woolwich.

In our opening pages we said that many of the musical experiments of our time are made by people who are unafraid of a final verdict that the experiments are sterile. The church is likewise beginning to say things that sound bold and dangerous and even damaging to its own faith, but to say them at least with less fear of contradiction than more cautious statements of the past implied. It is not that they do not expect to be contradicted. It is that the makers of such statements are not afraid of contradiction because they believe that through contradiction, through the extinction, if necessary, of their human structures of belief, the general apprehension of truth will be forwarded.

When Vaughan Williams said good taste was a moral issue he said more than he knew. He meant primarily that in the *English Hymnal* he was stating not only aesthetic but moral convictions and that that book stood for a contribution to goodness and not only good taste. What would he have said about Geoffrey Beaumont, then? The church seems latterly to have been implying that even in the devil's brew of modern culture that produces "pop" there is something to converse with. It is a moral issue all right—but a more complex one than he thought in his early years.

When Saul's daughter rebuked David for his dance of joy she stood for the essential shockableness of conventional religion, for the "nothing in excess" decorum of popular piety. And David said that this was superstition. If the church is listening to such things as Tippett's *Magnificat*, Walton's *Gloria* and even Krenek's electronic oratorio, it is denying a certain rigid code of decorum to which in the nineteenth century it was committed. And there are some who are naturally alarmed. For they say, and reasonably, as many said on reading the Bishop of Woolwich's conclusions about traditional morality, "if you let it all go, what will be left?"

Responsible theologians are not quite sure that we have rightly stated the Christian teaching on chastity in our traditional assumptions and public speeches. Responsible musicians are far from sure that we have rightly stated the truth about musical beauty in what we have assumed for many generations. Those who hear the new teachings say "take out that king-pin and all morals will collapse", and similarly, "take out the common chord and we shall all be wandering in a wilderness of dry logical ugliness".

All that we can say at present is—we cannot be sure that the tradition is right and that the prophets are wrong. Conversation may become heated, and prospects may look bleak. We may become thirsty for Vaughan Williams under the stern leadership of Krenek, as men thirsted for Mendelssohn when Vaughan Williams took over.

All this is where we cannot judge, but can only make decisions from time to time on the evidence before us; and where we shall feel confident to speak only if we are sure that contradiction will be, however uncomfortable for us, in the end the means of progress.

But this we can say: that the age that has produced eccentricities which are so formidable and concessions to popular taste which are so disconcerting in one which has also produced an enormous amount of obviously fine music, an enhancement of the musician's social status, and an astonishing increase in the educational encouragement of music. In church music we have, in the past generation, seen the establishment of the Royal School of Church Music, the rise of denominational music-workshops, the recognition of music by the Student Christian Movement as a subject of Christian study, the establishment in Scotland (1962) of the Dunblane Ecumenical Music Group for inter-church research into the problems of contemporary church music; we have more recitals of music, more opportunities for hearing the finest church music there is, more appreciation of modern idioms, than there ever was. In the City of Edinburgh alone, which has a population of under half a million, and whose church music tradition is still very largely ruled by the customs of the Church of Scotland, one can hear excellently rendered programmes of secular music at Cramond Parish Kirk, equally fine recitals at Palmerston Place Parish Kirk, a weekly half-hour recital of church music, often modern and experimental, church music every Sunday night at the High Kirk of St. Giles, an occasional performance of Fauré's Requiem (of all things to expect in such a place) in the historic Parish Kirk of Greyfriars — and this is to say nothing of the energetic musical tradition at St. Mary's Episcopal Cathedral, and the highly creative work going on in St. Mary's Roman Catholic Cathedral, where Benjamin Britten's *Missa Brevis* was performed within a few months of its first performance in London, and for the first time in Scotland. And that is to take a few of the more conspicuous examples from what was, thirty years ago, surely the most musically philistine city (at any rate where church music was concerned) in the world.

No doubt the conversation will get heated, and more so. The publication of Peter Maxwell Davies's *Ave Maria* in the *Musical Times* of October 1961 marked a new move in that journal towards the encouragement of "far-out" vocal music, and provoked a stormy correspondence. The more the ordinary people of the churches become aware of what is going on, the more decisive we may expect their reactions to be. But Messiaen cannot now say that nobody appreciates him; and the Coco-Cola drinking maiden may well be embarrassed and surprised by the church's efforts to supply her with warm oatmeal. The conversation continues.

Nothing, perhaps, is more important than that the conversation should not stop. Disagreement and dissent will not stop it; patronage and contempt will. It will probably remain true that those who contribute most fruitfully and successfully to church music will tend to be those who listen most openly to the music of the past and of their neighbours: who, like Herbert Howells, are soaked in the music of their time and of other times and yet evolve a style of their own. Deafness to other music may bring, as it did to Bartok and as perhaps it does to some *avant-garde* musicians of our own time, a piercing and prophetic originality without which the world and the church will be the poorer. But history and one's neighbours matter; and it is the creative counterpoint between different musical cultures, and different classes of men, and between the sacred and the secular, which will in the end determine the course that church music takes. There is at present no reason for supposing that that course will not take us through more exciting country, and more vital experience, than it has passed through up to now. All the signs are that it will, perilous though the journey will be from time to time.

APPENDIX

An Experiment in Church Music

THE Student Christian Movement held its fourth International Congress at Bristol, 1st–7th January, 1963. For the first time at an international congress, music was a subject of study in one of the study-commissions. Each morning and evening the 1,600 students at the congress (about 400 of whom were from overseas) met for worship in the Colston Hall (the city's chief concert-hall). There the music was directed by the Rev. Ian Mackenzie and Mr. Peter Cutts. (Mr. Mackenzie was formerly assistant organist at St. Giles, Edinburgh, and Mr. Cutts is an honours graduate in music at Cambridge university).

The praise-list at these sessions was as follows (at each session, two congregational hymns being sung).

WEDNESDAY MORNING: "Sing, my tongue, the glorious battle"
(Jan. 2)   REGENT SQUARE (H. Smart, 1813–79).
           "Every star shall rise", words and music
           (unpublished) by Sydney Carter.
EVENING: "Love divine, all loves excelling".
           CLARITAS (sung for the first time).
           "One who is all unfit to count".
           WIGTOWN (Scottish Psalter 1615).
THURSDAY MORNING: "Let all mortal flesh keep silence".
(Jan. 3)   PICARDY (French carol tune).

Ex. 65   *Peter Cutts.*

"Ride on, ride on in majesty",
> tune from Malcolm Williamson's *Procession of Palms*.

EVENING: "In the Cross of Christ I glory",
> tune by Peter Cutts, sung for the first time. (Ex. 65.)

"Dieu, nous avons vu ta gloire",
> sung in French to the tune by Jean Langlais from *Bible et Liturgie*, 1957 (see p. 137).

FRIDAY MORNING: Psalm 150, from the *Folk Mass* by Geoffrey Beau-
(Jan. 4)   mont.

"The head that once was crowned".
> ST. MAGNUS (English, early eighteenth century).

EVENING: "Lord of the dance", unpublished, by Sydney Carter.

"The strife is o'er", to an arrangement of the "pop-song", "Wonderful Land", made by Ian Mackenzie.

EXAMPLE 66——

SATURDAY MORNING: "Wake, awake, for night is flying".
(Jan. 5)
> WACHET AUF, in the original version of Philipp Nicolai, 1599.

"A toi la glorie",
> sung in French to the tune from Handel's *Judas Maccabaeus*, "See the conquering hero comes".

EVENING: "Christ is made the sure foundation".
> WESTMINSTER ABBEY (Purcell).

A newly composed hymn for the "pop-song" *Telstar*.

BIBLIOGRAPHICAL INDEX OF MUSIC
AND MUSICIANS

THIS does not pretend to be a comprehensive bibliography of any of the composers here listed, although in the case of the *20th Century Church Light Music Group* it is reasonably complete. All it claims to provide is (1) a reference index for the present work, and (2) publishers' references for all the works mentioned in the text, and often for a few other representative works of the same composers which are not mentioned in the text. In most cases the latest examples are given. From a study of the music here mentioned the reader will gain a working knowledge of twentieth century church music: but of course there is far more to be discovered and browsed in than is, or could possibly be, given here.

Where a work is recorded in a reasonably accessible disc, a reference to the record number is given in the index: a list of records thus mentioned is in the discography at the end, made out alphabetically by index-letters.

Abbreviations:

A.	—	Abingdon Press, 201 Eighth Avenue South, Nashville, U.S.A.
B.	—	Boosey and Hawkes Ltd.
C.	—	J. & W. Chester Ltd.
E.	—	Epworth Press.
H.W.G.	—	H. W. Gray Co., New York (associated with Novello, London).
M.	—	Merseburger, Berlin.
N.	—	Novello (Ad: *Festal Voluntaries for Advent*: F.A.: *Festival Album*): Col.—*Colours of the Organ*).
O.U.P.	—	Oxford University Press.
P.	—	Paxton.
S. & B.	—	Satiner & Bell.
U.	—	Universal Edition.
W.	—	Weinberger Ltd.
Y.B.P.	—	Year Book Press.

Letters in roman capitals following publishers' initials are part of the order number of the piece referred to.

ALDRIDGE, Richard
Organist, Purley Congregational Church
"He came all so still" (1957), N. CA 615.
"Let us rejoice, the fight is won" (1959) N. Anth. 1383.

ALLDIS, John
Member of 20th Century Light Music Group.
Festival Te Deum 1961), *W.*   Rec. CLM 202.

ANDREWS, H. K. (b. 1903).
Faculty of Music, Oxford University.
Evening Service, D minor (1940), *O.U.P.*
Evening service, G (1958), *N.* PCB 1359.
"My song is love unknown" (1941), *O.U.P.*
"The spacious firmament" (1949), *O.U.P.* E. 54.
"O sing the glories" (1956), *O.U.P.* E. 78.

APPLEFORD, Rev. Patrick.
Member of 20th Century Light Music Group.
Mass of Five Melodies (1961), *W.*   Part Rec. CLM 202.
Hymns and tunes in *20th Century Hymn Tunes* (*W* 1960, 1962) and in
    Rhythm in Religion (*W.* 1960). Part Rec. CLM 201 CB 1629, 1630.

ARMSTRONG, Sir Thomas (b. 1898).
Principal, Royal Academy of Music.
Missa Aedis Christi (1940), *O.U.P.*, OCM 502.
"Lord, it belongs not to my care" (1959), *O.U.P.* A. 161.
"Creator Spirit" (1937), *O.U.P.* A.74.

ASHFIELD, Robert (b. 1911).
Rochester Cathedral.
"Fairest of morning lights" (1948), *O.U.P.* E. 50.
ORGAN
Sonata (1956) *N.* OCNS 237.
Carillon, Plaint and Paean (1962) *N.* OMC 30.

BAIRSTOW, Sir Edward (1875–1946).
Organist, York Minster.
Communion Service, E flat (1923) (U), *O.U.P.* OCM 402.
Evening Service in G (1940), *O.U.P.* OCM 501.
"Save us, O Lord, waking" (1902), *N.* Anth. 740.
"Come, ye gentles" (1902), *N.* M.T. 717.
"Let all mortal flesh keep silence" (1925), *S. & B.* CCL 204.
                                        Rec. on RG 340.
"Blessed city" Banks (York) Y. 659. In R.S.C.M. Festival Choir Book,
    1951, p. 62.
"The day draws on" (1930), *O.U.P.* E. 1.
"As Moses lifted up the serpent" (1931), *O.U.P.* A. 44.
"Though I speak with the tongues" (1934), *O.U.P.* A. 63.
"Let my prayer come up" (1937: Coronation), *O.U.P.* A. 77.

BAKER, Robert.
Director, School of Sacred Music, Union Theological Seminary, New
    York.
"O Lord God to whom vengeance belongeth" (1941), *H.W.G.* 1741.

BEAUMONT, Rev. Geoffrey ("Father Gerard") (b. 1903).
Founder of the 20th Century Light Music Group.
A 20th Century Folk Mass (1956), *W.*   Rec. LPR. 201 and MG 20019.
Eleven Hymn Tunes (1957), *W.*   Some rec. on CLM 205.
Three Hymn Tunes from the 20th Century Folk Mass (1957), *P.*
    Rec. on CLM 205, all on LPR 201 and MG 20019.
Tunes in *Rhythm in Religion* (1960), *W.*   Rec. on CB 1629–30.
Tunes in *20th Century Hymn Tunes* (1960, 1962), *W.*
    Some rec. on CLM 203.

BERKELEY, Lennox (b. 1903).
Domini est Terra, C.
Thou has made me, C.

BINGHAM, Seth (b. 1883).
Distinguished American musician and teacher.
Four Marian Litanies (1955), New York: St. Mary's Press.

BIRTWISTLE, Harrison (b. 1934).
Monody for Corpus Christi (1961), *U.* UE 12928.

BLAKE, Leonard J. (b. 1907).
Director of Music, Malvern College.
Morning & Evening Service in E flat (1940), *N.* PCB 1274–7.
Evening Service in D (1949), *O.U.P.* CCM 517.
Communion Service in D (1961), *N.* PCB 1390.
"And now another day is gone" (1937), *N.* MT 1129.
"Consecration" (1949), *O.U.P.* E. 52.
"Lord of the worlds above" (1959), *N.* CS 107.

BLISS, Sir Arthur (b. 1891).
Master of the Queen's Musick.
The Beatitudes' (1962), *N.* 19080.
"Stand up and bless the Lord your God" (1960), *N.* Anth. 1387.

BRENT SMITH, Alexander (1889–1950).
Director of Music, Lancing College, 1912–34).
Elegy (1939), *N.* 16731.
"My soul, there is a country" (1920), *S. & B.* CCL 206.

BRITTEN, Benjamin (b. 1913).
A boy was Born, Op. 3 (1932/58), *B.*   Rec. LXT 5416.
Ceremony of Carols, Op. 28 (1943), *B.*   Rec. RG 179, LW 5070.
Rejoice in the Lamb, Op. 30 (1943), *B.*   Rec. LXT 5416.
St. Nicolas, Op. 42 (1948), *B.*   Rec. LXT 5060.
A Wedding Anthem, op. 46 (1950) *B.*
Hymn to St. Peter, Op. 56a (1955), *B.*
Noye's Fludde, Op. 59 (1958), *O.U.P.*   Rec. NF 1.
Missa Brevis in D, Op. 63 (1959), *B.*   Rec. CEP 654.
War Requiem, Op. 66 (1962), *B.*   Rec. MET 252–3.

Jubilate (1945), *O.U.P.* S. 551.   Rec. on RG 340.
Festival Te Deum, Op. 32 (1945).   Rec. on RG 340.

BROCKLESS, Brian (b. 1926).
R.A.M.
"Now blessed be thou" (1959), *N.* MT 1401.
ORGAN
Prelude, Toccata and Chaconne (1959), *N.* ISCOM 5.

BROCKLESS, George F. (1887–1953).
Organist, Central Hall, Westminster.
Tunes in *Methodist Hymn Book* (1933).

BULLOCK, Sir Ernest (b. 1890).
Formerly Principal Glasgow Academy of Music.
"Give us the wings of faith" (1925), *O.U.P.* A. 1.
"Christ the fair glory" (1926), *O.U.P.* A. 8.
"Alleluia: the Lord keep you" (1934), *O.U.P.* A. 65.
"Give laud unto the Lord" (1937), *O.U.P.* E. 31.
"Holy is the true light" (1945), *N.* MT 1334.
"Lift up your heads" (1949), *O.U.P.* E. 51.
Evening Service in G minor (1952), *O.U.P.* OCM 527.
"We saw him sleeping" (1961), Arnold A. 535.

BUSH, Geoffrey (b. 1920).
Christmas Cantata (1948), *N.* 17362.
"O Love, how deep, how broad" (1956), *N.* MT 1360.
"Praise the Lord, O my soul" (1956), *N.* Anth. 1344.
In praise of Mary, Elkin.
Two Latin Hymns (1963), *N.* MT 1448

CAMPBELL, Sydney S. (b. 1909).
Organist, St. George's, Windsor.
"Sing we merrily" (1962), *N.* MT 1438.

CASHMORE, Donald (b. 1926).
Ealing Music Centre; Kingsway Hall, London.
"Give unto the Lord" (1959), *N.* MT 1400.
"Jesus comes with all his grace" (1960), *N.* MT 1406.
"God is ascended up on high" (1961), *N.* Anth. 1403.
This child behold (Cantata: 1962), *N.* 19127.
"Sing to the Lord" (1962), *E.* EP 390.

COOK, John.
Evening Service in G (1952), *N.* PCB 1310.
ORGAN
Invocation & Allegro Giojoso (1956), *N.* OMC 6.
Five studies in form of a Sonata (1958), *N.* OCNS 283.
Flourish & Fugue (1962), *H.W.G.*

COPLEY, Evan (U.S.A.).
"Salvation belongeth unto the Lord" (1961), A. APM 145.
"Four Anthems for Treble Voices" (1962), A. APM 213.
ORGAN
Prelude on "Ein" Feste Burg" (1961), A. APM 282.
Three Chorale-Preludes (1961), A. APM 253.

DARKE, Harold (b. 1888).
St. Michael's, Cornhill.
"In the bleak midwinter" (1911), S. & B. Car. 8.
"Even such is time" (1929), O.U.P. A. 30.
Communion service contributed to Coventry Cathedral celebrations (ms. 1962).
ORGAN
Three Chorale Preludes (1919), N. OCNS 60.

DAVIES Peter Maxwell (b. 1934).
"Ave Maria" (1961), N. MT 1424.
O magnum Mysterium (1961), Schott.

DIERCKS, John (U.S.A.).
"Clap your hands" (1960), A. APM 103.
ORGAN
Six Sacred Pieces (1963), A. APM 255.

DIETTERICH, Philip.
"O Love that triumphs over loss" (1961), A. APM 126.
"Wilt thou not turn again?" (1961), A. APM 134.

DISTLER, Hugo (1908–42).
From Geistliche Chormusik, Op. 12 (1934).
"Ich wollt dass ich daheine war"   Rec. 643229.
                                          Lobe den Herren Rec. 643232.
Setting of "Die Helle Sonn", verse 3.   Rec. TN 71678.
                                       Singet dem Herren Rec. on 643211.
Choral Passion (1933) Op. 7.   Rec. 642205–6.

DYSON, Sir George (b. 1883).
Formerly Principal, Royal College of Music.
"Praise" (1919), Arnold 29.
"Confortare" in Coronation service, 1953, p. 70.   Rec. on ALP 1057.
"I will worship" (1954), N. MT 1337.
"Hail, Universal Lord" (1958), N. Anth. 1370.
Benedicite in F (1958), N. PCB 1360.
ORGAN
Prelude & Postlude (1956), N. OMC 3.
Variations on Psalm Tunes (1960), N. OCNA 308–9.

ELDRIDGE, Guy H.
"Let us with a gladsome mind" (1952), *O.U.P.* A. 133.
" 'Tis the spring of souls today" (1958), Elkin 2563.
ORGAN
Four Impressions (1959), *N.* OMC 16.

FINZI, Gerald (1901–56).
Dies Natalis (1939), *B*
FORTNER, Wolfgang (b. 1907).
Die Schöpfung (1956).   Rec. DGM 18405.

GARDNER, John L. (b. 1917).
Morley College.
Cantiones Sacrae, (1952) *O.U.P.*
"Hail the day that sees him rise", *O.U.P.*
GÉLINEAU, Père Joseph.
Psalmody scores from The Grail, 58 Sloane St., London, W. 1.
                                        Rec. GR 3–4, 5–6, 7–8, 24: SM 33.50.
GIBBS, Armstrong (b. 1889).
"Most glorious Lord of life" (1926), *O.U.P.* A. 3.
"Bless the Lord, O my soul" (1934), *O.U.P.* E. 14.
"I the prisoner of the Lord" (1948), *O.U.P.*
"O Praise God in his holiness" (1953), *O.U.P.*
Behold the Man (Cantata, 1955), *O.U.P.*
GOODMAN, Joseph (U.S.A.).
Motets for Mixed Voices (1954).
Christmas Office Hymn (1956).
Missa Brevis (1959).
All from St. Mary's Press, New York.

HARRIS, Sir William (b. 1883).
Formerly Organist, St. George's, Windsor.
Praise the Lord (1938), *N.* 16637.
"King of glory" (1925), *O.U.P.* A. 2.
"O what their joy and their glory" (1931), *O.U.P.* A. 48.
"Love of love and Light of light" (1934), *O.U.P.* A. 62.
"Vox Ultima Crucis" (1937), *O.U.P.* E. 21.
"Laudamus" (1945), *O.U.P.* A. 112.
"I heard a voice" (1947), *O.U.P.* A. 117.
"Be strong in the Lord" (1948) *Black* A. 98.
"Sing a song of joy" (1946), *N.* MT 1236.
"Holy is the true light" (1956), *N.* MT 1259.
"Lord of the worlds above" (1961), *N.* Anth. 1411.
"The Lord my pasture" (1945), *N.* MT 1222/C.S. 116.

"Bring us, O Lord God" (1959), *N*. Anth. 1368.
"Let my prayer come up" (1953).
Coronation service, p. 23.   Rec. on ALP 1056

ORGAN
Sonata in A minor (1938), *N*. OCNS 173.
Four Short Pieces (1938), *N*. OCNS 170.
Flourish for an Occasion (1952), *N*. OCNS 203.
Epilogue on "Dix" (1956), *N*. OCNS 270.
Elegy and Postlude (1959), *N*. TS ii.
Three Voluntaries (1957), *N*. OCNS 284.
Miniature Suite (1957), *N*. OMC 9.
Processional March (1960), *N*. OCNS 312.

HARWOOD, Basil (1859–1949).
Service in A flat (undated), *N*.
"O sacred banquet" (1937), *O.U.P.* A. 76.
"All my heart this night" (1942), *N*. MT 1196.
"I sing the birth" (1943), *N*. MT 1207.
"Draw nigh to God" (1944), *N*. MT 1216.
"O how glorious is the Kingdom".

ORGAN
Sonata in C sharp minor.
Paean (1902), *N*. 11698 (out of 24 Original Compositions published in a series).
Eight Pieces (1935), *N*. OCNS 156.

HOLST, Gustav (1874–1934).
Two Psalms (1920), Augener.
This have I done for my True Love (1930), Augener.
Hymn of Jesus (1928), Op. 37.   Rec. LXT 6006.
Hymns in *Songs of Praise*, 1931.

HOWELLS, Herbert (b. 1892).
Faculty of Music, London University.
"When first thine eyes" (1927), *O.U.P.* A. 10.
"Mine eyes for beauty pine" (1928), *O.U.P.* A. 14.
Four Anthems (1943)
  "O pray for the peace of Jerusalem".
  "We have heard with our ears".
  "Like as the hart".
  "Let God arise", *O.U.P.* A. 107–110.
  "Behold O God our defender" (1953).
Coronation service, p. 16.   Rec. on ALP 1056.

Services

Te Deum and *Jubilate*. (E flat) (1950) N. PCB 1277.   Rec. RG 120

Magnificat and *Nunc Dimittis*. (G minor)(1947(N. PCB 1280. Rec. LX 1572.

Canterbury Cathedral, Te Deum and Benedictus (1951) N. PCB 1278.

St. George's Windsor, Te Deum and Benedictus in F sharp minor (1952)
N. PCB 1281.

Worcester, A minor (1953), N. PCB 1324.

New College, Oxford, G major (1953) N. PCB 1288

St. Paul's, G minor (1954), N. PCB 1322.

Westminster, B minor (1956), N. PCB 1350.

Westminster, F sharp minor (1957) N. PCB 1367.

Collegium Sancti Johanni, D minor (1958), N. PCB 1375.

Missa Aedis Christi (1961), N. 18959.

Missa Sabrinensis (1955) N. 17948.

An English Mass, (1956) N. 18285

God is gone up (1958), N. 18680.

Hymnus Paradisi (1950), N. 17468.

Sequence for St. Michael (1961), N.

ORGAN

Rhapsodies, Op. 17/1–3 (1918–19), Augener.

Psalm Preludes, First Set (1915), N. OCNS 82–84.

Psalm Preludes Second Set (1938–39), N. OCNS 177–79.

Sonata (1933), N. OCNS 150.

Six Organ Pieces (1951)

Preludio Sine Nomine (1940).

Sarabande for the Morning of Easter (1940).

Master Tallis's Testament (1940).

Fugue, Chorale and Epilogue (1940).

Sarabande in modo Elegiaco (1945).

Paean (1940), N. OCNS 220–25.

Sicilano for a High Ceremony (1953), N. OCNS 276.

HUTCHINGS, Arthur (b. 1906).

Faculty of Music, Durham University (Professor).

"Grant them Rest" (1952), N. MT 1314.

"Victim Divine" (1957), N. MT 1374.

Service in G (1958), N. PCB 1364.

IRELAND, John (1879–1962).

These things shall be (1937), Boosey.

"Greater love hath no man" (1912), S. & B. CCL 140.

Rec. on RG 340.

Service in F (1912), N. PCB 882–4.

JACKSON, Francis (b. 1917).
Organist, York Minster.
Service in G. minor (1958) N. PCB 1296.
'How bright those glorious spirits" (1948), *Y.B.P.* A. 97.
ORGAN
Three Pieces (1955), N. OMC 4.
Toccata, Chorale and Fugue (1955), N. OCNS 275.
Diversion (1960), N. Col. 3.
Toccata-Prelude on Wachet Auf, N. OCNS 267.

JACOB, Gordon (b. 1892).
"The spacious firmament" (1931), *O.U.P.* OCS 150.
"To my humble supplication" (1945), N. MT 1228.
"The 23rd Psalm" (1952), *O.U.P.* E. 59.
"O Lord I will praise thee" (1952), *O.U.P.* E. 62.
"Sing a song of joy" (1957), *O.U.P.* A, 150.
The New-Born King (Christmas Cantata) (1960), *O.U.P.*
ORGAN
Prelude, Meditation & Fanfare (1958), N. OMC 13.

JANACEK, Leos (1854–1928).
Večñe Evangelium (1916), Artia, Prague.
M'sa Glagolskaja (1928), U. 9544a.   Rec. SUA 10265.

JIRAK, Karel B. (b. 1891).
Professor, Roosevelt University, Chicago.
ORGAN
Five Little Preludes & Fugues, Op. 77 (1960), N. ISCOM 7.

JOUBERT, John. (b. 1927)
Faculty of Music, University of Birmingham.
"O Lorde the Maker of al thing" (1953), N. Anth. 1319.
"*Libera Pledem*", Op. 19 (1956), N. Anth. 1326.
"Great Lord of lords" (1957), N. Anth. 1329.
"Welcome Yule" (1957), N. MT 1375.
"*O Tristia Secla Priora*", Op. 32 (1959), N. Anth. 1371.
Missa Beati Joannis, Op. 37 (1962), N. 19122.

KODALY, Zoltan (b. 1882).
Psalmus Hungaricus, Op. 13 (1924), U.   Rec. ALP 152.
Te Deum (1936), Score: Hawkes 702.   Rec. ALP 152, XWN 18455.
Missa Brevis (1951), Score: Philharmonia 276.   Rec. ALP 1687.
Jesus and the Traders, U.   Rec. 640217.
KRENEK, Ernst (b. 1900).
Spiritus Intelligentiae Sanctus (1956).   Rec. LPE 17244.
ORGAN
Sonata (1941), N.

LANG, C. S. (b. 1891).
Formerly Director of Music, Christ's Hospital.
A Cradle Hymn (1943), N. MT 1209.
"Save us, O Lord, waking" (1951), N. MT 1298.
"Sing Alleluia Forth" (1957), N. CS 97.
"Set up thyself" (1958), *Elkin* 2562.

Evening service in B flat, Op. 16 (early) (1961), N. PCB 1400.
Te Deum in E flat, Op. 73 (1958), N. PCB 1341.
Communion Service in F Op. 78 (1959), N. PCB 1369.

ORGAN
Voluntary on Winchester New (1956), N. Ad.
Pastorale (1957), N. T.S.
Prelude and Fugue in G minor (1960), N. OCNS 307.
Prelude, Pastorale and Fugue (1962), N. OMC 28.

LANGLAIS, Jean (b. 1907).
St. Clothilde, Paris.
Missa in Simplicitate (1953).   Rec. 270 C 003.
"Dieu, nous avons vu ta gloire".   Rec. SM 33.50.

ORGAN
Three Characteristic Pieces (1957), N. OMC 10.
Triptyque (1958), N. ISCOM 1.
American Suite (1961), H.W.G.

LANGSTROTH, Ivan (b. 1887).

ORGAN
Fantasy and Fugue (1953), N. OCNS 240.
At the Cradle (1956), Op. 34, N. OCNS 278.
Interlude on Winchester Old (1956), N. OCNS 273.
Three Chorale Preludes (1957), N. OCNS 292.
Theme with Variations (1961), N. ISCOM 6.

LEIGHTON, Kenneth (b. 1929).
Faculty of Music, University of Edinburgh.
The Light Invisible, Op. 16 (1958), N. 18660.
Crucifixus pro Nobis, Op. 18 (1960), N. 19028.
"A Hymn of the Nativity" (1960), N. Car. 633.
"Alleluia, Amen" (1962), N. Anth. 1416.

LOVELACE, Austin.
Washington, D.C., U.S.A.
"O Thou eternal Christ" (1960. A. APM 105.
"Dear Lord and Father" (1961), A. APM 140.
"Prayer for Families" (1962), A. APM 267.
and many other anthems in the same series.

MARTIN, Frank (b. 1890).
Swiss composer.
Golgotha (1949), U.
La Mystère de la Nativité (1959), U.
In Terra Pax (1953), U.

MARTINŮ, Bohuslav (1890–1959).
Czech composer.
Polni M'še (Field Mass) (1947).
Melantrich, Prague.   Rec. SUA 10387.
The Prophecy of Isaiah (1959).
Israeli Music Publications, Tel Aviv and Leeds Music Corp. New York.
Gilgamesh (1957) U. UE 12701.

MARVIN, The Rev. Ernest.
Presbyterian Minister, Lockleaze, Bristol with Ewan Hooper.
A Man Dies, Television-Mime on the Life and Death of Christ. Text and
music published by A.B.C. Television Ltd., 1961.
Rec. (2 songs) DB 4660.

MESSIAEN, Olivier (b. 1908).
"*O sacrum convivium*" (1935).   Rec. on 270 C 003.
ORGAN
Apparition de l'Église Éternelle (1932). Lemoine, Paris, 22673 H.
Rec. on 270 C 003.
L'Ascension (1934), Leduc, Paris, AL 18.826.   Rec. RG 339.
Le Banquet Céleste (1928), Lemoine.   Rec. MMA 11127.
La Nativité du Seigneur (1936), 4 vols. Leduc. Rec. MMA 11127 and ("Les
Bergers") on 270 C. 003.
Livre d'Orgue (1951).

MICHEELSEN, Hans (b. 1902).
Nunc Dimittis.   Rec. on 643239.

MILNER, Anthony (b. 1925).
Morley College and University of London.
Salutatio Angelica Op. 1 (1948), U. 12736 L.
The City of Desolation (1955), U. 12336 L.
The Water and the Fire (1963) N. 18862.
"Blessed are all they" (1957), N. Anth. 1353.
"Praise the Lord of heaven", Op. 13/3 (1960), N. MT 1407.
Turbae I (1960), N. II 1963 N.
ORGAN
Rondo Saltato Op. 6/1 (1957), N. ISCOM 2.

MILNER, Arthur (b. 1894).
Faculty of Music, University of Durham.
"Blessed is the man" (1959), N. Anth. 1378.
"Sweet was the song" (1962), E. EP 393, no. 2.
ORGAN
Saraband for a Solemn Occasion (1959), N. OCNS 300.
Galliard for a Festive Occasion (1960), N. OCNS 303.

Prelude, Siciliano and Ricercare (1960), *N.* OMC 21.
Two Meditations on Psalms (1960), *N.* OCNS 304.

NAYLOR, Bernard.
  Nine Motets (1960)
    Advent: Christmas: Epiphany: Ash Wednesday; Good Friday: Easter:
    Ascension: Whitsun: Trinity.
    N. Anth. 1393–1400, 1402.
  "I sing the birth" (1962), *N.* Car. 647.

NICHOLSON, Sir Sydney (1875–1947).
  Founder of the Royal School of Church Music.
  Service in D flat.
  "God be in my head".
  "In numbers but these few".
  "Love divine".
  "Let us with a gladsome mind".
    and in the Sydney Nicholson Commemoration Book (R.S.C.M., 1951).
  Hymns in *Hymns Ancient and Modern*, 1950.

NIELSEN, Carl (1865–1931).
  ORGAN
  Commotio, Op. 58 (1931), Dania, Copenhagen.

OLDHAM, Arthur (b. 1926).
  St. Mary's Catholic Cathedral, Edinburgh.
  Laudes Creatuarum (1961).   Rec. LLP 1011.

OLDROYD, George (1893–1956).
  Stabat Mater, *O.U.P.*
  "Song of the Passion", *O.U.P.* A. 81.

ORR, Robin (b. 1909).
  Faculty of Music, University of Glasgow (Professor).
  "They that put their trust in the Lord" (1948), *O.U.P.* Rec. on RG 340.

PARRY, Sir Hubert (C. H. H.) (1848–1918).
  Ode on the Nativity (1912), *N.* 13695.
  Blest pair of Sirens, *N.*
  Songs of Farewell
    "I know my soul hath power" (1916).
    "My soul, there is a country" (1916).
    "At the round earth's imagined corners" (1917).
    "Never weatherbeaten sail" (1916).
    "There is an old belief" (1916).
    "Lord, let me know mine end" (1918), *Y.B.P.*

"I was glad" (1911), N. Coronation, p. 2.   Rec. on ALP 1056.
Te Deum (Coronation, 1910).
ORGAN
Fantasia & Fugue in G (1913), N. OCNS 22.
"Wanderer" Toccata and Fugue (1920), N. OCNS 76.
Chorale-Preludes 2 books (1912, 1916), N. OCNS 1 and 45.
Three Chorale-Fantasias (1914), N.

PEETERS, Flor (b. 1903).
Belgian Organist and Composer.
Thirty Chorale-Preludes, Op. 68, 69, 70, Peters 6023.
Prelude on Stuttgart (1956), N. OCNS 271.
Chorale-Fantasy on "Christ the Lord is risen" (1961), H.W.G.
Prelude, Canzona and Ciacona (1957), N. OMC 5.

PEPPING, Ernst (b. 1901).
German composer.
Drei Evangelien—Motetten (1938), Schott, BSS 35567.
Te Deum (1956).   Rec. LPM 18409.
St. Matthew Passion (1951),   Rec. 642208-9.
"Lobet Ihr Knechte".   Rec. 643232.
ORGAN
Kleines Orgelbuch (1941).
   Schott (Vienna) BSS 36306.

POULENC, Francis (1899-1963).
French Composer.
Mass in G (1937), Salabert, Paris.
Gloria (1959), Salabert.   Rec. CX 1798.
ORGAN
Organ Concerto (1938).   Rec. CX 1798,
      RB 1627.

POWELL, Robert (U.S.A.).
"From the rising of the sun" (1960), A. APM 116.
"Let saints on earth" (1960), A. APM 112.
"O Trinity of blessed light" (1961), A. APM 146.
ORGAN
Four Psalm Preludes (1962), A. APM 254.

PRITCHARD, Arthur (b. 1908).
Professor, Royal Academy of Music.
"In heavenly love abiding" (1952), N. MT 1309.
"O praise God in his holiness" (1953), N. MT 1321.
"O Lord I will praise thee" (1960), N. Anth. 1384.
ORGAN
Elegy and *Fancy* (1957), N. OCNS 281-82.

P

RATCLIFFE, Desmond.
>Editorial Staff, Novello & Co.
>"In Salutation" (1947), N. MT 1257.
>Evening service in C minor (1949), N. PCB 1285.
>Give us the wings of faith (1960), N. CS 110.
>"At the Lamb's high feast" (1960), N. MT 1415.
>ORGAN
>*Preamble, Contrast & Hosanna* (1960), N. OMC 22.
>*Caprice* (1960), N. Col. 5.

READ, Gardner (U.S.A.).
>"Vital spark of heavenly flame" (1963), A. APM 276.

RIMMER, Frederick (b. 1914).
>Faculty of Music, University of Glasgow.
>"Sing we merrily" (1963), N. MT 1443.

ROWLEY, Alec (1892–1957).
>"Christ the Lord is risen" (1943), N. MT 1210.
>"Sweet was the song" (1947), N. MT 1256.
>"Here at thine altar" (1953), N. Anth. 1165.
>"My spirit longs for thee" (1957), N. MT 1368.
>ORGAN
>*Symphony no. 2 in F* (1959), N. OCNS 290.
>*Sonatina* (1959), N. OCNS 298.
>*Triumph Song* (1952), N. OCNS 210.

RUBBRA, Edmund (b. 1901).
>Faculty of Music, University of Oxford.
>*Festival Te Deum*, Op. 71 (1951), Lengnick 3732.
>*Lauda Sion*, Op. 110 (1961), Lengnick 4093.
>*Missa Cantuarensis.*   Rec. on HLP 27 (part).

SOMERVELL, Arthur (1863–1937).
>*The Passion of Christ* (1914), B. H. 8480.
>*Christmas* (a Cantata: 1926), B. H. 11935.

SOWERBY, Leo (b. 1895) (U.S.A.).
>"Psalm 96" (1963), H.W.G. CMR 2784.
>"My Son, if thou wilt receive" (1963), H.W.G. CMR 2792.
>*Te Deum* in B flat (1963), H.W.G. CMR 2787.
>ORGAN
>*Holiday Trumpets* (1960), N. Col.

STANFORD, Sir Charles (C. V.) (1852–1924).
>*Three Motets*, Op. 135 (1911).
>"Ye choirs of new Jerusalem" in R.S.C.M. Triennial Festival Service Book, 1954.
>*Service in G* (1904).   Rec. on RG 99.
>ORGAN
>*Six Preludes*, Op. 88 (1903), S. & B.
>Preludes and Fugues, Op. 193 (1910), N. OCNS 98–9.

STANTON, W. K. (b. 1891).
Formerly Professor of Music, University of Bristol.
"By the waters of Babylon" (1940), *O.U.P.*
"Christ if the world's true light" (1943), *O.U.P.* E. 36.
"Hast thou not known" (1953), *O.U.P.* A. 134.
"Of one that is so fair (1956), *O.U.P.* X. 28.
"Service and Strength" (1957), Joseph Williams CM 123.
"Sing we triumphant hymns of praise" (1961), *O.U.P.* OCS 795.

STATHAM, Heathcote (b. 1889).
Organist, Norwich Cathedral.
Te Deum in F (1956), *N.* PCB 1355.
"Ye that know the Lord is gracious" (1956), *N.* Anth. 1342.
"There were shepherds" (1958), *N.* NT 1388.

ORGAN
Four Diversions (1957), *N.* OMC 8.
Fantasia on "Veni Immanuela" (1956), *N.* OCNS 266.
A Sketch (1960), *N.* Col.

STRAVINSKY, Igor (b. 1882).
Symphony of Psalms (1930).   Rec. LXT 5639.
Mass (1948). *B.*   Rec. LXT 6001.
Threni (1958). *B.*   Rec. ABL 3329.
A Sermon, a Narrative and a Prayer (1961), *B.*
The Flood (1962) *B.*

SZYMANOWSKI, Karol (1883–1937).
Stabat Mater (1928), *U.* 8743.

THALBEN-BALL, G. T. (b. 1896).
Organist, the B.B.C. and the Temple Church, London.
Laudate Dominum, (1954) *N.* 18041.
Service in C.   Rec. CLP 1529.

THIMAN, Eric (b. 1900).
Organist, the City Temple, London.
The Last Supper (1930), *N.* 15532.
The Temptations of Jesus (1952) *C.* 3727.
"Sing Alleluia forth" (1925), *N.* MT 989.
"Lo round the throne" (1930), *N.* MT 1051.
"Christ hath a garden" (1931), *N.* MT 1061.
"O Lord support us" (1934), *N.* MT 1095.
"O love of God" (1942), *N.* MT 1195.
"I will lay me down in peace" (1944), *N.* MT 1215.
"I praised the earth" (1947), Curwen.
"My soul, there is a country" (1957), *N.* Anth. 1341.
"Blessed city" (1961), *H.W.G.* CMR 2679.
"The pilgrim's prayer" (1951), *N.* MT 1304.

ORGAN
Four Chorale-Improvisations (1933), N. OCNS 147.
Six Pieces in Various Styles (1960), Curwen.
Prelude on "Adeste Fideles" (1956), N. OCNS 269.

THOMAS, Mansel (b. 1909).
"One generation passeth away" (1962), N. Anth. 1424.
"I will lift up mine eyes" (1963), N. Anth. 1419.

TIPPETT, Michael (b. 1905).
Formerly Director of Music, Morley College.
Magnificat & Nunc Dimittis (1962), Schott.   Rec. on RG 340.

TYNSKY, Richard (b. 1909).
Czech composer and conductor.
ORGAN
Phrygian Toccata (1960), N. ISCOM 3.

VAN HULSE, Camil (b. 1897).
Formerly Belgian, now U.S.A. composer.
ORGAN
Four Short Pieces, Op. 94 (1957), N. OCNS 28.
Biblical Sketches, Op. 107 (1958), N. OMC 14.
Christmas Rhapsody, Op. 103/2 (1958), N. ISCOM 4.
Seven Preludes & Fugues, Op. 106 (1961), N. ISCOM 8.

VAN IDERSTINE, A. P. (U.S.A.).
"Garden Hymn" (1962), A. APM 227.
"Wondrous Love" (1962), A. APM 193.

VAUGHAN-WILLIAMS, Ralph (1872–1958).
Toward the Unknown Region (1907), S. & B.
"Lord thou hast been our Refuge" (1921), Curwen, 80592.

Rec. on RG 340.

Sancta Civitas (1925), Curwen, 3663.
Te Deum in G (1928), O.U.P.
Benedicite (1929), O.U.P.
Mass in G minor (1930), O.U.P.   Rec. RG 179, 7 eg 8614.
"O how amiable" (1934), O.U.P. A. 94.
Dona nobis Pacem (1936), O.U.P.
The Pilgrim's Progress (1941), O.U.P.
"My soul, praise the Lord" (1947), O.U.P.
"Prayer to the Father of Heaven" (1948), O.U.P.
"O Taste and See" (1953), Coronation p. 127.

Rec. on ALP 1058 and on CX 1193.

Hodie (1954), O.U.P.
A Vision of Aeroplanes (1956), O.U.P.
ORGAN
Three Preludes on Welsh Hymn Tunes (1920), S. & B.
Prelude & Fugue in C minor (1921), S. & B.

VILLA-LOBOS, Heitor (1881–1959).
Brazilian Composer.
Mass in Honour of St. Sebastian (1937).
Associated Music Publishers, New York.

WALTER, Samuel (U.S.A.).
"How firm a foundation" (1962), *A*. APM 125.
"The Lord reigneth", *A*. APM 203.

WALTON, Sir William (b. 1902).
"A Litany" (1915/1930), *O.U.P.* OCS 733.   Rec. on RG 340.
"Set me as a seal upon thine heart" (1938), *O.U.P.* A. 86.
Te Deum (1953), Coronation Service, p. 146.   Rec. on ALP 1058.
Gloria (1961), *O.U.P.*

WARREN, Raymond.
The Strife is o'er (1960), N. 18766.

WEBBER, W. S. Lloyd (b. 1914).
Organist, Central Hall, Westminster.
The Divine Compassion (1954), Francis, Day and Hunter.
The Saviour (1961), N. 19050.
"O for a closer walk" (1957), N. Anth. 1349.
"Most glorious Lord of life" (1959), N. MT 1391.
"Unite to praise" (1961), N. MT 1419.
ORGAN
Chorale, Cantilena & Finale (1958), N. OMC 11.
Rhapsody on "Helmsley" (1956), N. OCNS 265.
Benedictus (1960), N. Col.

WELLESZ, Egon (b. 1885).
Mass in F minor, Op. 51 (1949), Lengnick, 3683.
WERNER, Franz (b. 1898).
Der Herr jat euch gebracht.
Settings of Easter hymns.   Rec. 643254.

WESTRUP, Sir Jack (b. 1904).
Faculty of Music, University of Oxford (Professor).
"God be merciful" (1962), N. Anth. 1427.

WILLAN, Healey (b. 1880).
"Christ whose glory" (1950), Concordia 98–2006.
"Rise crowned with light" (1950), Concordia 98–2001.
"O Lord our Governor" (1953), Coronation service, p. 95.
                                                Rec. on ALP 1057
ORGAN
Rondino, Elegy and Chaconne (1957), N. OMC 7.
Prelude and Fugue in C. minor, N. LRO 36.

WILLIAMSON, Malcolm (b. 1931).
Planctus (1961), *W.*
"Wrestling Jacob" (1962), *N.* Anth. 1437.
"Let them give thanks" (1962), *W.*
Symphony for Voices (1962), *W.*
ORGAN
Vision of Christ Phoenix (1962), Chappell.
"Light Church Music".
Adoremus (1961), *B.*
Procession of Palms (1962), *W.*   Rec. CLM 204.
Harvest Thanksgiving (1962), *W.*   Rec. CLM 206.
The Morning of the Day of days (1963), *W.*   Rec. CLM 208.
Twelve Hymn Tunes (1962), *W.*   Some rec. on CLM 204, 206.
"Easter Carol" (1962), *W.*   Rec. on CLM 204.
WILLS, Arthur (b. 1926).
Missa Eliensis (1960), *N.* PCB   1381.
Evening Service, G minor (1960), *N.* MV 143
ORGAN
Elevation (1960), *N.* Col.
Postlude (1960), *N.* OCNS 306.
Introduction & Allegro (1961), *N.* ISCOM 9.
WOOD, Charles (1866–1926).
"O Thou the central Orb" (1915), *YBP* A. 9.
"O Lord, that seest" (1919), *YBP* A. 12.
"Hail gladdening Light" (1919), *YBP* A. 11.
"Glory and honour and praise" (1921), *YBP* A. 32.
"Exspectans Exspectavi" (1919), *YBP* A. 25.
St. Mark Passion (1921), Faith Press.
(posthumous)
"God omnipotent reigneth" (1927), *YBP* A. 50.
"How dazzling fair" (1929), *YBP* A. 64.
"O be joyful" (1929), *YBP* A. 63.
"Once he came in blessing" (1935), *YBP* A. 88.
Communion service in F (1926), *YBP*
ORGAN
Sixteen Preludes (1912), *S. & B.*

ZIMMERMANN, Heinz Werner (b. 1930).
Lobet, ihr Knechte (1956), *M.*   Rec. 643235.
Uns ist ein Kind geboren (1956), *M.*   Rec. 643235.
Das Vater Unser (1957), *M.* 451.   Rec. 643235.
"Herre, mache mich zum Werkzeug deines Friedens" (1959), *M.* 452.
Psalmkonzert (1958), *M.* 521.   Rec. 640229.
Gelobt sei der Herr Taglich (1959), *M.* 478.

ALP 152.	KODALY: *Psalmus Hungaricus*, Op. 13 and *Te Deum*.	
(deleted 1963)	Budapest Choir, Hungarian Concert Orch./Composer.	ARTIA
ALP 1687.	KODALY: *Missa Brevis*. Budapest Choir, Soloists, Hungarian State Orch./Composer.	H.M.V.
CB 1629–30.	20TH CENTURY CHURCH LIGHT MUSIC GROUP: *Rhythm in Religion*.	(45) PAXTON
CEP 654.	BRITTEN: *Missa Brevis*, Op. 63. Westminster Cathedral Choir.	(45) DECCA
CLM 201.	20TH CENTURY CHURCH LIGHT MUSIC GROUP: *Songs for Saints and Sinners* (from *Thirty 20th Century Hymn Tunes*, various composers). Bob Brown Singers/W. Davies.	(45) TOWER
CLM 202.	20TH CENTURY CHURCH LIGHT MUSIC GROUP: ALLDIS: *Festival Te Deum*. APPLEFORD: *The Lord's Prayer*, from *Mass of Five Melodies*. C. Keyte and vocalists/W. Davies.	(45) TOWER
CLM 204.	WILLIAMSON: *Procession of Palms* and *Two Hymns and Agnus Dei*. John Alldis Choir/W. Davies.	(45) TOWER
CLM 205.	BEAUMONT: *Hymn Tunes*.	(45) TOWER
CLM 206.	WILLIAMSON: *Harvest Thanksgiving* and *Four Hymns*. John Alldis Choir/W. Davies.	(45) TOWER
CLM 208.	WILLIAMSON: *The Morning of the Day of days* and *Te Deum & Let Them Give Thanks*. Elizabeth Singers/Halsey.	(45) TOWER

(N.B.—TOWER label from Josef Weinberger, 33 Crawford Street, London, W.1.)

CX 1193.	Recital by St. Paul's Cathedral Choir, including Howells: *A spotless rose.* Vaughan Williams: *Five Mystical Songs* and *O Taste and see*.	COLUMBIA

CX 1798.	POULENC: *Gloria* and *Organ Concerto*. French National Radio Chorus, Soloists, Orch./Prêtre.	COLUMBIA
DB 4660.	MARVIN & HOOPER: *A Man Dies*. Two songs, "Go it Alone" and "Gentle Christ". V. Mountain.	(45) Columbia
GR 1–2.		
GR 3–4.	GÉLINEAU: Psalms 23†, 112†, 135†, 138†. The Blessings of Daniel, Magnificat. St. Edmonds College, Ware, Brannigan/Wells.	(45) GRAIL
GR 5–6.	GÉLINEAU: Psalms 4, 62†, 83†, 102†, 125†. Canticle of Simeon (Nunc Dimittis). Choirs of St. Luke's, Pinner and (part of) Digby-Stuart College/Trotman.	(45) GRAIL
GR 7–8.	GÉLINEAU: Psalms 22†, 32†, 41†, 136†, 138†, Magnificat. Cy Grant, Waxwell Singers/Trotman.	(45) GRAIL
GR 24/1–2	GÉLINEAU: Psalms 8, 22†, 41†, 42†, 50†, 90†, 99†, 129†. Children's choir, Monks of Downside, Edgar Fleet Quartet/Malcolm.	GRAIL
HLP 27.	HISTORY OF MUSIC IN SOUND, containing among other modern secular music, RUBBRA: *Missa Cantuarensis*, excerpts.	H.M.V.
ILP 500.	CLEALL: *Songs from Sankey*. Echelforde Singers/Cleall.	PILGRIM
LLP 1011 SLLP 1012.	} OLDHAM: *Laudes Creaturarum*. McLoughlin, Choir. Scottish National Orch./Composer.	WAVERLEY
LPE 17244.	KRENEK: Spiritus Intelligentia Sanctus.	DGG
LPM 18405.	FORTNER: *Die Schöpfung*. (The Creation). Fischer Dieskau/Norddeutscher Rundfunk Orch./Schmidt-Isserstedt, with Author Narrating.	DGG
LPM 18409 SMLP 138020	} PEPPING: *Te Deum*. Chorus of Kirchenmusikschule, Dresden, Soloists/Flämig.	DGG
LPR 201	BEAUMONT: *20th Century Folk Mass*. John Alldis, Choir, W. Davies.	PAXTON

LX 1572.	HOWELLS: *Collegium Regale*, Magnificat and Nunc Dimittis (Kings College, Cambridge).	(78) COLUMBIA
LW 5070.	BRITTEN: *A Ceremony of Carols*. Copenhagen Boys' Choir.	DECCA
LXT 5060.	BRITTEN: *St. Nicolas*, Op. 42. Pears, Hemmings, Aldeburgh Festival/Composer.	DECCA
LXT 5416.	BRITTEN: *Rejoice in the Lamb*, and *A boy was born*. Purcell Singers, Malcolm/Composer.	DECCA
LXT 5639 ⎱ SLX 2277. ⎰	STRAVINSKY: *Symphony of Psalms*. Geneva Motet Chorus/Ansermet.	DECCA
LXT 6001	STRAVINSKY: *Mass*.	DECCA
LXT 6006. ⎱ SXL 6006. ⎰	HOLST: *Hymn of Jesus*. B.B.C. Chorus & Orch./Boult.	DECCA
MET 252–3 ⎱ SET 252–3 ⎰	BRITTEN: *War Requiem*.	DECCA
MG 20019.	BEAUMONT: *20th Century Folk Mass*. Frank Weir & his Concert Orch., Peter Knight Singers, Charles Young (cantor).	ORIOLE
MMA 11127 ⎱ AMS 16074 ⎰	MESSIAEN: *Le Banquet celeste* and *La Nativité du Seigneur*. Dupré (Les Bergers).	MERCURY
NF 1.	BRITTEN: *Noye's Fludde*. English Chamber Orchestra, Soloists, Choirs/del Mar.	ARGO
RB 1627 ⎱ SB 2147 ⎰	POULENC: *Organ Concerto*. Boston Sym. Orch.	RCA
RG 99.	KING'S COLLEGE CHOIR: Evensong, including *Stanford in G*, and Hadley: "My Beloved Spake".	ARGO
RG 120.	KING'S COLLEGE CHOIR: Easter Matins, including Howells: *Collegium Regale* (Te Deum & Jubilate).	ARGO
RG 179. ⎱ ZRG 5179 ⎰	BRITTEN: *A Ceremony of Carols* amd VAUGHAN WILLIAMS: *Mass in G minor*. Canterbury Cathedral Choir/Campbell.	ARGO
RG 339 ⎱ ZRG 5339. ⎰	MESSIAEN: *L'Ascension*. Simon Preston.	ARGO

RG 340 ⎱ ZRG 5340. ⎰	ST. JOHN'S COLLEGE, CAMBRIDGE: *Modern Church Music.* Britten: *Festival Te Deum.* *Jubilate.* "Hymn to the Virgin". Bairstow: "Let all mortal flesh keep silence". Howells: "Like as the hart". Ireland: "Greater Love hath no man". Orr: "They that trust in the Lord". Tippett: *Magnificat* and *Nunc Dimittis.* Vaughan-Williams: "Lord, thou hast been our refuge" Walton: "A Litany".	ARGO
SM 33–50.	STRASBOURG CATHEDRAL: *Vigiles* —*Bible et Liturgie* (1957), containing psalmody by J. Gélineau (Pss. 46†, 116†, 135†, canticle by J. Langlais, and lit- urgical music by M. Chapuis and D. Julien.	STUDIO
SUA 10265.	JANACEK: *Slavonic Mass.* Moravian Mixed Choirs, Brno Radio Symphony Orch./Bakala.	SUPRAPHON
SUA 10387.	MARTINŮ: *Field Mass* (Military Mass). Czech P. Orch., Choir/Liska.	SUPRAPHON
XWN 18455.	KODALY: *Te Deum.* Vienna Chorus & Sym. Orch./ Swoboda.	WESTMINSTER
270 C 003	LANGLAIS: *Missa in Simplicitate.* Collard/Langlais. MESSIAEN: *Les Bergers.* *Apparition de l'Eglise Eter-* *nelle.* *O sacrum Convivium.*	
		DUCRETET-THOMSON
33 CX.	See CX.	
45 DB.	See DB.	
640208–9.	PEPPING: *St. Matthew Passion.* St. Thomas Choir, Leipzig.	CANTATE
640217.	Recital by St. Thomas's Choir, Leipzig, including KODALY: "Jesus and the Traders".	CANTATE
640229.	ZIMMERMANN: *Psalmkonzert.*	CANTATE

642205–6.	DISTLER: *Choral-Passion*, Op. 7.	
	Westphalian Singers.	CANTATE
643211.	DISTLER: *Singet dem Herren*.	
	Windsbach Children's Choir.	(45) CANTATE
643232.	DISTLER: *Lobe den Herren*.	
	PEPPING: *Lobet ihr Knechte*.	
	St. Thomas Choir, Leipzig.	(45) CANTATE
643235.	ZIMMERMANN: *Lobet ihr Knechte*.	
	Uns ist ein Kind ge-boren.	
	Das Vaterunser.	(45) CANTATE
	Heinrich Schutz Choir.	
643239.	MICHEELSEN: *Nunc Dimittis*.	
	Westphalian Singers.	(45) CANTATE
643254.	WERNER: *Easter Music*.	
	Heinrich Schuts Choir.	(45) CANTATE
7 EG 8614.	VAUGHAN WILLIAMS: "O Taste and See".	
	Temple Choir/Thalben-Ball.	(45) H.M.V.

Index